IØ16Ø313

On Stage Alone

UNIVERSITY PRESS OF FLORIDA

Florida A&M University, Tallahassee
Florida Atlantic University, Boca Raton
Florida Gulf Coast University, Ft. Myers
Florida International University, Miami
Florida State University, Tallahassee
New College of Florida, Sarasota
University of Central Florida, Orlando
University of Florida, Gainesville
University of North Florida, Jacksonville
University of South Florida, Tampa
University of West Florida, Pensacola

University Press of Florida

Gainesville/Tallahassee/Tampa/Boca Raton

Pensacola/Orlando/Miami/Jacksonville/Ft. Myers/Sarasota

ON STAGE ALONE

SOLOISTS AND THE MODERN DANCE CANON

Edited by Claudia Gitelman

and Barbara Palfy

First cloth printing, 2012
First paperback printing, 2014

Library of Congress Cataloging-in-Publication Data
On stage alone : soloists and the modern dance canon /
edited by Claudia Gitelman and Barbara Palfy.
p. cm.
Includes bibliographical references and index.
ISBN 978-0-8130-4025-7 (cloth: alk. paper)
ISBN 978-0-8130-6034-7 (pbk.)
1. Dancers. 2. Dancing—Psychological aspects. 3. Modern
dance. I. Gitelman, Claudia. II. Palfy, Barbara.
GV1594.O53 2012
792.8—dc23
2012001071

University Press of Florida
15 Northwest 15th Street
Gainesville, FL 32611-2079
http://www.upf.com

Contents

Illustrations

On Stage Alone

Introduction

Claudia Gitelman

Soloists ignited the modern dance movement and they have been a source of its constant renewal, inhabiting space between the new and the not-yet-known. Soloists, however, have received less attention in dance literature than have performers and choreographers associated with large companies. *On Stage Alone* broadens the dance canon by bringing to light modern dance soloists with significant sustained careers performing full programs of their own choreography. Courageous, self-fashioning dance artists represent the individuality that is the domain of modernism and its sequel, postmodernism.

Modernism in this context refers broadly to that movement within the arts that took hold in the late nineteenth century. Abstraction replaced representation and individualism replaced obeisance to a unified worldview, whether religious or secular. Modernism exposed tensions between conformity and individualism and between nature and the embrace of technology. In the mid-twentieth century, American theorist and art critic Clement Greenberg embraced abstraction, not as an end in itself but as a means of directing the viewer's eye to where it should be: the formal aspects of a work. In many ways the solo dancer epitomizes modernism, as becomes apparent throughout this volume.

Everyone with an interest in dance knows the big names—Loïe Fuller, Isadora Duncan, Ruth St. Denis, Maud Allan—but there is a longer, richer, more diverse phenomenon to be explored. This book presents an international roster of male and female soloists who worked from the late nineteenth century into the twenty-first, and who offer opportunities to launch arguments about what it means to be modern.

Eight scholars contributed essays. Although they worked independently, a common theme emerges from their work. That solo artists shape cultural attitudes is the volume's overarching topic. In the early years of the twentieth century dance soloists gave intellectuals an opportunity to react to modernism. One essay contends that soloists in the 1920s affected the public's confidence in the freedom of bodies that are alone. In another essay readers follow Daniel Nagrin's solo career as he led American audiences in the 1940s and 1950s to broaden their perspectives on the male dancer, and in another we watch Ann Carlson's tribute to spontaneity as she performs with live animals. Readers meet soloists who carry culture across borders and see careers that offer solutions to the dilemma of individuality and aloneness.

Largely absent from dance literature, soloists also face public policy in the United States that works to direct attention away from solo artists. In the 1980s the National Endowment for the Arts refocused its original mission to foster artistic creation and initiated a program to acquaint Americans with the best of their cultural and artistic legacy. Irving Sandler, former chair of the Oversight Committee for the Visual Arts, laments that the NEA has become the "National Endowment for education about the Arts."[1] The American Masterpieces funding program, laudable for supporting education and reconstruction of past work, has in effect drawn funds away from innovative and experimental artists, among whom solo performers must be numbered.

Despite this neglect there is today renewed interest in the solo form. A pilot master's degree program in Solo Dance Authorship is being tested at Universität der Kunste in Berlin.[2] A meeting convened in Paris by Le Centre

National de la Danse in 2000 was dedicated to solo dancing and led to the publication of a collection of essays, *La Danse en solo*.[3] The American scholar Susan Leigh Foster has written about methods of training dance soloists by master educators Louis Horst, Daniel Nagrin, and Douglas Dunn.[4] *On Stage Alone* contributes significantly to this ongoing international discourse.

Accounts of modern concert dance place its beginning at the end of the nineteenth century in the achievements of the Americans Fuller, Duncan, St. Denis, and Allan. Elizabeth Kendall writes about them in *Where She Danced: The Birth of American Art Dance*, published in 1979, the same year that Nancy Lee Chalfa Ruyter's *Reformers and Visionaries: The Americanization of the Art of Dance* appeared. Ann Daly's focused *Done into Dance: Isadora Duncan in America* is one of many biographies of individual forerunners, recent among them Rhonda Garelick's *Electric Salome: Loïe Fuller's Performance of Modernism*.[5] These fine scholarly works have been used by some teachers and students as a means of demonstrating American authorship of modern dance.

Recent scholarship has confronted this notion. Writing in 1993, Susan Manning quotes critics and dancers in the 1930s who, she argues, mythologized the American genesis of the form.[6] In his 1998 book *Alien Bodies* Ramsay Burt convincingly establishes connections between European and American modern dance, placing them in political context.[7] Carrie Preston's new book, *Modernism's Mythic Pose: Gender, Genre, Solo Performance*, reminds us that modern dance and other new arts of the twentieth century were aesthetically justified by the French theorist of acting technique François Delsarte.[8]

On Stage Alone is not a polemic that directly confronts the notion of American exceptionalism, but its international format significantly complicates the idea. Readers meet European soloists whose careers overlapped, or even preceded, those of the American precursors. In the middle decades of the twentieth century, while modern dance practitioners, audiences, and critics in the United States turned their attention to dance companies created by skilled, charismatic performers, soloists continued to be a major stage presence elsewhere in the world. In the twenty-first century, audiences in the United States are drawn to soloists from Asia, South America, and Africa as well as from Europe and the United States. Several find a place in this volume.

The lone dancer-choreographer is granted a flexibility denied to dance companies burdened with corporate apparatus—managers, agents, publicists, fundraisers, and so forth. Choreographer–company directors are responsible for maintaining the allegiance of audiences they have attracted in the past. Readers learn that soloists, too, are influenced by audience expectations and managerial requirements, their own or a promoter's. Removing oneself from the support of other performers and from the relative safety of learning and presenting choreography created by a leader, however, requires courage and permits risk taking. Reviewing a solo recital in 1944, Edwin Denby, dean of dance critics in mid-twentieth-century America, recognized the versatility required of a soloist, remarking that serious solo programs call for risks in expression. He warned one dancer, Merce Cunningham, that he was too cautious to carry a solo program.[9]

The interlacing of aesthetic and social discourse becomes starkly apparent from time to time. Paul Taylor's well-known four-minute 1957 solo *Epic* incited a "review" of four inches of blank space in a prominent dance publication.[10] Karen Finley's 1989 solo performance in which she slathered her nearly naked body with melted chocolate so enraged the United States Congress that a grant approved by the National Endowment for the Arts was withdrawn.[11]

On Stage Alone groups essays by relevant themes. First, Carrie Preston, Ramsay Burt, and Janice Ross build theory arising from the solo. Launching from the solo career of the Japanese-American dancer Michio Ito, Preston takes a wide-angle view of dance historiography. She maintains that critical desires of soloists, audiences, and dance writers shape how each confronts master narratives of self-expression, nationality, and race. Burt launches his essay from a coincidence in 1919 Switzerland where Vaslav Nijinsky gave a solo concert in St. Moritz as he was going mad, and in Davos Mary Wigman performed the first solo concert of her many solo tours. Burt's deeply textured argument raises questions about bonds connecting aloneness, relationality, and becoming ecstatic. Ross confronts the dilemma of a soloist's aloneness by studying works that Ann Carlson creates with and about animals, contrasting spontaneity and the carefully scripted. Carlson's solos, contends Ross, also have the power to destabilize assumptions about gender identity.

Karl Toepfer and Julie Malnig focus attention on the modern body. In his text and with many photographic images, Toepfer proposes that by frankly exposing their bodies, soloists in 1920s Europe took a crucial and necessary step toward the individuality inherent in modernism. Malnig concentrates on Maud Allan, who, Malnig argues, legitimized aspects of women that threatened Victorian values lingering in the early twentieth century. Allan danced the carnal woman in her solo *The Vision of Salome*; the chaste in her symbolist-inspired union with nature; and the self-aware "new woman" of the 1920s in her life and the management of her career.

Sandra Meyer, Deborah Jowitt, and Renée D'Aoust address questions of racial, gender, and national difference. Meyer studies pioneer soloist Eros Volúsia, who helped to construct a new Brazilian dance by promoting Afro-Brazilian culture and connecting it to dance modernism, an objective carried on today by Luiz de Abreu. Jowitt, in her essay about Daniel Nagrin, describes a repertory of solos about men, which broadened audience experience of masculinity on stage. Launching from contemporary Swiss choreographer Anna Huber, D'Aoust explores differences in arts funding in Europe and the United States. She argues that Huber's innovative conceptual work is not possible without the financial stability provided by several levels of government support.

No single book can recognize all soloists who design and perform concerts exclusively of their own work. From readers who miss an artist who fits within the book's parameters, we beg forbearance. This book is a paean to all modern dance soloists who both author and mediate their work through performance. Reading about cultural attitudes shaped by the artists studied here valorizes the work of all who dance alone.

Notes

1. Sandler responds to William Safire's op-ed column "A Gloria to Behold," *New York Times*, March 8, 2004, praising NEA action. Sandler's rebuttal, "The Government and 'Edgy' Artists," appeared March 10, 2004, as a letter to the editor.

2. A two-year, full-time performance-oriented MA focused on "the making, composition, critical understanding and dissemination of body-based performance

work and its contextualization within the wider field of contemporary arts and cultural practices" is described in an online prospectus, www.udk-Berlin.de.

3. Claire Rousier, ed., *La Danse en solo: Une Figure singulière de la modernité* (Pantin: Centre National de la Danse, 2002). At this writing there are no plans for an English translation.

4. Susan Leigh Foster, "Making a Dance/Research through Movement," in *Landscapes for Performance as Research: Scholarly Arts and Creative Cartographies*, ed. Shannon Rose Riley and Lynette Hunter (New York: Palgrave Macmillan, 2009).

5. Elizabeth Kendall, *Where She Danced: The Birth of American Art Dance* (Berkeley: University of California Press, 1979); Nancy Lee Chalfa Ruyter, *Reformers and Visionaries: The Americanization of the Art of Dance* (New York: Dance Horizons, 1979); Ann Daly, *Done into Dance: Isadora Duncan in America* (Bloomington: Indiana University Press, 1995); Rhonda K. Garelick, *Electric Salome: Loïe Fuller's Performance of Modernism* (Princeton, N.J.: Princeton University Press, 2007).

6. Susan Manning, *Ecstasy and the Demon: Feminism and Nationalism in the Dances of Mary Wigman* (Berkeley: University of California Press, 1993), 257–65.

7. See chapter 6, "Dancing Across the Atlantic," in Ramsay Burt, *Alien Bodies: Representations of Modernity, "Race" and Nation in Early Modern Dance* (London: Routledge, 1998).

8. Carrie Preston, *Modernism's Mythic Pose: Gender, Genre, Solo Performance* (New York: Oxford University Press, 2011).

9. Denby reviewed (favorably) Merce Cunningham's debut solo concert in the *New York Herald Tribune*, April 11, 1944, reprinted in *Dance Writings/Edwin Denby*, ed. Robert Cornfield and William Mackay (New York: Alfred A. Knopf, 1986), 284.

10. Louis Horst, *Dance Observer*, November 1957, 139.

11. For a summary of congressional debate and Supreme Court deliberation, see Allison O'Brien, "Government Watch," *Dance/USA*, Summer 1998.

one

Michio Ito's Shadow

Searching for the Transnational
in Solo Dance

Carrie J. Preston

Michio Ito (1893–1961) included more than two hundred
dancers in his Pageant of Lights at the Rose Bowl, but the *Pasadena Star
News* of September 21, 1929, claimed that the massive ensemble was over-
shadowed by his ninety-five-second closing solo, *Pizzicati* or *Shadow Dance*.[1]
The audience demanded an encore of Ito's signature solo to a section of Delibes's ballet *Sylvia*, as had the audience for his first concert in the United
States in December 1916.

The *New York Sun* review complained that music by Delibes and other
"Occidentals" undermined the "national peculiarities" of the Tokyo-born
performer's so-called "Japanese Dancing."[2] Ito's *Pizzicati* demonstrates few
"national peculiarities," and a spectator not looking for the advertized "Japaneseness" might have recognized the choreography as an example of the
"music visualizations" common in Euro-American modern dance of that
period.[3] The feet remain planted in a wide second position while the arms
and hands thrust and circle with flicking wrists to the vigorous and playful

7

rhythms. As the music shifts to a more melodious and legato section, the arms sweep across the body and the torso twists and lifts. Ito's student Kyoko Ryutani reported that Ito taught dancers to imagine a "marionette" moved by strings attached to fingers.[4] The plucked strings of the pizzicato section figuratively control the body, which falls as the music ends like a puppet when the lines are cut. At the Rose Bowl, Ito was lit from below so that his shadow loomed over the stage; a solo, or perhaps a dancer's duet with his shadow, eclipsed the Pageant of Lights.

Early reviews of Ito's work were preoccupied with his "Japaneseness" or "Oriental dance" and the relative value of his solos and ensemble pieces. Current critics have not resolved these tensions in discussions of a career that traveled from Japan to Germany, Britain, and the United States and included Hollywood films, versions of Japanese *noh* and *kyogen* dramas, and orientalist revues. Ito produced many of the latter for the United States military after he was imprisoned as a spy (although never criminally charged) and deported in 1943 to Japan, where he was hired to entertain postwar occupying forces. After long neglect, Ito's choreography, but primarily his solos, began to be reintroduced to the United States in the late 1970s. Reviews of this "rediscovery" celebrate Ito as an expressive soloist and insist that his choreography is not "ethnic" but "a marriage of East and West."[5] This construction of Ito's career fulfills two critical desires related to anxiety about culture, nationality, and ethnicity: as a soloist, Ito fits comfortably into the standard narrative that American modern dance originated as a solo genre; second, his solos are more easily understood as choreographies of cultural fusion or transnationalism than as dances employing exoticism and orientalism.

Edward Said's classic study, *Orientalism* (1978), describes "a style of thought" in which academics, artists, and politicians define the so-called West against a generic East in a manner that supports Western imperialism.[6] Transnationalism is thought to designate a very different engagement with cultural diversity, one that examines how cultural forms cross borders to reveal affiliations transcending national identities; it is one of the most exciting and productive methodologies for studies of dance and modernism more generally.[7] While it is tempting to suggest that Ito's dance theories anticipated current models of transnationalism, such claims often suppress the ways in which his choreography both adopted orientalist tropes and troubled our pieties about "bad" orientalism and "good" multiculturalism.

Ito's desire for cultural fusion coexisted with his orientalism. His career suggests that transnational approaches can be usefully applied to cultural representations that do not comply with current standards of sensitivity, including the many orientalist dances that were at the center of American modern dance innovation. As my discussion of Ito's current critical reception reveals, standards have not changed since his first performances to the degree we might wish. I do not intend to provoke shame about our struggles to approach global cultures or propose a new "good" diversity. I suggest that transnational perspectives are problematic but necessary, shaped by misunderstanding and, as Ito demonstrates, remarkable creativity.

Ito is often described as the "all-but-forgotten pioneer of American modern dance," but his choreography is beginning to be remembered after several reconstructions and important critical assessments by Mary-Jean Cowell, Midori Takeishi, and Yutian Wong.[8] My summary of Ito's career focuses on his work in the solo form. While the "recovery" of his solos by American dance companies fulfills the assumptions of dance history, it marginalizes his multidisciplinary art. Ito's early but brief training in *nihon buyo,* or Japanese dance, from 1911 to 1912 may have stimulated his interest in solo performance.[9] Nihon buyo and other traditional Japanese performance arts such as noh are usually taught in private lessons; the student masters a set repertory, and solos dominate both amateur and professional performances.[10]

In the first example of Ito's transnational aesthetic studies, he traveled to Germany in 1912 to study opera, but—partially inspired by Isadora Duncan—he shifted his aspirations to dance and attended Émile Jaques-Dalcroze's school in Hellerau for a year. Dalcrozian eurhythmics emphasized improvisational movement, individual bodily experiences of musical rhythms and forms, and unique compositions, rather than a particular dance technique or repertory.[11] This pedagogy was very different from Ito's nihon buyo lessons, but both emphasized solo performance.

At Hellerau, Ito would also have come into contact with the ideology of individualism and emphasis on self-expression that suffused this period in modern dance and early twentieth-century performance more generally. A celebration of the individual is prevalent in Isadora Duncan's famous description of "Art" as "an effort to express the truth of my Being in gesture and movement."[12] Ito similarly claimed in a 1919 brochure for his school, "My dance is an expression of my feeling through the medium of the movement of my body.... Every one has his own feeling and his own expression; dance as you feel and as you want—that is a better dance for you than any other kind."[13] As the contributions to this book reveal, solos were the perfect genre for dancers hoping to remake their art and their self.

Less acknowledged is the role of popular Delsartism from about 1880 to 1920 in promoting expressive solo performance. Delsartism was an international movement loosely derived from the work of French performance theorist François Delsarte (1811–71).[14] Initially Delsarte popularized solo declamation and attitudes displaying the "passions," but the diverse trajectories of the movement developed additional solo forms; statue-posing in postures imitating Greek art was particularly popular.

Most trajectories of Delsartism shared a commitment to recovering an "authentic" and "expressive" self that was thought to have been present in ancient Greece but to have been destroyed by Western modernity. Henrietta Hovey, an early American exponent, claimed that Delsartism would liberate a "real self" that "may struggle in vain for expression through the one body [man's], which labor has narrowed down to a machine only speaking of labor; or the other [woman's], which respectability has stiffened up, till it can only express 'respectability.'"[15] Ted Shawn had studied Delsartism extensively with Hovey and invited her to teach at the school he and Ruth St. Denis founded in 1915, where she influenced a generation of modern dancers.[16] Delsartism also shaped Dalcroze's teachings, particularly his emphasis on how bodily motion could express music.[17] As Delsartism linked the solo with "true" expression, soloists became popular among audiences, which in turn affected the publicity for modern dancers. Duncan's first American tour in 1908 was billed as "a feat of endurance never previously seen outside of Europe . . . the first example of a single artist devoting a whole evening to dancing."[18] Of course, a number of solo dancers and Delsartean performers, including Hovey, had previously occupied stages wearing the "Greek" tunics Duncan promoted.

The popularity of solos and their association with shaping identity were a crucial part of the performance milieu Ito encountered at Hellerau and after he moved to London in 1914. If Delsartism and Duncan advocated mythic Greece as an escape from the stultifying effects of modernity, other artists sought new modes of expression in the aesthetic traditions of Asia, the Middle East, and Africa as well as the "folk."[19] Both profiting from and encouraging these interests, Ito began his professional performing career as a soloist in the fashionable salons of London, initially for Lady Ottoline Morrell in November 1914. Ito's memoir describes how he attempted to refuse to dance because he did not have a costume, but Morrell produced "magnificent sheiks costumes . . . the gold thread glistened."[20]

Ito would continue to encounter audience expectations of a generically "oriental" costume, in this case one loosely derived from the Middle East. He wrote of his first professional engagement in May 1915 at the Coliseum Theatre, a music hall in London, "Because I was billed as 'The Japanese Dancer' I had to create a 'Japanese' atmosphere. All my dances were original however. I danced a programme based on *Shojo* and *Kitsune* and sometimes even wore *eboshi* [formal black hat] and *nagabakama* [a long, pleated split skirt] as well."[21] Kitsune refers to the fox featured in Japanese folklore and theater, such as a kyogen play Ito translated in 1923 as *The Fox's Grave*.[22] *Shojo* is a noh play about the Chinese spirit of wine, and a photograph by Alvin Langdon Coburn shows Ito in Japanese costume and holding a wine ladle, Shojo's customary prop.[23] The stage designer Charles Ricketts and the painter and illustrator Edmund Dulac probably created the costume for Ito's 1915 solo recitals in London (fig. 1.1).

The tension Ito suggests between his "original" choreography and the "'Japanese' atmosphere" expected by music hall audiences led him to privilege his solos very early in his career. In a 1915 letter to Lady Ottoline Morrell, Ito announced that he would be giving three evenings of performances "alone" at a "theatre studio in Melbury Road in Kensington. The little theatre studio is charming [and] much better than the Coloseum [sic] for my work."[24] As if to assure her further that he had not become a music hall performer, he insisted, "I am still very faithful to my Art." Ito's solo recitals in Kensington and at the Margaret Morris Theatre in London (1916) were primarily promoted and attended by artists who were exploring non-Western art and culture, such as Ricketts, Dulac, Ezra Pound, and W. B. Yeats. If they, like Coliseum audiences, expected a "Japanese atmosphere," these artists also requested his help in experiments and adaptations involving the performance traditions of Japan. They viewed Ito as a reliable source of information and inspiration in spite of his protests; when Pound asked him to help translate noh plays, Ito replied that "as far as I'm concerned there's nothing more boring. Besides I couldn't presume to assist you."[25] Ito is mentioned in studies of modernism primarily owing to his choreography and performance in *At the Hawk's Well* (1916), Yeats's noh-inspired dramatization of Irish legend. Much work remains to clarify his collaboration with Yeats and later contributions to modernist drama.

Ito's transnational journey continued when, shortly after his dance in *At the Hawk's Well*, the United States producer Oliver Morosco offered Ito a contract for a play in New York. He managed to be released from the engagement, which he claimed was a lewd comedy far below his artistic standards.[26] As in London, Ito's United States career from 1916 to 1943 was characterized by tensions surrounding his desire to be a solo concert dancer, performing an "original" and "universal" art, rather than a "Japanese dancer" or the diverse performer/entertainer/director he actually became. His multifaceted career is not fully accounted for by dance history or performance studies, partially because Ito tended to celebrate his solo work but also because of critical discomfort with the exoticism in his popular performances.

Even in his solo dances, Ito appealed to the common orientalist tropes that postulated a mystical East as a counterpoint to the West as well as the similar but slightly more specific fascination of Japonisme. He mixed both with his desire to represent the Japanese performance traditions that were a formative part of his early training and cultural experience, a desire encouraged by Euro-American modernist artists such as Yeats and Pound. All these modes appear, often in a single performance, suggesting that his entire career is best understood through a flexible transnational perspective, rather than an orientalist or Americanist approach.

Ito's first New York concert in December 1916 introduced *Pizzicati* along with four other solos that developed Japanese themes, listed in the program as *Japanese Fisher Song, Mai no Hagime: Introduction to Dancing, Hangia: Female Demon, Fox Dance,* and *Shojo: The Spirit of Wine, a Symbol of Happiness* (see fig. 1.1).[27] Throughout 1916 and 1917 he expanded his repertory

1.1. Michio Ito in Japanese costume, 1915. Photograph by
Alvin Langdon Coburn. Courtesy of George Eastman House,
International Museum of Photography and Film.

with solos such as *Sword Dance*, which included noh-style chanting by the painter Ri-ichiro Kawashima, and others like *Golliwog's Cake Walk* (1917), which exploited the fascination with folk and African American dancing.[28] In August 1917 Ito joined Ballet Intime, a company established by former Ballets Russes dancer Adolph Bolm to feature soloists in "ethnic dances," all celebrated for their "Mystic Oriental Atmosphere."[29] Demonstrating the flexibility with which the construct could be applied, "Oriental" appears repeatedly in the promotional material and reviews that identify Bolm as a "Russian," describe Tulle Lindahl as "a Scandinavian dancer," and celebrate the "East Indian dances" of "Roshanara," the daughter of a British official in the colonial government of India.[30]

Ito also staged his own adaptations of Japanese kyogen plays and the Ezra Pound/Ernest Fenollosa translations of noh at the Neighborhood Playhouse and Greenwich Village Theater, and he restaged Yeats's *At the Hawk's Well* with new music by the Japanese composer Koscak Yamada in New York in 1918, Los Angeles in 1929, and Japan in 1939. He danced in revues like the *Greenwich Village Follies* (with Martha Graham), worked on orientalist productions including the operetta *The Mikado* and the opera *Madame Butterfly* (both in 1927), and choreographed lavish spectacles such as the Pageant of Lights. As Mary-Jean Cowell has detailed, he worked on six Hollywood films, which generally supported orientalist stereotypes and Western colonial enterprises.[31]

Ito continued to perform concerts of his own choreography along with these diverse performance ventures, and Cowell suggests that "Ito probably considered his film work a financial convenience unrelated to his career as a concert dance artist and teacher."[32] She points out that José Limón, Lester Horton, Martha Graham, most of the Denishawn company, and many other modern dancers performed in films and the popular theater. Dance historians often echo the dancers in privileging concert work and dismissing the popular performances undertaken for economic and other reasons, but they may need to revise definitions of what a dance career meant at this time. Ito's memoir claimed that very few could make a "profession of dancing" and distinguished between "artistic work," when he could be "completely absorbed," and "subsistence employment" or "bread-and-butter jobs" that forced him to follow the "requirements" of an employer. He appears to have been surprised by early assessments of his career: "Recently, when I was reading the section on Michio Ito in a book called *History of American Dancing*, I discovered that I was considered a pioneer of American artistic dance, responsible for introducing Modern French Music to America through dance."[33] He contradicts the assessment: "Actually, I had only danced seriously to Debussy and Ravel. . . . Broadway took up more of my time." The tendency for critics to treat him as a "concert dancer" and avoid both his popular work and his contributions to modernist performance has become even more prominent with the recent "recovery" of Ito's choreography, which has featured his solos.

In the late 1970s Satoru Shimazaki began performing Ito's work in New York, and in 1979 he presented a full-evening concert of twenty-four pieces from Ito's repertory. Solos dominated the program, and several of the small group compositions originated as solos but were later expanded by Ito or his Tokyo students.[34] Ito's *Ecclesiastique I* (1922, Schumann) and *Ladybug* (1923 and 1929 for an ensemble, Chopin) originated as solos, and *En Bateau* (1929, Debussy) was performed in 1923 as a solo entitled *The Blue Waves*.[35] Shimazaki performed in 1996 with Dana Tai Soon Burgess, director of the Washington, D.C.–based Asian American dance company, and as recently as 2004–5 Burgess included *Four Solos by Michio Ito* with his own *Tracings*, a long piece exploring Korean immigration to the United States.[36] University of Washington professor Hannah Wiley worked with Taeko Furushu and Kumiko Komine to reconstruct five solos for the University of Washington's Chamber Dance Company in 2001, with performances repeated in 2006.[37] Most recently, Kyoko Ryutani and Kumiko Komine set eleven pieces on Utah's Repertory Dance Theatre, and although they staged several as small group pieces, all but one were originally performed as solos.[38] Responses to these performances of Ito's choreography and an analysis of several better-known solos reveal prevalent assumptions about American modern dance history and its representations of culture.

Most reviews of the reconstructed Ito dances attempt to situate Ito as a forgotten pioneer in the established history of American dance, and this task is far easier in relation to his solo pieces than large pageants or the mixed genre of dance plays. The "modern dance master narrative," as summarized by Mark Franko, describes the first generation of modern dancers as self-expressive soloists "typified by Isadora Duncan"; they were replaced by a second generation of dancers who expunged "self-expression" to produce systematic training techniques and choreographies of modernist innovation.[39] This story ignores the continuing influence of Delsartism and related movements emphasizing self-expression. As Franko points out, it adheres to prevalent narratives of modernism, which often cite such claims as T. S. Eliot's: "The progress of an artist is a continual self-sacrifice, a continual extinction of personality."[40] The influence of the "modern dance master narrative" is evident in reviews such as Jack Anderson's "Satoru Shimazaki, Soloist," which positions Shimazaki in the "tradition" of "such choreographic pioneers as Isadora Duncan, Mary Wigman and Michio Ito [who] often presented solo concerts notable for their emotional candor."[41] The narrative suggests that self-expression had to be abandoned for modernist technique, and as if to advance Ito in this narrative, Cowell claims that Ito actually beat the second generation to a system: "Ito seems to have had a systematic, if eclectic, approach to training before the development of Graham or Humphrey-Weidman technique."[42] Framing Ito as more advanced than his contemporaries reinforces rather than undermines the master narrative of modern dance—which, of course, "forgot" Ito. As Yutian Wong powerfully argues, the "rehabilitative move" suggests that Ito is "worthy of canonization" but implies that the source of his "exclusion" was the failures of contemporaneous critics rather than "the continued practice of writing dance history," a practice that has not interrogated its own "politics of whiteness."[43]

In a related attempt to position Ito comfortably (and we should be wary of comfort) in American modern dance history, reviewers attempt to establish his choreography as more individualist and less orientalist than that of other modern dancers. Describing Ito as "a charismatic soloist in an age of soloists," the influential dance historian Marcia B. Siegel critiqued Shimazaki's performance for lacking "Ito's passion, his magnetism" and for failing to understand "how possessed" a soloist must be in "this genre."[44] Although she refers to Ito's "Japanese origin" as "unique," she presents him as a typical soloist and suggests, "Everyone was doing exotica, so his choice of subject matter from foreign and ancient cultures wasn't unusual." She even argues that he exploited "exotic" dance less than his contemporaries, contrasting his work with the "personality-blitz solos of Ruth St. Denis," continuing,

"Although Ito staged some Noh-style spectacles . . . his [solo] concert work appears little touched by Orientalisms." Ito's presentation of noh plays, such as the Pound/Fenollosa translation of *Tamura* at the Neighborhood Playhouse (1918 and 1921), contributed to American orientalism, but so did Ito's solo pieces like *Shojo*, which may have drawn from the Pound/Fenollosa translation.[45] Ito had performed a version of *Shojo: The Spirit of Wine* in London, but he remade the dance in collaboration with the composer Charles Griffes, whose innovative score reworked the Japanese melodies "Nen nen korori" and "Chidori no Kyoku," probably supplied by Ito.[46] Such collaborations, utilizing Ito's familiarity with Japanese music, often produced interesting performances, but his choreographic impressions of Japanese and other Asian themes did not depart markedly from those of his contemporaries. The difference in audience responses, both then and now, is largely because Ito was Japanese; our assumptions about the importance of his country of birth give him the authority to reinterpret Japan's performance traditions.

Siegel did not see Ito's *Shojo* or many other choreographies of Japanese themes on Shimazaki's program. Cowell suggests that Ito preserved few of what she calls his "Oriental works" because they "would seem too pseudo-Oriental in his native land."[47] Yet Ito staged spectacular revues such as *Fantasia Japonica* as director of the Ernie Pyle Theater (formerly the Tokyo Takarazuka Gekijo) for the American military forces occupying Japan after his repatriation; he appears to have been concerned about the desires of his audience rather than "pseudo-Orientalia."[48] Ito's *Warrior*, also known as *Prelude VI* (1927, Scriabin), does demonstrate the influence of Japanese performance techniques, but Siegel's review claims it "looks less Japanese than Ted Shawn's." The comment indicates that Shawn's piece conforms to conventional styles of performed orientalism that have little to do with nationality. Siegel appears to attribute orientalism to the costumes, props, and dramatic narrative of Shawn's *Japanese Spear Dance* rather than to the choreographed movement.

Fascinated by samurai culture, Shawn created the dance to music by Louis Horst in 1919. As reconstructed by Jeffrey B. Hankinson, the warrior wears a white mask and carries a large halberd, both resembling those used in noh performance.[49] A headband and loincloth vaguely resembling Native American dress complete the costume and mix primitive stereotypes from different cultures. The choreography, dominated by leg extensions with a flexed foot and deep pliés from second position with heels and halberd raised high, does not resemble either samurai swordplay or its theatrical representation in noh. In the dramatic conceit of the piece, the warrior is injured, bandages his arm, and then, in a gesture that made the audience for the reconstruction laugh, pulls out a fan and performs a lyrical dance before taking up the halberd again. The piece is an early example of Shawn's work to adapt modern dance primitivism for choreography that would emphasize strength and aggression, movement qualities traditionally associated with masculinity.

Ito's *Warrior*, as reconstructed most recently by Ryutani and Komine for Repertory Dance Theatre, includes some choreography that might have been drawn from Japanese performance traditions, particularly movement forms or *kata* from the warrior dances in noh and nihon buyo. That audiences do not respond with laughter is not because the choreography is "less Japanese" but because it is less like other contemporaneous orientalist choreographies. Instead of including props like a halberd, Ito choreographs arm positions that mimic holding a spear and shield. Rather than a dramatic story of injury and recovery, the piece uses these positions and the physical strength and tension associated with the warrior to create complex bodily shapes and floor patterns. The prevailing leg movement consists of stamping, which is also common in noh and nihon buyo choreography, and a distinctive march with toe hitting first and heel following to create a syncopated rhythm, which may show the influence of Ito's Dalcroze training. Throughout the piece, the torso is thrust forward with head raised and knees slightly bent to create a low, grounded quality, resembling the standard posture in both noh (called *kamae*) and nihon buyo (*katachi*). In *Warrior* this posture contributes to the impression of a continuous, contained energy driving the movement forward; Shawn's choreography, in contrast, resembles a sequence of distinct poses. Ito's dance ends with a leap and fall to the knee, and while the knee plant in noh and nihon buyo often marks a vigorous battle, the closing movement of *Warrior* conveys strength without being linked to narratives of defeat or triumph.

Shawn's *Japanese Spear Dance* must be analyzed in relation to danced orientalism, but Ito's *Warrior* could be described without reference to nihon buyo and noh. The comparison between Ito's dance and these traditional performance forms is potentially useful because Ito studied buyo and adapted noh plays, and because bodily techniques, training regimens, and cultural habits can shape choreography. Ito was aware that audiences would associate his work with Japanese art, and like most performers, he worked to fulfill the desires of his audience. Still, determining the extent and significance of the influence of nihon buyo and noh is difficult, and I am wary of assuming a culture-of-birth determinism that would bind Ito's nationality to his choreography in spite of many other transnational influences. This concern, along with an awareness of how artists are marginalized by the prejudices invoked by national labels, leads Siegel to claim that Ito's choreography is "less Japanese" than Shawn's but also to elide "Japaneseness" and orientalism problematically. National, ethnic, and other identity categories lack ontological coherence, as poststructuralism has taught us, but they still have very real functions in the world. They can be used precisely for their descriptive value and with awareness of their potential pitfalls.

One such pitfall is the ahistorical assumption that Ito's choreography, unlike Shawn's, must demonstrate what we might now call "cultural sensitivity" and a commitment to "authenticity." Ito did not share the current critical preoccupation with distinguishing the appropriation and exploitation of cultural forms from their "legitimate" reinterpretation—concerns that stem from a history of Western imperialism that stole art objects and destroyed traditions as well as from continued racism and political inequality. Although she does not mention Ito, Nancy Lee Chalfa Ruyter provocatively addresses these problems in her analysis of the American dancer La Meri (1898–1988); she suggests that La Meri's performances of East Indian dance differed from the "'Orientalist' presentations" of Shawn, Ruth St. Denis, and others because she attempted to study the dances with what Ruyter calls "native teachers" and present them as authentically as possible.[50] According to Ruyter, authenticity is not an "absolute" or inherent trait of a performance but a quality that audiences interpret and a "conception that may be understood and used in different ways."[51]

Ruyter's formulation of "authenticity" is compelling, but all discussions of cultural representation, "ethnic" dance, and traditional performance tend to bear an ethnocentric if well-intentioned bias: we rarely ask about an "authentic" ballet dance in the same way we concern ourselves with "authentic" noh or nihon buyo movement. Owing to asymmetric political and cultural influence, it would seem absurd to claim that Ito as a Japanese native appropriated American modern dance. Ito disturbs the categories we have used to negotiate the orientalism of modern dance ("native teacher," "authentic performance," "reinterpretation or fusion," "cultural appropriation") because he worked across all of these categories and combined them in unique ways. Ito occasionally presented himself as a "native teacher," offering a long, not always correct history on the noh theater to the *Boston Post* in 1921 and promising to use the "Japanese system" to train American performers capable of producing noh. In the same interview, he insisted that his art was "'Michio Itow's dance' rather than 'Japanese dance.'"[52] Ito also took up the dance forms of foreign cultures in choreographies that complicate simplistic ideas of "reinterpretation" and "appropriation," three of which were included in Shimazaki's program: *Tango* (1927, Albeniz), *Impressions of Persia* (date unknown, to an unspecified Persian folk song), and *Spanish Fan Dance* (1929, Sarasate).

Ito's surprising and popular *Tango* has been a feature of nearly every reconstruction of his choreography in the past decades. He made a solo of the tango, a duet form that emerged in the late nineteenth century from the Río de la Plata regions of Argentina and Uruguay, influenced by African, Spanish, and South American popular dance forms. Ito's choreography responds to the tango enthusiasm then gripping Europe and the United States, but as Marta E. Savigliano points out, "Tango's international popularity, dating to the 1910s, has been associated with an erotic scandal: the public display of passion performed by a heterosexual couple, the symbol of which is a tight embrace and suggestive footwork."[53] Ito dispensed with both partner and tango-esque footwork but wore a black suit with wide-bottom pants and brimmed hat reminiscent of the Argentinean *compadrito* style. Ito's choreographic innovation is his ability to retain the passion and erotic interest of the tango in the solo form.

Throughout the piece the dancer repeatedly looks intently along the forward right diagonal, a gaze that seems to position the missing partner in that corner. Indicating the gravity of this focus, the dancer carves the stage into lines, stepping alternately along the vertical and diagonal with low leg extensions and twists of the upper body that reinforce its linearity. A similar alternation between forward movement and a stationary, deliberate shifting of weight from leg to leg creates a feeling of contained energy and suppressed desire. The hands remain on the hips for the first half of the dance, so it is surprising and exciting when, following an abrupt change in the music, the dancer snaps his fingers above his head and flicks his foot back with quick shifts of direction and low lunges. This brief sequence bears some resemblance to tango steps, but as the music repeats the opening rhythm, the dancer returns his hands to hips and replicates the first measured steps. The choreography surprises again when, after an almost continuous diagonal focus, the soloist abruptly looks out to the audience and extends a hand, as if to say, "Come dance with me. It's you I've wanted all along." Ito's solo manipulates the passion associated with the tango so that the audience becomes the object of that desire.

Ito created innovative and crowd-pleasing choreography by drawing from the various performance traditions available to him: modern dance's exoticism and enthusiasm for ethnic dances like the tango, his training in Japanese performance forms and Dalcrozian eurhythmics, and the popular interest in expressive solo performance. In *Pizzicati*, described at the beginning of the chapter, Ito wore a belted jacket and baggy cinched pants, a costume that resembled the uniform of a martial artist and was perceived as "oriental" by reviewers. Ito's focus on movements of the arms and upper body may have been influenced by a similar emphasis in nihon buyo, noh, and other Japanese performance forms, but the alternately angular and curving arm motions were also influenced by Dalcrozian exercises in the gestural interpretation of music. Ito's marionette image and shadow effect reflect modernist theatrical innovations, which he connects with Japanese performance, claiming "the ideas of European stage-artists of that time such as Gordon Craig and Max Reinhardt were really nothing but Noh."[54]

Craig's famous essay associated "The Actor and the Über-Marionette," and he constructed screens for Yeats's *At the Hawk's Well* and other modernist performances, a design that may have influenced Ito's screen in *Pizzicati*.[55] Regardless of these modernist influences, the widely repeated, probably apocryphal myth of the origins of Ito's famous dance opposed his "Eastern" aesthetics to Anna Pavlova's "Western" balletics. After Pavlova danced to

Delibes's *Pizzicati* "on her toes" for Ito, she invited him to perform: "Having no music, he asked the pianist to play the same piece again and planting his feet firmly on the floor he danced the entire dance using only his arms and hands."[56] Benefiting from the star power of Pavlova and the trope of improvisational genius, the story also reinforces the assumed opposition between East and West, a rhetoric that continues to shape interpretations of Ito's dance today.

A 1916 New York review of Ito's solos announced, "East is East and West is West, but—Kipling notwithstanding—next week the two will meet."[57] Listing the primitivisms touring American stages with "Hawaiian," "Salomé," "Apache," and "classic dancers," the reviewer claims, "Now for the first time we shall see a new Terpsichore, with eyebrows slanted and wearing a kimono." The persistence of the overgeneralized constructs in the first line of "The Ballad of East and West" (1898) is evident in George Jackson's review of a 2002 performance that included four Ito solos: "'Oh, East is West and West is East, and ever the twain shall merge' is how Dana Tai Soon Burgess might rewrite Kipling's much-quoted poem."[58] Mystique: East Meets West was the title of Repertory Dance Theatre's 2010 concert. The laudable effort to stage a "meeting" actually maintains underlying assumptions about the essential qualities and differences of East and West. As contemporary reviewers, dance companies, and audiences mirror Ito's early twentieth-century context, they demonstrate the prevalence of a thought pattern that carves the world into two polarizing halves. Critics are not exempt, and Edward Said's retrospective *Orientalism* warns that it is "a structure of attitudes that cannot simply be waved away or discounted," even as it takes new political, artistic, and scholarly forms.[59]

How then to best analyze Ito's work and that of other dancers and artists who represent cultures with indecipherable mixtures of authenticity, essentialism, appropriation, and creativity? The best critics writing on Ito have tried to absolve him of orientalism and applaud his vision of cultural fusion or, in contrast, have attempted to remove him from an international context into that of a single ethnic group. Transnational approaches, in spite of their own potential dangers, are the most promising methodologies for discussions of Ito and for dance studies more generally.

Orientalism and various other kinds of exoticism served as malleable sources of inspiration for dancers in the early twentieth century, and they were crucial components of the modern dance innovations of Shawn, St. Denis, Ito, and others. They are also sources of embarrassment for dance historians, especially those who turn to Ito looking for an example of diversity in the early modern dance scene. Cowell's foundational discussion of Ito's representation of culture and ethnicity demonstrates the understandable desire to retrieve him from orientalism in order to establish him more firmly in dance history. She argues that although Ito's discussions of his art "echoed contemporaneous Orientalist stereotypes, his objective was an art more perfect because it rose above the limiting assumptions embodied in those constructs."[60] Cowell even attributes Ito's erasure from dance history to his audience's inability to "appreciate his effort to integrate East and West," speculating that this failure, not his internment and deportation, was "the greatest tragedy in Ito's life."[61] Yet reviewers as early as 1916 were discussing the meeting of East and West in Ito's dance. Ito repeatedly provided interviewers with a familiar formula about East and West that echoes the modernist desire—which he encountered in his collaborations with Yeats, Pound, Dulac, and Griffes—to fuse the two; he claimed, "Eastern art is three-fourths spiritual; Western art is three-fourths material. True art should be one-half spiritual, one-half material."[62]

In a performance for the magazine *Shadowland* that might gloss Ito's own *Pizzicati* or *Shadow Dance*, he cast a shadow on the wall with his hand:

> The East sees the shadow and does not question about the hand. The West knows exactly what the hand is for and understands its composition but dismisses utterly the perception of the shadow. . . . The world cannot be divided against itself like that. These two, together, must grow to comprehend that when you move the hand away, you move the shadow away, and that when you toy with your fingers, the shadow dances also.

Cowell reads this passage as a critique of the "supposed supremacy of Western culture," but it also replicates common associations of the East with dancing shadows and the West with scientific inquiry.[63] Ito emphasizes the value of stereotypes about the East, but in doing so he adheres to a common trajectory of orientalism. Said summarizes centuries of enthusiasms and longings for fusion in the "interchange between the academic and the more or less imaginative meanings of Orientalism" and argues that both uphold imperialist doctrines.[64]

Said focuses on writers and texts, and although he includes analysis of complex political, economic, and cultural institutions, many contemporary critics following his lead neglect the embodied practices and bodily art forms that are a crucial part of cultural constructions and negotiations. Cowell and other dance critics have begun to redress this neglect. Moving beyond the discursive, Cowell examines how Ito choreographs culture and ethnicity, but she also demonstrates a tendency common in modern dance criticism: to privilege the solo. Cowell recognizes that Ito's "syncretic ideal" may have been undermined when he "participated in the vogue for Orientalia" and that audiences often assumed a Japanese theme because of "the reality of Ito's Japanese body," but she claims that he "realized his goal of fusing East and West most obviously in his choreography to Westernized arrangements of Japanese music and in his work in America with Japanese composers"— that is, in his solos.[65] Cowell provides a fascinating reading of Ito's *Tone Poem II*, a solo to music by Yamada, convincingly arguing that the choreography is syncretic in its "combination of sound both Western and vaguely Asian with a relatively abstract movement vocabulary"; but this combination does not necessarily promote what Cowell calls Ito's "self-ascriptive ethnicity," his attempts to "locate himself and his work in a supranational artists' realm, where he was neither Japanese nor American."[66] The solo, at least since popular Delsartism, has been idealized as a genre in which the performer could construct new subjectivities, but Ito's work demonstrates the limits of this implied agency. Audience assumptions of Ito's Japaneseness were crucial to the perception of his ability to unite cultures or to serve as "Japan's spiritual ambassador," in one reviewer's assessment.[67] He capitalized on such assumptions throughout his career in promotional material, interviews, and dance themes, not just in his film work, which Cowell describes as "ironical" because it subverted "his vision of an art combining 'East' and 'West.'"[68]

Cowell's idea of Ito's "supranational ethnicity" problematically combines national, ethnic, and racial categories, and as Yutian Wong points out, "For Asian American subjects, the politics of ethnic identification are loaded and subject to misuse, and the terms 'ethnicity' and 'race' are frequently used interchangeably in the interest of tokenization and aestheticized multiculturalism."[69] Wong powerfully argues that an elision of nationality, ethnicity, and race is inscribed in such juridical codes as U.S. Executive Order 9066, which sent Ito along with 110,000 Japanese and Japanese Americans to internment camps, regardless of legal citizenship. Demonstrating the very different assumptions about nationality for people of European descent, Italian and German Americans were detained only if they were suspected of ties to enemy governments. Wong uncovers the utopian impulse behind the desire to frame Ito as an "international artist" who bridges cultural misunderstandings: "Ito's 'internationalism' becomes historically illegible within a modern dance history premised on neo-liberal understandings of multiculturalism when it comes to the dancing Asian American body."[70] Wong provides an important critique, yet the desire for a "multiculturalism" she calls "neo-liberal" is not new but evident in the early reviews of Ito as the "internationally famous" solo dancer and "cosmopolitan individualist." Wong's preferred approach also has a long history; she fractures the master narrative into smaller identity-based categories by recommending that Ito be positioned in an "Asian American history." Acknowledging that many critics might counter that this position marginalizes Ito and undermines his influence on modern dance, she argues that it is a "centralizing move" and one recognizing the "conditional nature of racialized migrations."[71]

Many identity categories (racial, ethnic, and gendered) inform Ito's career, and all are complicated by his transnational performances and identifications. The desire to recover Ito for a strictly "Asian American" history reflects as many utopian critical impulses as attempts to recover him from orientalism. "Asian American" is an awkward label for, as Wong recognizes, the Japanese American community in Los Angeles was suspicious of Ito as an elite artist married to an American woman. Wong says nothing of the response of an Asian American community, a category that combines many racial and ethnic groups while leaving out the national identifications that may have been more important to many the rubric attempts to include, especially given Japanese military encroachments into China and Korea during Ito's period. I have found no evidence to suggest that Ito claimed an Asian American identity, and the rubric does not easily accommodate his training and diverse performances in Japan and Europe. Nor is it clear that positioning Ito in "Asian American" history would help us to analyze better his choreography or contributions to modern dance; tellingly, Wong does not provide a reading of Ito's art. The category cannot elucidate Ito's participation in transnational modernist movements that crossed the boundaries of Japanese, American, and European identities and aesthetics.

The orientalism and exoticism of modern dance and modernism must not be ignored, but our critical strategies should diversify, not reconsolidate identity categories. Said argues against "any attempt to force cultures and peoples into separate and distinct breeds or essences" as riddled with the same "misrepresentations and falsifications" that construct "East" and "West."[72] Only a transnational perspective can accommodate the fact of Ito's international career and collaborations, all of which were enmeshed in orientalist assumptions and aesthetics. This is not to say that Ito anticipated transnationalism or that he was ahead of his time. Ito was very much within the modernist period that represents an early phase in the increasing globalization of the world. It was a moment in which orientalist themes and reinterpretations of cultural traditions would make dance careers, a fact that is part of the same complex of assumptions that would result in Ito's internment. If Ito had refused to capitalize on orientalist fascinations, it is more likely that he would have fallen into obscurity than that he would have received more recognition in dance history. To frame his experiences as ironical or exceptional further marginalizes him from his centrality within the American dance scene, which applauded the "exotic oriental" as much as the solo.

A transnational approach considers how identities, genres, and aesthetic influences go on tours that exceed national boundaries to establish some surprising affiliations and collaborations. Powerful studies by Kwame Anthony Appiah, Arjun Appadurai, Susan Stanford Friedman, and Jahan Ramazani as well as Said and many others have transformed approaches to modern culture. Modern dance studies can contribute much to this field owing to its early international circuits and its aesthetic practices shaped by the use of ethnic material and orientalist desire. Modern dance prompted transgeneric collaborations among dancers, poets, musicians, designers, and filmmakers, and it attends to embodied experiences of the world. Far more exceptional than Ito's entrenchment in orientalism is his participation in so many of the venues of transnational modernism.

For dance studies to benefit from the insights of transnational studies, it must focus less on modern dance as a solo form and more on the diversity of dancers' careers and collaborations. It must also avoid a tendency evident in other fields of transnational studies to turn orientalism and exoticism into conversation-stopping accusations or equally unproductive dissections of various degrees of authenticity in cultural representation. I understand transnationalism as an approach to contact, collaboration, and conflict across cultures, not a cure for the many ills of globalization; that masquerade would turn Ito into the marionette he performed in his *Shadow Dance*. Transnationalism indicates a challenge we cannot ignore and one that Ito embraced with a good deal of creativity and innovation and with an impulse, choreographed into *Tango*, to hold out his hand and invite his audience to join the solo.

Notes

I would like to thank Kyoko Ryutani and Kumiko Komine for valuable instruction in Michio Ito's technique and choreography and Michele Ito for sharing her personal collection of her grandfather's artifacts. I am also indebted to Mary-Jean Cowell for providing biographical information, Kevin Riordan for research assistance, and David Crandall for translation and interpretation.

1. Helen Caldwell, *Michio Ito: The Dancer and His Dances* (Berkeley: University of California Press, 1977), 88–89.

2. "Japanese Dancing," *New York Sun*, December 11, 1916, Michio Ito Clippings, The Jerome Robbins Dance Division, The New York Public Library for the Performing Arts (hereafter JRDD, NYPL).

3. Ruth St. Denis, "Music Visualization" (1925), in *Dance as a Theatre Art*, 2nd ed., ed. Selma Jeanne Cohen (Princeton, N.J.: Princeton Book Company, 1992), 129–34.

4. Kyoko Ryutani, Repertory Dance Theatre class, Salt Lake City, Utah, July 3, 2009.

5. Anna Kisselgoff, "Dance: Michio Ito Salute," *New York Times*, October 4, 1979, Ito Clippings, JRDD, NYPL.

6. Edward Said, *Orientalism* (New York: Vintage, 1978), 2–3.

7. Susan Leigh Foster, ed., *Worlding Dance* (Basingstoke, U.K.: Palgrave Macmillan, 2009); Jahan Ramazani, *A Transnational Poetics* (Chicago: University of Chicago Press, 2009); Kwame Anthony Appiah, *Cosmopolitanism: Ethics in a World of Strangers* (New York: Norton, 2006).

8. Anna Kisselgoff, "Michio Ito, An All-But-Forgotten Pioneer of American Modern Dance," *New York Times*, February 26, 1978, D10; Mary-Jean Cowell and Satoru Shimazaki, "East and West in the Work of Michio Ito," *Dance Research Journal* 26, no. 2 (Autumn 1994): 11–23; Yutian Wong, "Artistic Utopias: Michio Ito and the Trope of the International," in *Worlding Dance*, 144–62.

9. Midori Takeishi, *Japanese Elements in Michio Ito's Early Period (1915–1924): Meetings of East and West in the Collaborative Works*, ed. David Pacun (Tokyo: Gendaitosho, 2006), 9–14.

10. Tomie Hahn, *Sensational Knowledge: Embodying Culture through Japanese Dance* (Middletown, Conn.: Wesleyan University Press, 2007).

11. Selma Landen Odom, "Delsartean Traces in Dalcroze Eurhythmics," in *Essays on François Delsarte*, ed. Nancy Lee Chalfa Ruyter, *Mime Journal* (2004–2005): 137–52.

12. Isadora Duncan, *My Life* (1927; reprint, New York: Liveright, 1995), 8.

13. "Michio Itow's School: Season of 1919," personal collection of Michele Ito.

14. See Nancy Lee Chalfa Ruyter, *The Cultivation of Body and Mind in Nineteenth-Century American Delsartism* (Westport, Conn.: Greenwood, 1999); Carrie J. Preston, *Modernism's Mythic Pose: Gender, Genre, Solo Performance* (New York: Oxford University Press, 2011).

15. "What Is Delsartism?" in *A Delsartean Scrap-Book*, ed. Frederic Sanburn (New York: Lovell, 1891), 4.

16. Ted Shawn, *Every Little Movement* (New York: Dance Horizons, 1954).

17. Odom, "Delsartean Traces," 137.

18. Peter Kurth, *Isadora: A Sensational Life* (Boston: Little, Brown, 2001), 232.

19. Elin Diamond, "Deploying/Destroying the Primitivist Body in Hurston and Brecht," in *Against Theatre: Creative Destructions on the Modernist Stage*, ed. Alan L. Ackerman and Martin Puchner (New York: Palgrave Macmillan, 2006): 112–32.

20. Ian Carruthers, "A Translation of Fifteen Pages of Ito Michio's Autobiography 'Utsukushiku Naru Kyoshitsu,'" *Canadian Journal of Irish Studies* 2, no. 1 (1976): 32–43.

21. Carruthers, "A Translation," 39.

22. Michio Ito and Louis V. Ledoux, "*Kitsune Zuka* or *The Fox's Grave*: An Ancient Japanese Farce," *Outlook*, February 14, 1923, 306–8.

23. A similar costume appears in a drawing of Ito as "Sho-jyo" in Marguerite Mooers Marshall, "Woman of 70 Is Not Too Old to Dance, Says Terpsichore with a

Kimono, Symbolizing Emotions of Far East," *Evening World* (New York), December 2, 1916, n.p., collection of Michele Ito.

24. Michio Ito, letter to Ottoline Morrell (n.d., ca. 1915), Harry Ransom Humanities Research Center, University of Texas.

25. Carruthers, "A Translation," 39.

26. Takeishi, *Japanese Elements*, 27.

27. Ito Clippings, JRDD, NYPL. Tulle Lindahl performed in four additional solos.

28. Takeishi, *Japanese Elements*, 38.

29. "Orientals Lend Weird Art," *Musical America*, September 1, 1917, 17.

30. "Ballet Intime," Ito clippings, JRDD, NYPL.

31. Mary-Jean Cowell, "Michio Ito in Hollywood: Modes and Ironies of Ethnicity," *Dance Chronicle* 24, no. 3 (2001): 263–305.

32. Ibid., 291.

33. Carruthers, "A Translation," 40.

34. "Satoru Shimazaki Performing Works of Pioneer Choreographer," program, Theatre of the Open Eye, New York, October 2–7, 1979, collection of Michele Ito.

35. Ito programs, JRDD, NYPL.

36. George Jackson, "A Celebration of Michio Ito: When Modern Was New," *Dance Magazine*, May 1996, 86–87.

37. "The Dances of Michio Ito," dir. Hannah C. Wiley, 2001, Chamber Dance Company Archive, University of Washington.

38. Ito programs, JRDD, NYPL.

39. Mark Franko, *Dancing Modernism/Performing Politics* (Bloomington: Indiana University Press, 1995), ix.

40. T. S. Eliot, "Tradition and the Individual Talent," *The Egoist* (1919), in *T. S. Eliot: Selected Prose*, ed. Frank Kermode (London: Faber, 1975), 40.

41. Jack Anderson, "Satoru Shimazaki, Soloist," *New York Times*, November 20, 1983.

42. Cowell and Shimazaki, "East and West," 14.

43. Wong, "Artistic Utopias," 156, 149.

44. Marcia B. Siegel, "Dusting the Curio Cabinet," *Soho Weekly News*, October 11, 1979, collection of Michele Ito.

45. Ezra Pound and Ernest Fenollosa, *The Classic Noh Theatre of Japan* (New York: New Directions, 1959); first published as *'Noh' or Accomplishment* (1916).

46. Takeishi, *Japanese Elements*, 42–43.

47. Cowell and Shimazaki, "East and West," 19.

48. "Review of Eighth Army Special Services Productions," collection of Michele Ito.

49. *Denishawn Dances On!* (video), presentation by Michelle Mathesius, narr. J. L. Moody, Kultur, 2002.

50. Nancy Lee Chalfa Ruyter, "La Meri and the World of Dance," *Anales del Instituto de Investigaciones Estéticas* 22, no. 77 (2000): 169–88.

51. Ibid., 179.

52. "Noh Dramas, Once Sacred to Shinto Gods, Coming to Boston," *Boston Post*, January 16, 1921, Yeats Archives, National Library of Ireland.

53. Marta E. Savigliano, "Whiny Ruffians and Rebellious Broads: Tango as a Spectacle of Eroticized Social Tension," *Theatre Journal* 47 (1995): 83–104.

54. Carruthers, "A Translation," 35.

55. Edward Gordon Craig, *On the Art of the Theatre*, ed. Franc Chamberlain (1911; reprint, New York: Routledge, 2009): 27–48.

56. "In the Spotlight," *American Dancer*, June 1929, n.p., collection of Michele Ito.

57. Marshall, "Terpsichore with a Kimono," n.p.

58. George Jackson, "Three Times a Charm: Dana Tai Soon Burgess & Company," *Dance Magazine*, April 2002, 76–77, 93.

59. Said, "Afterword," in *Orientalism*, 341.

60. Cowell, "Michio Ito in Hollywood," 301.

61. Cowell and Shimazaki, "East and West," 19–20.

62. "Noh Dramas."

63. Cowell and Shimazaki, "East and West," 13.

64. Said, *Orientalism*, 3.

65. Cowell, "Michio Ito in Hollywood," 266–67.

66. Ibid., 268, 272.

67. "Michio Ito, Internationally Famous Dancer and Group of Noted Solo Dancers," 1933, collection of Michele Ito.

68. Cowell, "Michio Ito in Hollywood," 301.

69. Wong, "Artistic Utopias," 153.

70. Ibid., 155–56.

71. Ibid., 156, 161.

72. Said, *Orientalism*, 347.

two

Alone into the World

Reflections on Solos from 1919
by Vaslav Nijinsky and Mary Wigman

Ramsay Burt

According to Romola Nijinsky, her husband Vaslav began his program of solos at the Suvretta Hotel in the Swiss resort St. Moritz in January 1919 by sitting still in a chair for an uncomfortably long time.[1] While Romola interpreted this as a sign of Nijinsky's deteriorating mental health, the psychologist Peter Ostwald disagrees, noting in his 1991 book on Nijinsky that "for a dancer to come on stage, sit down, not move, and simply stare at the audience was unheard of in 1919. Today, we would not be shocked by it."[2] Although the start of Nijinsky's solo program was undoubtedly disturbing, it was not entirely unprecedented. There are other moments in his choreography when he confounded audiences by using stillness, and this is something about which some critics complained. Thus, for example, at the moment in *L'Après-midi d'un faune* when Debussy's music is at its most intense, the faun and principal nymph freeze in an intense interlocking of gazes. The Chosen One in *Le Sacre du printemps*, after she has been selected, stands and stares for most of the second half of the ballet while the company dance around her until she finally begins her sacrificial solo. Nijinsky's solo program in St. Moritz should not be taken as an isolated phenomenon. It can be placed alongside other radical experimental performances of its own time by Mary Wigman and others and, as Ostwald infers, from later in the twentieth century. By pushing in an avant-garde way at the boundaries of the form, these solos enacted a process of becoming alone in the world. This was a diminution of the self that critiqued ideologies of individuality and self-expression in order to find new ways of reconnecting art and modern life.

Nijinsky's solo program was presented in aid of the Red Cross, and one of his solos explored, in a highly expressive way, his response to the horrors of the war that had just ended. Later that year at another Swiss resort, Davos, Mary Wigman performed a solo program at a sanatorium, her audience consisting of psychiatric patients and shell-shocked veterans as well as people staying in the resort's hotels. Writing toward the end of her life, she described them as suffering patients, sportsmen, gamblers, and adventurers. She began the performance with lyrical dances set to music by classical composers but then moved on to her more radical, modernist pieces performed without music. To her surprise, "this audience of the sick and blasé applauded my dances wildly."[3] There is a suggestion here that Wigman was prepared to perform her more difficult works regardless of any fears she may have had about their reception. She was convinced of the power and importance of her radical new approach to dance. Here, and elsewhere in her writing, Wigman describes her work as an almost spiritual quest—something only she could do on her own, having renounced aspects of worldly existence. In a society for whom a belief in God was becoming increasingly marginal and being supplanted by a commitment to rationality, and scientific and technological progress, artists found themselves taking on some of the roles previously performed by priests and priestesses. According to Romola, just before the start of his performance at the Suvretta Hotel, Nijinsky surprised her by announcing, "This is my marriage to God."[4] This suggests a religious renunciation of worldly things that is comparable to Wigman's view of her role as an artist. Wigman and Nijinsky both seem to have found that it was only by being alone on stage that they could find ways of expressing the important truths that, in 1919, they felt they were discovering.

Little scholarly attention has been paid to these two performances, and there is little evidence about them. Nijinsky mentions the Suvretta Hotel concert in his notebooks, subsequently published as his *Diaries*, and Romola wrote about it in her 1933 book. Maurice Sandoz published reminiscences of the concert in 1954, thirty-five years after the event.[5] There is even less information about Wigman's Davos concert. She wrote about it in an autobiographical fragment published at the end of her life. It was the first of a series of solo concerts she gave that year, which started in Switzerland and continued in Germany. During these, having distanced herself from Rudolf Laban, she established her reputation as an important artist in her own right. It is assumed that the program in Davos closely resembles those she presented later in the year.[6] What evidence there is suggests some significant correspondences between Nijinsky's and Wigman's concerts. Both artists were opposed to the war, both had avant-garde sensibilities, and spiritual ideas informed the creation of the work performed in these concerts. Their juxtaposition, I believe, is useful because taken together, the concerts highlight a significant stage in the development of the solo as one of the central forms in twentieth- and twenty-first-century choreography.

Compared with the solos of Isadora Duncan, Loïe Fuller, Ruth St. Denis, and others during the first decade of the twentieth century, Nijinsky's and Wigman's performances in 1919 were challenging and uncomfortable in an avant-garde way. Contemporary writing about these earlier solo artists often valued their ability to attain self-fulfillment through self-expression. As Julie Malnig has shown, women's magazines in the early twentieth century promoted the idea that dancing was a consumer leisure activity through which women readers could aspire to ideals of natural beauty. This was something that figures ranging from the exhibition ballroom dancer Irene Castle to the modern dancer Isadora Duncan exemplified. Malnig points out that in 1917, Duncan contributed an essay, "What Do Modern Women Want?" to *Modern Dance Magazine*. Dance was becoming a commodity within the development of aspirational consumer lifestyle choices.[7] Nijinsky and Wigman's performances in St. Moritz and Davos were avant-garde modernist in a radical and uncompromising way that was implicitly critical of the social and economic context of early twentieth-century modernism and the accompanying development of consumer culture. The freedom of expression Nijinsky and Wigman claimed in 1919 signaled something more demanding than the freedom to consume. Whereas Duncan's dancing could be promoted as the epitome of self-fulfillment, Nijinsky's and Wigman's 1919 solos suggested that a diminution of self was necessary in order to try and find new ways of reconnecting art with the world.

The historical context of the solos that Nijinsky and Wigman performed in St. Moritz and Davos was the aftermath of World War I. Both artists had been philosophically opposed to war. Their rejection of the more conventional ways of thinking and behaving that they believed had led to the war was accompanied by the development of an interest in spirituality. New forms of abstraction promised to offer access to pure, intense, unmediated experiences of a quasi-spiritual nature. In Nijinsky's case this derived from his Tolstoyan view of art and from Tolstoy's Christian pacifism. Where Wigman's dance is concerned, this spiritual view of abstraction underlay the idea of "absolute dance," which, as Susan Manning has pointed out, was developing at this time around Wigman's work.[8]

The following discussion addresses three topics: the development of the solo dance in relation to tensions between ideas of freedom and concerns about the impact of modernization; an analysis of Nijinsky's and Wigman's relation to classical European music in order to clarify what was modernist about their 1919 concerts; and an examination of the way pacifist views led both Nijinsky and Wigman to the spiritual ideas that underpinned these concerts. It ends with a discussion of the exceptional aloneness of the solo dancer by considering what these two concerts in 1919 can tell us about the solo dance as a key twentieth- and twenty-first-century form.

The solo modern dancer is on his or her own as a performer in a way that distinguishes dance from the other arts. Musicians performing solos are not entirely alone in the same way as the modern dance soloist. The violinist playing a concerto performs with an orchestra, while in jazz a solo emerges from ensemble playing. Whereas solos in eighteenth- and nineteenth-century ballets usually occurred as items within an evening that involved a company of dancers, modern dance emerged around the beginning of the twentieth century as a form where the dancer was entirely alone on the stage. The majority of the early modern solo-dance artists also worked on their own creating choreography. Although painters work alone in the studio, the paint they use and the canvas to which it is applied are separate from themselves.

Solo modern dancers, however, characteristically dance material that is created on and by themselves. About working alone in the studio in his house in St. Moritz generating the material for his solo concert and shows, Nijinsky writes in his *Diaries* that he was aware of the awkward atmosphere in the house at the time. Wigman, having suffered a physical and mental breakdown in 1918, retreated to a sanatorium in Walensee, where she danced every day out of doors, creating the solos that she subsequently performed in Davos. Each, therefore, produced solos in situations of extreme isolation.

The dancer's exceptional aloneness, as philosopher Jean-Luc Nancy recently observed during a dialogue with the dance artist Mathilde Monnier, is unique among the arts.[9] The title they chose for their dialogue—"Seul(e) au monde"—is one that cannot easily be translated into English. It concerns being alone in the world but suggests a relation between dancer and world. The French preposition *au* might be literally translated as *at* or *toward*, but I suggest taking *au* to mean *into*; this suggests translating Monnier and Nancy's title as "Alone into the World," hence my using this as the title of my essay. Elsewhere in his philosophy Nancy has repeatedly used the phrase "thrown into the world" (which comes from Heidegger) to explain the freedom of being. The title *Alone into the World* also resonates with "the essential solitude and solitude in the world," the title of an essay by the French novelist and critic Maurice Blanchot, another writer Nancy often cites. Blanchot's essay begins, "When I am alone, it is not I who am there, and it is not from you that I stay away, or from others, or from the world. . . . When I am alone, I am not there."[10] Art, for Blanchot, comes from this solitude, this vacating of the self that is the duty of the artist. I argue that in their 1919 solos, Nijinsky and Wigman vacated the self in the way Blanchot described in order to go beyond themselves and heal a rupture between art and the world.

Wigman's performance in Davos was evidently highly expressive. Nijinsky's solo performance was so expressive that it appears to have disturbed its audience. Romola, who seems to have been unable to understand or sympathize with her husband's avant-garde sensibility, interpreted the intensity of his solos as a sign of his mental instability. Ostwald, however, argues that nothing in Nijinsky's behavior prior to his institutionalization should be interpreted as psychotic. In his view Nijinsky's psychosis was produced by the treatment he received in mental hospitals. The disturbing intensity of

Nijinsky's and Wigman's performances in 1919 nevertheless raises questions about the relation between genius and madness, in this case between expressionist art and the art of the mentally ill. The psychologist Hans Prinzhorn, with whom Wigman had a relationship in Dresden in the early 1920s, published a very influential book, *Bildnerei der Geisteskranken* (Artistry of the Mentally Ill), in 1922. In this he explained the difference between artist and mental patient in terms of their engagement with human society. While recognizing that expressionist painters often renounce the outside world in order to turn inward upon themselves, he argued that they always maintain some kind of relations with others:

> The loneliest artist still remains in contact with humanity, even if only through desire and longing, and the desire of this contact speaks to us out of all pictures by "normal" people. The schizophrenic, on the other hand, is detached from humanity, and by definition is neither willing nor able to re-establish contact with it.[11]

The kind of expressionist artist that Prinzhorn is discussing here is one who senses a rupture between artist and society and who struggles with the problem of finding a way to reestablish contact. This, for Blanchot, depends on a necessary vacating of the self. The disturbing intensity of Nijinsky's and Wigman's solos in 1919 should not therefore be seen as a sign of mental disturbance but as testimony to the urgency they felt about the need to communicate the experiences informing the creation of their work, and the difficulty of doing so. Underlying these difficulties was the impact of modernity.

One of the most destabilizing motors for social transformation at the beginning of the twentieth century was the transition from a mode of capitalism in which the creation of wealth necessitated a disciplined and obedient work force to a situation in which further industrial growth necessitated the development of consumer society. Raymond Williams proposes that this arose as a result of "the planning and attempted control of the markets [through] the creation of needs and wants and of particular ways of satisfying them."[12] The industrial base could grow only if customers were encouraged to express their individuality through developing new kinds of consumer lifestyles; Zygmunt Bauman notes that consumerism promised "that a cure for all the troubles you may suffer is waiting somewhere in some shop and can be found if you search earnestly enough."[13] Bauman has pointed out that from the beginning of the twentieth century, sociologists have identified the development of a particular form of modern individualism. Thus Georg Simmel believed that as the individual tries to make sense of diverse and fragmented experiences, "the only solid ground the person can hope for (and even this is in vain) in the whirlwind of chaotic impressions the modern urban environment never tires of supplying, is his own 'personal identity.'"[14] This led to a more complicated set of new demands. Bauman argues:

> The poignant experience of being a "self" and "having" a self at the same time (i.e., being obliged to care, defend, "keep clean" etc. one's self, much as one is regarding other possessions) are a necessity imposed upon certain classes of people by the social context of their lives, and the most relevant aspect of such context is the absence of an unequivocal and comprehensive behavior recipe for the "life project" as a whole, as well as for the ever changing situations of daily life.[15]

This curious formulation of a split between being and having a self suggests that individuality is in some ways like private property. Although it is intangible, it is nevertheless something that one has the freedom to own and look after. Bauman implies, however, that one may be judged on how well one looks after it.

Dancers are very much aware of being a "self" and "having" a self at the same time as they work with their own bodies. They are particularly aware of how much effort it takes to develop and maintain their technical abilities through regular classes and rehearsals. Bauman stresses the uncertainty of modern life and the ambivalence that individuals feel toward modernity. Malnig identifies the ways in which women's magazines encouraged their readers to identify with celebrity dancers like Isadora Duncan and thus aspire toward the supposed stability and fulfillment these celebrities seemed to have achieved. Nijinsky's and Wigman's 1919 solos made problematic these ideals about stability and instead pursued ideals that radically conflicted with those of the emerging consumer culture. The dancing body was becoming a key site within which the struggle took place to find, amid the uncertainty of modern life, elusive qualities of truth and meaning. As Nancy and Blanchot argue, it is the artist's role to reveal this. By renouncing conventional aesthetic properties and qualities, Nijinsky and Wigman reveal an ambivalent relation to modernity—one that is critical of it while at the same time dependent on it. The 1919 solos by Nijinsky and Wigman can be seen as a necessary response to the increasingly complex, fragmented, and contradictory demands of a newly developing consumer society. This is something that an examination of their approach to music reveals.

Nijinsky and Wigman each emerged as modernist artists within very different social and cultural contexts. Nijinsky came from a Polish family of ballet dancers who were resident in Russia, and he trained at the Imperial Theater School in St. Petersburg. Whereas Nijinsky, in becoming a ballet dancer, was in effect following a family tradition, Wigman was born into a middle-class family in Hanover, Germany, whose expectations that she would marry an eligible husband conflicted with her own desire to become an artist. Nijinsky developed a highly refined technical ability as a ballet dancer, whereas Wigman denounced ballet and developed herself as a dance artist by studying with Émile Jaques-Dalcroze in Hellerau and then with Rudolf Laban in Munich and Switzerland.

I noted earlier that Nijinsky and Wigman had similar modernist sensibilities. Through Diaghilev, Nijinsky became acquainted with the modern movement in the arts, particularly music. Nijinsky was personally acquainted with not only Stravinsky but also Debussy, Ravel, and Richard Strauss. Wigman became acquainted with the expressionist painter Emil Nolde while still a student in Hellerau. In Zurich, during the 1914–18 war, she attended and on at least one occasion contributed to Dada performances. One ability that Nijinsky and Wigman had in common was their musicianship. As a young woman Wigman took lessons in singing, revealing such talent that her teacher suggested she could take it up as a career.[16] Nijinsky learned to play the piano as part of his course at the Imperial Theater School. According to his sister, Bronislava Nijinska, he had a very good ear for music and could play complex, difficult pieces from memory.[17] A photograph taken by Stravinsky in May 1913 shows Nijinsky seated at a piano beside Ravel playing a duet.

Key to understanding their 1919 programs are their distinctive attitudes toward music. According to Maurice Sandoz, one of the pieces of music played during Nijinsky's performance in St. Moritz was a Bach fugue.[18] In 1917 Wigman began a concert in Zurich with two new pieces she had created, each to a piece from Bach's series of forty-eight preludes and fugues: *Praeludium VIII* and *Arie*. Bach's keyboard music at the time was an unusual choice for dancing. In the nineteenth century, ballet music constituted a separate genre. While Tchaikovsky's ballet music is now considered among the finest work he composed, ballet music was generally more lightweight and repetitious, and was regarded as a minor genre. In the early 1900s Isadora Duncan and, following her example, Michel Fokine made what was for some a daring innovation by using music not written for dance but taken from the concert repertory. Thus Duncan used Romantic music by Beethoven, Brahms, Chopin, and Mendelssohn that was characteristically richly harmonic. In contrast with this, Bach's keyboard music was polyphonic and exploited a use of counterpoint that was largely absent from nineteenth-century Romantic music. In the early twentieth century, modernist composers like Schoenberg, Webern, and Hindemith found in Bach's work an example of polyphony and handling of complex formal structures that supported their own attempts to break away from the lushness and sensuality of late Romantic chromaticism. When Duncan danced to Chopin, as Ann Daly notes, she demonstrated her uncanny instinct for musicality: "Instead of dancing squarely on the beat, she played with the elasticity of her accompaniment's rhythm, embedding hesitancy or fear or longing or a whole host of inner states in the way she variously quickened or suspended her movement through time."[19] Through emotional expressiveness Duncan therefore conveyed her oneness with the music and by doing so suggested a coherent subjectivity. This was not something to which Bach's keyboard music easily lent itself.[20]

According to Sandoz, while Nijinsky's piano accompanist Bertha Asseo played a Bach fugue during the St. Moritz concert, Nijinsky "went to a side table and there, whilst half-listening to the music, went through a series of gestures the meaning of which escaped me."[21] Sandoz says at first he thought they were like the movements of a medium trying to raise a table in the air. Then he says it was as if Nijinsky was balancing invisible cubes of wood one on top of another until they fell down and he began again from the start: "It seemed to us strange, then tiresome, and eventually it became disquieting."[22]

The pianist stopped in surprise before the end of the fugue, saying to Nijinsky that what he was doing was not dancing.[23] According to Sandoz, the pianist then began to play a Ballade by Chopin, only for Nijinsky to complain that it was too well known and to ask her to play "something that nobody knows."[24]

Sandoz prefaces his account by admitting that what he remembers was very different from Romola's description of the concert. There is a possible explanation for the differences between their accounts. Romola missed the first part of the concert. Embarrassed by the way her husband began by sitting, surveying his audience, she suggested that he dance part of *Les Sylphides*, which was set to music by Chopin. Following his abrupt refusal, she says she was so upset that she left the room. There seems to be more at stake in Romola's and Sandoz's accounts than a clash between traditional and modernist musical tastes. Underlying this were differing ideas about what constitutes dance. Chopin's piano pieces belong to a genre of Romantic music that lends itself to a conventionally expressive danced interpretation, like those choreographed by Duncan and Fokine that offered the promise of stability within the uncertainty of modern life. Unable or unwilling to appreciate her husband's modernist sensibilities, Romola saw in Nijinsky's performance signs of incoherence and instability. It could also, however, be interpreted as a modernist investigation of fragmentation that suggests a rejection of the values mediated through the kind of aspirational consumer dance culture Malnig has identified.

There is another mention of Chopin in Sandoz's account that also points to Nijinsky's interest in fragmentation. Nijinsky's concert, he writes, began with a dance set to Chopin's Prelude in C Minor, No. 20 (opus 28, no. 20).

This is a short, stately piece that consists of a simple melodic phrase repeated twice. It has a consistent, stable, but slightly halting 4/4 rhythm in which a shorter note on the third beat is followed by an even shorter note before the final beat—one, two, three, *and* four—so that there is a slight accent on the short third beat before the "*and*." Here is Sandoz's description:

> First of all he extended his two arms in front of him in an attitude of defence which was emphasized by his keeping the palms of his hands vertical; then he opened them with a gesture of welcome, raised them as though in prayer, and at the fourth and fifth beats [i.e., the notes on the "*and*" and the fourth beat] let them suddenly fall as though the joints that held them had snapped. He did the same for each sequence till the final chord was reached.[25]

Sandoz goes on to say how surprising he found Nijinsky's interpretation of this music: "I, who had hitherto considered this prelude a homogenous work, was surprised that a dancer should in this way underline its fragmentary nature."[26] We might now say that by emphasizing fragmentation, Nijinsky was deconstructing the prelude. In deconstructing Chopin he was surely, by implication, also disrupting the aesthetic underlying works by Fokine and Duncan that were set to Chopin's music. What marked Nijinsky's sensibility as modernist was not just this attraction to fragmentation but its use as a way of critiquing the kinds of solutions to the problem of individuality that consumer culture offered.

If Nijinsky's modernist sensibility reveals itself within the tensions about the kind of music played for the dancer and how that music can be interpreted, Wigman's modernism manifests itself as a desire to explore what dance movement can itself express independent from music. At her first public appearance performing her own work, in Munich in 1914, Wigman presented two pieces—*Lento* and *Hexentanz*—danced in silence. Susan Manning discusses at length a review of this performance by Rudolf von Delius, who applauded Wigman for revealing for the first time the true essence of dance as an autonomous art form that was at last independent of music.[27] Manning states that while Wigman's concerts in 1919 began and ended with pieces set to music by classical composers, between these she presented her more intense, expressive cycle *Ekstatische Tänze* (Ecstatic Dances), which were not set to any music. Writing in 1926 about *Götzendienst* (Idolatry), one of the Ecstatic cycle, Fritz Böhme said it raised questions about the relationship between dance and music: "In that solo the relationship between music and dance was newly solved: music as sound, an ascending yet subservient means for understanding the sequence of movement. Movement was no longer moving picture or moving sculpture. Dance without music was born."[28] No composer is credited in the programs for *Ekstatische Tänze*. It is not altogether clear here whether *Götzendienst* was performed entirely without music and, if so, what role sounds like the rustling of Wigman's costume, a straw cape, may have played. In a contemporary description of the piece Wigman's friend Berthe Trümpy writes that the straw-clad apparition hissed, and she mentions at one moment a drum.[29] In the 1920s and 1930s Wigman developed a process of creating movement on her own in the studio and then collaborating with her accompanist, initially Will Goetz and after 1929 Hanns Hasting, to create a supporting musical accompaniment, sometimes with a gong or percussion instrument. Something similar may have accompanied sections of *Ekstatische Tänze*. The composer Carl Orff, who later collaborated with Wigman, wrote, "Mary Wigman sought dance in its absolute state. Not a kind of dance that, like ivy, needed music as a house to climb on."[30] If Wigman did not, therefore, abandon music altogether, this poses the question: from which aspects of it did she feel she needed to distance herself?

Wigman's initial decision to make her earliest dances without music seems, in part at least, to have been a reaction against the tasks she had had to undertake as a student of Jaques-Dalcroze. She enrolled in 1910 at his academy, the Bildungsanstalt für Musik und Rhythmus in Hellerau. Jaques-Dalcroze's stated aim was to run "a preparatory school for the arts and for the enjoyment of life," and he sought to reunite musical and bodily rhythm which, in his view, modern life had impaired.[31] At his school he aimed to teach "the expression of the order of all human beings, [which] penetrates through the body into the soul, and harmony is taught through the gymnastic dance." His approach subsequently became known as eurythmics. Dance movement, for Jaques-Dalcroze, was a means for getting back in touch with a natural, harmonious sense of rhythm and "bring[ing] out the music that is sleeping inside."[32] His large-scale production of *Orpheus und Euridice*, with the innovative stage designer Adolphe Appia, demonstrated this sense of harmony through the graceful dancing of Euridice and her accompanying nymphs. Wigman, however, was one of the Furies, along with Rosalia

Chladek, Bertha von Zoete, Grete Wiesenthal, and Michio Ito. All these students, as Tamara Levitz has pointed out, went on to have significant careers as dancers, while nothing more was heard of those who had played the more graceful, harmonious roles.[33]

There was evidently no room in Jaques-Dalcroze's system for a dance that was not grounded in preexisting music, and his notions of order and harmony seem not to have appealed to his most talented students. Susanne Perrotet, who left Jaques-Dalcroze for Laban at the same time as Wigman, acknowledged that at Hellerau she had learned to listen: "But at the same time I was looking for dissonance in order to express my character and that was not possible within his altogether harmonious structure."[34] While working at Hellerau, Wigman found she had to get away from music in order to find her own dance. As she wrote in 1931:

> My first tentative attempts to compose were made when I was studying the Dalcroze system. Though I have always had a strong feeling for music, it seemed from the very start most natural for me to express my own nature by means of pure movement. Perhaps it was just because there was so much musical work to be done at the time, that all these little dances and dance studies took form without music.[35]

While Jaques-Dalcroze aimed to use dancelike movement as a system for teaching music by trying to "bring out the music that is sleeping inside," Wigman focused on movement for its own sake, seeking within for its source, but doing so in a musical way.

Writing about the creation of her 1926 piece *Drehmonotonie* (Monotony: Whirl Dance) she remembered listening to a Chinese gong while alone in a room and waiting "until the deep sound of the gong began to leave its metallic shell. The whole room seemed to wait in a peculiar state of tension for the growing of this sound. I too waited for it, ready with all my senses, as if I expected an apparition to manifest itself at any moment."[36] Her senses here seem to have been tuned not only toward her own physical responses to the sound but also outward to the room within which she seems almost to lose herself. Jaques-Dalcroze saw music and dance as equivalents in a way that was in line with late nineteenth-century ideas about synesthesia. Wigman's modernist sensibility made her seek out the autonomous, kinesthetic qualities of dance movement as an independent art form. Wigman's turn from synesthesia to kinesthesia thus led her to a different way of relating to the world.[37] While fragmentation of musicality offered Nijinsky a new way of performing subjectivity, Wigman found something comparable through merging with something outside herself. In each case, this was a modernist disruption of artistic conventions and traditions. By embracing what might have seemed irrational behavior, they were, in effect, refusing to comply with ideas about individuality and self-expression that were underpinning the development of a consumer culture. In 1919 this refusal would have seemed particularly compelling when supposedly rational behavior had led to the catastrophic events of a war from which the Western world was only just beginning to recover.

Both Romola and Sandoz describe a piece that Nijinsky danced in the Suvretta Hotel, which he specifically introduced as a dance about the war. Romola says Nijinsky "filled the room with horror-stricken suffering humanity . . . taking his audience away with him to war, to destruction, facing suffering and horror."[38] Sandoz suggests a more explicit narrative: "a funeral march on a field of battle, striding over a rotting corpse, avoiding a shell," that ended with him dying riddled with bullets.[39] Romola describes a scenic element made from cloth that Nijinsky arranged into a cross on the floor. Nijinsky recalls in his *Diaries* collecting this from the local dressmaker who had made it for him. Significantly, this would have been abstracted and symbolic, in contrast with the more conventional use of decor in the ballets he had created and danced in with the Ballets Russes. Romola says the piece was so moving that it was greeted with thunderous applause, while Sandoz says that "we were too overwhelmed to applaud."[40] The piece clearly had an intensely emotional impact and seems from both accounts to have been the most important one in the concert.

In Romola's account, Nijinsky introduced his war piece in an accusatory way, saying he would dance "the war which you did not prevent and so you are also responsible for."[41] Who exactly might such an accusation have been aimed at? Switzerland had, after all, been a neutral country during the war. Did Romola herself feel guilty? She was Hungarian; her country had been on the opposite side from Russia and had placed Nijinsky under house arrest as an enemy alien. On his release to perform in the United States he ignored call-up papers from the Russian army. Having not fought and thus having survived at a time when so many of his contemporaries had died, Nijinsky would have felt guilty for surviving. Whatever Nijinsky's intentions for the piece, it was clearly antiwar. By performing it, he was taking up the role of someone who reveals truths. His pacifist stance at the time was informed by his interest in Tolstoy's moral teachings. An example of these can be found in Tolstoy's defense of the Doukhobors, a pacifist Christian community who were persecuted by the Russian government for their men's refusal to do military service.[42]

When Nijinsky was growing up, Tolstoy had been acclaimed as Russia's greatest living writer. Nijinsky was presented with a complete set of Tolstoy's books as a graduation present from the Imperial Theater School. Romola complained, in several places in her book, about Nijinsky's adoption of Tolstoyan ideas, lamenting what she saw as the malign influence on him during the Ballets Russes tour of the United States from two members of the company, Dmitri Kostrovsky and Nicolas Zverev, the three of them often talking about Tolstoy late into the night. As a member of the Hungarian aristocracy, Romola was no more likely to understand Tolstoy's Christian anarchist teachings than she was to appreciate aesthetic modernism. There is considerable evidence, in the *Diaries*, of Nijinsky's commitment to vegetarianism, anarchism, and pacifism, all of which can be traced to Tolstoy. As Hanna Järvinen has suggested, there are uncanny echoes in the *Diaries* of Tolstoy's essay "What Is Art?"; she notes that "Nijinsky appraised the Tolstoyan view of art as a religious or spiritual experience that would lead to understanding, peace and equality between men."[43] It is this kind of experience that Nijinsky surely aimed to create with his antiwar solo.

Romola and Sandoz both suggest that Nijinsky behaved in an erratic way during the concert. Rather than presenting himself as a stable, coherent individual, Nijinsky was deliberately and provocatively playing the idiot. As Joan Acocella observes in her discussion of the *Diaries*, "The paradox of the wise fool, 'jester of God,' sane madman, is . . . a standard Christian idea, and more than standard in Russia. Nijinsky mentions *The Idiot* [in his *Diaries*] and compares himself to Dostoevsky's hero."[44] This, too, fits with Romola's and Sandoz's accounts of the concert. Notions about the artist as utopian visionary were circulating at that time in discussions about expressionism.

As Rose-Carol Long notes, expressionist artists and architects "looked upon their work as instruments for transforming society and searched for a style that would effectively change the moral and ethical climate."[45] For Nijinsky, and for Wigman as well, this kind of progress was one driven by spiritual or metaphysical forces that could be detected only through a rejection of materialism and positivist rationality, and by opening oneself up to the new and unknown. In this way an avant-garde modernist sensibility coincided with a spiritual outlook that took the form of aesthetic mysticism.

During her concert in Davos, Wigman premiered a new version of her cycle *Ekstatische Tänze*. Susan Manning suggests that the first version in 1917 had been made while still under Laban's influence, reflecting in particular her involvement in his epic durational *Sang an die Sonne* (Song to the Sun). This was a three-part work performed outdoors on midsummer day in Monte Verità at sunrise, noon, and sunset, based on rituals derived from mystical and esoteric ideas. Whereas in 1917 Wigman's esoteric ideas took a dramatic, representational form, in the revised 1919 version they were more abstracted. In 1917 the cycle consisted of five pieces in which Wigman, as Manning puts it, impersonated roles that alternated between masculine and feminine. Manning deduces this from analyzing a description by Wigman's friend Bertha Trümpy of the 1917 cycle.[46] In *Die Nonne*, a nun prayed devotedly in a space that, in this first version, was set with candles and incense. In *Der Tänzer Unserer Lieben Frau*, a male acrobat/dancer performed before the Virgin Mary. Following this, in *Götzendienst* an apparition from the primeval forest twisted and whirled in a straw cape and cap. Next came a fervent dance from a humble priestess in *Opfer* (Sacrifice), followed by *Der Derwitsch*, in which Wigman became a male Dervish with false beard and trousers. Finally, the mystical, contemplative, female temple dancer in *Tempeltanz* gradually sank into blessed stillness. In 1919, Manning notes, the two "male" dances— of the acrobat and the Dervish—were dropped and in their place a new dance, *Gebet* (Prayer), was added. Without the contrast between masculine and feminine, the dances in the revised cycle seemed less gender-specific, some critics reviewing the 1919 performances describing an impersonal quality in the dancer's presence. Manning also notes that in 1919, rather than always performing the cycle as a whole, Wigman often programmed only a pair of pieces from it, so that what had been a continuous narrative became separate abstracted pieces. One can surmise that in 1917, the cycle had a dramaturgical coherence: a confrontation with an apparition led to a climactic spiritual frenzy (the Dervish) and ended with the reward of greater spiritual sensitivity (the temple dancer). In 1919, however, the emotional essences of each dance seem to have been condensed into an impersonal, abstracted form.

While Nijinsky presented an indisputably antiwar piece in St. Moritz, Wigman's 1919 program made no explicit reference to the war. Nevertheless her pieces were created in the context of pacifism. Her illness and retreat in 1918 followed a succession of serious personal problems. Isabelle Launay suggests these may have contributed to Wigman's mental and physical breakdown.[47] Wigman heard that her grandfather had died and discovered that her brother had been invalided out of the army, returning home an amputee. A romantic relationship broke up, and Wigman fell out professionally with Laban, who himself was in serious financial difficulties with his Zurich dance school. Then she was diagnosed as suffering from tuberculosis. While recovering, Wigman writes, she joined a religious community whose members were shocked when she rehearsed her dances out of doors in a state of undress.

Manning proposes that in *Götzendienst*, Wigman's straw costume functions like a mask. Her thesis is:

At times Wigman used actual facial masks, but more often her costume or her facial expression, or both, functioned like masks. And in another sense her dancing became a metaphorical mask, for she did not dramatize her autobiography on stage but rather staged her self-transformations into another.[48]

I have already suggested that Wigman refused to express a conventional individuality. Where critics found her performances impersonal, this surely demonstrates that, as Manning suggests, Wigman's facial expression could function like a mask. By not dramatizing her autobiography and by becoming what Manning calls "an other," Wigman was becoming ecstatic in the literal sense of standing outside oneself, in classical Greek *ek-stasis*. There are two ways during the dance cycle that Wigman became ecstatic in the Greek sense: by giving oneself up in a self-less act of sacrifice and through losing oneself to an irrational force. The former takes place in *Opfer* (Sacrifice). Her expression of grief, suffering, and self-sacrifice would have resonated strongly as people across Europe counted the personal cost of the war. This subject would become one of Wigman's long-running choreographic themes. *Götzendienst* exemplified losing oneself to an irrational force. In the 1917 cycle, the ecstatic nature of the dancing was signaled primarily through costumed, role-playing dances and dramaturgy. In the 1919 version, costume as mask, choreographic abstraction, and the impersonality of the dancer's performative presence created an ecstatic mood.

In the concert at Davos, Wigman set the moral example of *Opfer* alongside the power of *Götzendienst,* the irrational energy of which came from a rejection of rationality. There are parallels between the irrational, ecstatic mood of Wigman's dances and the work of the Zurich Dadaists with whom Wigman was in close contact during the war years. Most dance scholars stress the differences between Laban's school and the Dadaists. Thus Carol-Lynne Moore notes, "Laban's students found themselves drawn into Dada events. Laban's attendance at Dada performances is clearly documented although he appears not to have contributed personally to the sometimes outrageous proceedings."[49] Laban did, in fact, contribute on at least one occasion. The program for the Dada Soirée on April 28, 1917, included music by Schoenberg, possibly an arrangement of his *Three Piano Pieces* (opus 11, 1909) played by Laban and Perrotet. No doubt Perrotet found in Schoenberg the dissonance denied her at Hellerau. Moore goes on to suggest, "Laban's artistic sensibilities do not seem to have extended to provocative avant-garde movements like Dada, Futurism, and the politicised Expressionism of the 1920s."[50]

This is to assume that all the Dadaists were uniformly nihilist and thus had entirely different concerns from the dancers of Laban's school, whereas the situation in Zurich was more complex. Art historian Hal Foster warns against making an easy equation between the avant-garde and transgression. He points out that "the critical moment in modernist art is often a stressing of a given fracture in the symbolic order."[51] The Zurich Dadaists' attitude toward the war is an example of this. Some artists, Foster suggests, "do not strive to critique this order at all, but, rather, struggle to make it over, or at least to shore it up."[52] While Dada poets like Richard Huelsenbeck and Tristran Tzara, who became involved in left-wing politics after the war, created nihilistic provocations, other Zurich Dadaists were more affirmative. Jean Arp, for example, later remembered, "Revolted by the butchery of the 1914 World War, we in Zurich devoted ourselves to the arts. . . . We were seeking an art based on fundamentals, to cure the madness of the age."[53] One might see Wigman's Davos concert as an attempt to seek artistic fundamentals that could cure the madness of the age.

Art historian David Hopkins argues that some of the more extreme performances presented in the early stages of Zurich Dada at the Cabaret Voltaire had unexpected consequences: "Virtually re-enacting the traumatic and dislocating effects of the war they were opposed to, the Dadaists unleashed forces they themselves found unsettling."[54] Kenneth Silver makes a similar argument about cubism and trench warfare: "Cubism offered both a system for the breaking down of forms and a method for organising pictorial decomposition. For a war that—with its trench fighting, new incendiary devices, modern artillery, and poison gas—was unprecedented in every way, Cubism's lack of association with the past was the analogue of the *poilu*'s [ordinary French soldier's] general sense of dissociation."[55] Dadaism offered a similarly unprecedented approach to breaking down conventional form. So did Wigman's modernist approach to dance.

A passage in Laban's 1920 book *Die Welt des Tänzers* (The Dancer's World) called "The Birth of a Demon" expresses concerns about a dancer who unleashes unexpectedly unsettling forces. Although the dancer is unnamed, this must surely be a description of a solo performance by Wigman. The straw-caped apparition in *Götzendienst* could be called a demon, and there were other demonic dances in her repertory, including the witch of *Hexentanz*.

> Who has not been present at the birth of a demon? A room full of
> people. In front upon a raised platform the dancer moves. Sometimes
> considering, then passionately twirling, gestural strength speaks from
> him. The initial slumbering reverie of the audience is slowly kindled by
> these waves. Soon invisible currents appear from man to man and he
> who can see can see the tensions of an immense net of crystallised force
> which surrounds everything. Nobody, not even the coldest of observ-
> ers can escape this dance when rousing applause rushes through the

room. . . . A demon is born. Or was he only unchained and was present invisibly before that?[56]

Laban is perhaps a little ambivalent about this electrifying dance performance. He goes on to say, "No being on earth has greater power to unchain the demon than the dancer," but argues that this power carries responsibilities.[57] It should lead dancers to greater self-knowledge and they should never let themselves be taken over by it: "The stimulation of egoism destroys the power of gesture . . . the dancer knows that it is a basic law of gestural power that he must not be misused by egotistical purposes."[58] What Laban is saying here is that when a dancer allows the stimulation of egoism to destroy the power of dance material, he or she is closing down the potential for becoming ecstatic and thereby expressing deeper truths. Laban's ambivalence here suggests that he has other reservations as well. In Foster's terms, Laban surely reveals himself here as someone who tries to make over or shore up fractures in the symbolic order and is worried that Wigman's performance will do the opposite. His message is that one must always pay something back to society, whereas Wigman's ecstatic performance attempted to embrace the difficult truth of positive, absolute freedom.

Nijinsky and Wigman sought to express their own versions of this difficult truth, the aesthetic mysticism of Nijinsky's holy fool paralleling that of Wigman's demons and priestesses. Their solos enacted a modernist critique of dominant ideologies of freedom and individuality and, by doing so, stressed a fracture in the symbolic order. The efficacy of their critique was dependent on the fact that they were using their ecstatic mode of consciousness to seek new relations with the world.

I made a claim at the start of this essay that the 1919 concerts given by Nijinsky and Wigman in St. Moritz and Davos marked a significant moment in the development of the modern dance solo. Much of my analysis and interpretation of the archival traces left from these concerts has been concerned with understanding them in relation to their historical and artistic context. It was a context of disconcerting change, including the development of a consumer society that promoted aspirations of self-fulfillment through self-expression. Different approaches to the interpretation of Chopin's music, and tensions surrounding what can or cannot be expressed within Jaques-Dalcroze's harmonious system, reveal what was distinctively modernist in Nijinsky's and Wigman's aesthetic sensibilities. At stake is not just the distance separating Nijinsky from Duncan (or Fokine), and between Wigman and Jaques-Dalcroze, but also that between Wigman and Laban. Dance scholars are right to suggest that Laban did not approve of the more nihilistic tendencies of early twentieth-century avant-garde artists, but they nevertheless need to recognize how much his work had in common with theirs. The passage "Birth of a Demon" demonstrates how much he understood their radicalism. Wigman, up until her break with Laban, would have turned to him in particular for critical feedback on works like *Götzendienst*. What the two concerts in 1919 therefore mark is not just the existence of modernist sensibilities but the way these manifested themselves in ecstatic performances.

Like Nijinsky and Wigman, later dancers have discovered that being alone on stage can act as a powerful incentive for finding challenging new ways of relating to the world. This raises questions about the bonds connecting aloneness, relationality, and becoming ecstatic. It is here that the ideas of Jean-Luc Nancy and Maurice Blanchot about the artist's exceptional aloneness, introduced earlier, are useful. I noted that for Blanchot, art comes from solitude, and I have argued that in their 1919 solos, Nijinsky and Wigman vacated the self in the way Blanchot described. Blanchot could almost have been describing their solos when he wrote, "What approaches me is not my being a little less myself, but rather something which there is 'behind me,' and which this 'me' conceals in order to come into its own."[59] Nancy and Blanchot seek to express the existential meaning of the ecstatic relationship I have suggested Nijinsky and Wigman created between their dancing and the world. It is this radical kind of relationship, I suggest, that makes Nijinsky and Wigman, rather than Duncan, the initiators of a genre of radical solos that has continued through the twentieth and twenty-first centuries.

For Nancy the world is always a world of beings whose primary existence is that of being "with," being outwardly directed to others. He says that the meaning of "Seul(e) au monde"—alone into the world—is that the solo dancer makes a world though performing movement. "The movement of opening up the self," he says, "is for me immediately the nature of dance," of bringing the dancer's presence, which is always something fluidly flowing from what precedes it into what succeeds it.[60] Whereas Laban and Wigman discussed the meaning of the relation in mystical terms, and Nijinsky understood it through the anarchist Christian ideas he found in Tolstoy, Nancy and Blanchot have developed ways of discussing "relationality" in terms of a secularized and demystified metaphysics. Within the genre of radical solos that I suggest Nijinsky and Wigman initiated, the relation the dancer creates with and toward the world is one that links the singularity of aloneness to the plurality of the world, which is always a world of others.

Notes

I am grateful to Hanna Järvinen and Claudia Gitelman for their comments on an earlier draft.

1. Romola Nijinsky, *Nijinsky* (London: Sphere Books, 1970), 336.

2. Peter Ostwald, *Vaslav Nijinsky: A Leap into Madness* (New York: Carol Publishing, 1991), 180.

3. Mary Wigman, *The Mary Wigman Book: Her Writings*, ed. and trans. Walter Sorell (Middletown, Conn.: Wesleyan University Press, 1975), 51.

4. Romola Nijinsky, *Nijinsky*, 336. In his own account, he told her in the carriage on the way home after the concert. Vaslav Nijinsky, *The Diaries of Vaslav Nijinsky: Unexpurgated Edition*, ed. Joan Acocella (New York: Farrar, Straus and Giroux, 1999), 7.

5. Indeed, none of the three sources can be considered to be entirely reliable.

6. See Susan Manning, *Ecstasy and the Demon: The Dances of Mary Wigman* (Minneapolis: University of Minnesota Press, 2006); Mary Anne Santos Newhall, *Mary Wigman* (London: Routledge, 2009); Hedwig Müller, *Mary Wigman: Leben und Werk der grossen Tänzerin* (Weinheim: Quadriga Verlag, 1986).

7. Julie Malnig, "Athena Meets Venus: Visions of Women in Social Dance in the Teens and Early 1920s," *Dance Research Journal* 31, no. 2 (Fall 1999): 34–62.

8. Manning, *Ecstasy*, 15–27.

9. Mathilde Monnier and Jean-Luc Nancy, "Seul(e) au monde," in *La Danse en solo: Une Figure singulière de la modernité*, ed. Claire Rousier (Pantin: Centre National de la Danse, 2002), 51–62.

10. Maurice Blanchot, *The Space of Literature* (Lincoln: University of Nebraska Press, 1989), 251.

11. Hans Prinzhorn, *Artistry of the Mentally Ill: A Contribution to the Psychology and Psychopathology of Configuration* (New York: Springer-Verlag, 1972), 266.

12. Raymond Williams, *Keywords* (London: Fontana Books, 1976), 79.

13. Zygmunt Bauman and Keith Tester, *Conversations with Zygmunt Bauman* (London: Polity, 2001), 114.

14. Zygmunt Bauman, *Freedom* (Milton Keynes, U.K.: Open University Press, 1988), 42.

15. Ibid., 41.

16. Wigman, *Mary Wigman Book*, 186.

17. Bronislava Nijinska, *Early Memoirs* (London: Faber, 1982), 122.

18. Maurice Sandoz, *The Crystal Salt Cellar* (London: Guilford, 1954), 74.

19. Ann Daly, *Done into Dance* (Bloomington: Indiana University Press, 1995), 66.

20. Although Duncan primarily danced to nineteenth-century music, she included works by seventeenth- and eighteenth-century composers in her repertory, among them a piece danced to an orchestral suite by Bach. See Daly, *Done into Dance*, 142–43.

21. Sandoz, *Crystal Salt Cellar*, 74.

22. Ibid.

23. Similar complaints had been made about his earlier choreography. See Hanna Järvinen, "Stillness and Modernity in Nijinsky's *Jeux* 1913," *Discourses in Dance* 5, no. 2 (2010): 15–31.

24. Sandoz, *Crystal Salt Cellar*, 75.

25. Ibid., 71.

26. Ibid. Hanna Järvinen points out that two constant criticisms regarding Nijinsky's choreographies (especially *Sacre*) were the "endless repetition of the same" ("jusqu'au irritation") and "following the musical structure too closely" (walking "between the notes"). E-mail to the author, December 7, 2009.

27. Manning, *Ecstasy*, 15–18.

28. Cited in Manning, *Ecstasy*, 68.

29. Ibid., 64.

30. Cited in Selma Odom, "Wigman at Hellerau," *Ballet Review* 14, no. 2 (1986): 51.

31. Cited in Hedwig Müller, "Émile Jaques-Dalcroze: The Beginnings of Rhythmic Gymnastics in Helerau," *Ballett-International* 8, no. 6–7 (June–July 1985): 24.

32. Ibid.

33. Tamara Levitz, "In the Footsteps of Euridice: Gluck's *Orpheus und Euridice* in Hellerau, 1913," *Echo* 3, no. 2 (2002), http://www.echo.ucla.edu (accessed August 14, 2008).

34. Cited in Martin Green, *Mountain of Truth: The Counterculture Begins* (Hanover, N.H.: University Press of New England, 1986), 96.

35. Cited in Odom, "Wigman at Hellerau," 50.

36. Mary Wigman, *The Language of Dance* (Middletown, Conn.: Wesleyan University Press, 1966), 37.

37. As art historian Maurice Tuchman notes, the painter Wassily Kandinsky derived from his close interest in the theosophical and anthroposophical movements an idea about vibrations in painting, which, in a synesthetic way, he associated with sound (German *Klang*). Kandinsky believed that "human emotion consists of vibrations of the soul set into vibration by nature." Maurice Tuchman, ed., *The Spiritual in Art: Abstract Painting 1890–1985* (New York: Abbeville, 1986), 35. Wigman, too, was concerned with finding the inner vibrations within experiences.

38. Romola Nijinsky, *Nijinsky*, 337.

39. Sandoz, *Crystal Salt Cellar*, 73.

40. Ibid.

41. Romola Nijinsky, *Nijinsky*, 337.

42. Lev Tolstoy, *Tolstoy's Writings on Civil Disobedience and Non-Violence* (London: Owen, 1968), 225–32.

43. Hanna Järvinen, *The Myth of Genius in Movement: Historical Deconstruction of the Nijinsky Legend* (Turku, Finland: Turun Yliopisto, 2003), 411.

44. Nijinsky, *Diaries*, xl.

45. Rose-Carol Washton Long, "Expressionism, Abstraction, and the Search for Utopia in Germany," in *The Spiritual in Art*, ed. Maurice Tuchman, 201.

46. Manning, *Ecstasy*, 62–65.

47. Isabelle Launay, *À la Recherche d'une danse moderne: Rudolf Laban, Mary Wigman* (Paris: Éditions Chiron, 1996), 18.

48. Ibid., 43.

49. Carol-Lynne Moore, *The Harmonic Structure of Movement, Music and Dance According to Rudolf Laban: An Examination of His Unpublished Writings and Drawings* (Lampeter, U.K.: Edwin Mellen Press, 2009), 20–21.

50. Ibid., 33, fn 46.

51. Hal Foster, *Prosthetic Gods* (Cambridge, Mass.: MIT Press, 2004), xii.

52. Ibid.

53. Hans Arp, cited in Hans Richter, *Dada: Art and Anti-Art* (London: Thames and Hudson, 1965), 25.

54. David Hopkins, *Dada and Surrealism: A Very Short Introduction* (Oxford: Oxford University Press, 2004), 32.

55. Kenneth Silver, *Esprit de Corps: The Art of the Parisian Avant-Garde and the First World War, 1914–25* (London: Thames and Hudson, 1989), 84.

56. Rudolf von Laban, *Die Welt des Tänzers* (Stuttgart: Walter Sieffert, 1920), 101.

57. Ibid., 102.

58. Ibid.

59. Blanchot, *Space of Literature*, 251.

60. Monnier and Nancy, "Seul(e) au monde," 62.

three

The Solo That
Isn't a Solo

Ann Carlson's
Dances with Animals

Janice Ross

Isadora Duncan, the great soloist progenitor of modern dance, famously declared that she had never danced a solo. "When I have danced I have tried always to be the Chorus: I have been the Chorus of young girls hailing the return of the fleet, I have been the Chorus dancing the Pyrrhic Dance or the Bacchic; I have never once danced a solo," Duncan wrote in her 1928 essay "The Dance of the Greeks."[1] Her statement has customarily been dismissed as part of the hyperbole accompanying her epic gesture of dancing the female body politic. As the initial architect of the solo female dancer in the twentieth century and the woman who negotiated what Duncan scholar Ann Daly has called "the complex semiotics of representation" of the female form in the cultural currents of her time, Duncan's proclamation is intriguing.[2] It hints at the complex signifying work of the solo female dancer's body on stage and its effort to be both particular and universal while resisting traditional historical associations of the unmannered or bestial.

This question of how one might read a female modern dancer performing alone as a "solo that is never a solo" offers a useful frame for this essay and its consideration of the solo work of Ann Carlson as an exposé of the mutual reinforcement and conflation of identity categories between the animal and human.[3] Carlson is a highly individual American postmodern choreographer who performs relatively infrequently but whose works are important wry movement expositions about the complex negotiations of being both author and text that surround the female soloist.

This essay considers the fraught negotiation of social, gender, and performance issues initiated by Carlson's solos with and about animals. In four of her signature dances—*Animals* (1988), *Sloss, Kerr, Rosenberg and Moore* (1986, 2007), *Grass/Bird/Rodeo* (1999), and *Madame 710* (2008)—she explores the interplay between gender identification and the volatilities of the social bodies and public identities we create. She uses our relationship with animals as one of the central paths into this investigation, ironically evoking the great essentialist myths displayed in Romantic ballets of the nineteenth century where women were seen as having a uniquely close connection to animals, spirits, and the natural world. In all four of these works Carlson also uses performance to inscribe multiple overlapping historical, social, and behavioral movement texts on the dancer's body. In all but *Sloss, Kerr, Rosenberg and Moore*, her quartet of simultaneous solos for four male lawyers, this body is female and contemporary, and its actual or metaphoric counterpart is animal.

Carlson, like her ghostly predecessor Isadora Duncan, occasionally breaks the fourth wall to speak directly to the audience from the stage—at times offering a cozy tutorial to live spectators on how we can watch her performances when she is the sole performer, choreographer, and narrator. Carlson has explained that she began conversing with her audiences as a way of folding the customary postperformance question-and-answer exchange into the performance itself.[4] In some works she solicits questions from the audience during the actual performance, and other times she chats amiably about specifics of the performance while changing costumes on stage. These talks become a part of a charting through performance of the "explicit body politic of the female dancer."[5] They simultaneously show and coach the spectator on how to connect with, what to attend to, and, implicitly, the agency and civilized control of the performer.

A talking female dancer is herself a radical intervention historically, and Carlson's vocalization productively challenges the power negotiation between spectator and performer in her solos. Carlson has said that between 1986 and 1988, as she was embarking on her major exploration of the solo form, she also began to think differently about how audiences were receiving her work. "I began to think of the audience as someone who was in the position of giving keen and loving attention, as opposed to critical judgment," she said, acknowledging that at the same time she was also developing a correspondingly gentle internal audience in herself.[6]

It was on the cusp of this shift in her perception of the audience as sympathetic and nonthreatening that in 1988 Carlson created *Animals*. This full-evening work is, in part, about the nonjudgmental and noncritical ethos of all (nonhuman) animals. It is her first dance with sentient nonhominoid partners on stage, fellow performers who in fact need precisely this kind of climate of kindness from the humans around them if they are to function effectively on display.

In each section of *Animals* she performs and in *Madame 710*, Carlson pairs herself with a live animal as a way of undoing her solo authorship. Yet she also paradoxically produces it by carefully scripting the performance as a container for the animal's natural behaviors read against her attempts to display human "naturalness." Dances such as *Madame 710* and Carlson's solos in *Animals*, specifically "Sarah" (with a goldfish), "Visit Woman Move Story Cat Cat Cat" (with a kitten), and "The Dog Inside the Man" (with a dog) complicate the category "solo" because they involve one person but two performers as well as one choreographed set of actions and another wholly unscripted but at the same time responsive to what is going on.

If one considers these dances across the more than twenty-year span of their making, beginning with the epic 1988 full-evening *Animals*, the persistence of Carlson's fascination with the layers of subjectivity one can pack into the dancing of a lone body is remarkable. It might be argued that she has steadily enlarged the category of the dance solo both in terms of the temporal references it includes and her revelation of the deceptiveness of its apparent transparency and simplicity. Carlson's solos rarely are about just the dancing human individual in the present moment. Instead she gives us snapshots over time, beginning with her early ideas for the dance—its autobiographical antecedents—and eventually showing us what these influences look like fully "brewed" into choreography. Throughout all this Carlson steadily shrinks the divide between presence and representation; that is, between embodiment and display. "The line between my life and my work is so thin that sometimes I long for the veil to be thicker," she once remarked in an interview.[7]

Most tellingly, the animals in Carlson's works are naturalistically "performing" themselves, the same goal she has for herself. Except for the boundaries of domestication that contain the cat, two goats, goldfish, and cow, Carlson's animal partners (beyond the trained dog in "The Dog Inside the Man" section of *Animals*) are not disciplined into any behavior other than the natural repertory of slow walking, chewing, standing, and lazy swaying actions a seasoned dairy cow might repeat (*Madame 710*) or the curious alert stillness of a tiny kitten measuring opportunity against potential danger on a cavernous empty stage (*Animals*). In all these instances Carlson elevates the animal body as she adumbrates the animal in the human.

In her solos with animals Carlson's choreography evolves from her movement response to each of her animal partners' physical vocabularies. In part she is engaged in what the theorist Michel de Certeau named his book, *The Practice of Everyday Life*: how people individualize mass culture in order to personalize it as she creates a nontraditional way to be a consumer of animals without eating them, to allow them some autonomy within the rules of being domesticated.[8]

Animals represents the beginnings of Carlson's solo dances with animals and as such it reflects its historical moment, a time when human and animal performances were not as freighted with associations of endangerment and abuse. In a postperformance discussion recorded at the time of this five-part work's 1988 premiere at Dance Theater Workshop in New York, Carlson remarked that she had originally begun working with live animals as "an observation technique," a "nonabusive" way to observe and reproduce their actions without ever intending to have them in the finished performance. "It was a performance experiment," she said. "I wanted to challenge my own ideas about performance. I wanted to give myself and others a context to be completely themselves."[9]

This impulse to deploy the vocabulary of the ordinary dates from the beginning of Carlson's training as an artist when, in a college art-history class in the late 1970s she happened upon the work of Carolee Schneemann, Chris Burden, Eleanor Antin, Vito Acconci, and Hannah Wilke. "Some kind of blinders fell off," Carlson said of that encounter. "I learned about what some visual artists were doing using the body in performance as a kind of canvas as opposed to a vehicle."[10] Carlson subsequently began working as a collagist on the canvas of her body in her solos, using a resonance of images to create meanings that accrue through assemblage and layering.

Indeed, *Animals* discloses a different relationship between human and animal than was usually depicted in 1970s and 1980s performance, a time less open to anthropomorphizing and more focused on the live animal as an inspiration for a new physical lexicon. What it also showcases much more than her later solos is Carlson "becoming animal," trying on the actions and identities of her animal associates. In keeping with the capacity of Carlson's solos to disclose the social moment of their construction, *Animals* was clearly made at a time of awareness about environmental and animal extinction that was far more rudimentary than what it would become by the second decade of the twenty-first century.

In her three solos in *Animals* Carlson represents the animals with which she co-inhabits the stage, encountering in shared time and space their presence on her own body. She has said she made "a couple of research trips to the Bronx Zoo" as she was creating "Visit Woman Move Story Cat Cat Cat," a portrait of Koko the Gorilla and her beloved kitten, and that for "Sarah," her movement portrait of a dolphin at Sea World in San Diego, California, she spent time at Martha's Vineyard listening to whale and other sea mammal sounds.[11]

In *Animals* Carlson is masterful at not just keen observation skills but kinesthetic expertise in transferring the weighted, swinging gait of a joyful gorilla onto her own unselfconsciously nude body, and in the instance of "Sarah," how to reshape her anatomy so that she presents herself upended, flexed feet and straight legs negotiating the air like a dorsal fin slicing through a watery current. In expressing the bond between Koko and her kitten, and the dolphin and her trainer, Carlson imbues her performance with that quest for a renewed relationship between humans and animals that Performance Studies theorist Una Chaudhuri identifies as a recent feature of animal representation in performance and part of the urgent search "in the arts and humanities to identify new means of seeing, showing and knowing the animals."[12] Carlson also charts new territory in the area of cultural representation of animals in performance that Chaudhuri deems the most deficient element in the field. "Whether approached with the tools of rationality or those of imagination, the lives of animals as currently configured generally resist meaningful cultural visitation on any significant scale," Chaudhuri has written.[13]

Carlson's use of her own nudity in "Visit" is not consciously theatrical or eroticized but rather a statement of emotional undress—a "cultural visitation" through dance and a means for her to present the complex emotions Koko displayed when her kitten companion eventually died. "Do you have to do it naked?" Carlson's mother asked her after seeing the dance for the first time. Carlson knew she was referring in particular to the moments when Carlson pauses in a deep squat, her backside fully exposed to the audience as she bats at her hair with one hand as if waving away insects. "I felt like on some level of the piece I was grieving *shame*," Carlson said later, remembering her mother's embarrassment at her naked bum juxtaposed with Carlson's deep immersion in her character of Koko grieving for the dead little cat. "Because the shame and the grief felt very close."[14] (fig. 3.1)

Isadora Duncan seems a shadow presence in "Visit" because, as in Duncan's early solos, it is the grandeur of the full-figured female, iconic, maternal, and sensually at ease with her body, that is the means as well as the subject of the dance. Swinging with her full weight spilling from both hands as she hangs on a bar at the foot of the stage or loping across the stage on all fours, a tiny gray kitten dangling by the scruff of her neck from Carlson's mouth, we understand the investment Carlson makes in reproducing the qualities of animalness she finds in the gorilla and discovers correspondingly in herself. "I was working with a movement therapist and I had experienced the image of a ball of black fur in my solar plexus," Carlson told the audience about another aspect of the dance's origins. "To me it is more about femaleness than humanness. . . . I kept trusting the idea that genetically along the line I would find the connection between myself and the Gorilla."[15]

"Visit" is performed to the elegiac sadness of Beethoven's Quartet No. 15 (opus 132), which supports the grandeur of its emotions. In the *Animal*

3.1. Ann Carlson and the kitten that shares the stage with her in "Visit Woman Move Story Cat Cat Cat" from *Animals*. Photograph by Lois Greenfield. Courtesy of Ann Carlson.

quintet, the tiniest animal Carlson has ever partnered—a three-inch goldfish in an oval glass bowl—precedes "Visit." This little fish is the smallest of the three Sarahs referred to in the eponymous dance. Carlson, dressed in a strapless black cocktail dress with a gill-like ruffled skirt, portrays the midsized Sarah and the recorded voice of a Sea World announcer coaxing the trained dolphin Sarah to perform for an amusement-park audience representing the life-sized one.

Wearing black stockings and high heels, and with her feet anchored to the floor, Carlson looks sleek, poised, and tragically trapped as she sweeps her outstretched arms through the air forcefully as if struggling to surface from deep underwater. "Sarah" is thus tinged with a different kind of animal sorrow, the remorse of being, or even watching, the trained animal compelled to perform. We read all these emotions and conditions on Carlson's glamorously clad body, which also registers the more familiar discomfort of watching a performing female. The pain is made more complex because of the density of these imperative performances—the trained dance soloist's body portraying a seductive woman as the proxy for the trained dolphin. Meanwhile, the tiny goldfish Sarah circles endlessly in her bowl atop a black pedestal in the center of the stage, while the Carlson Sarah churns her arms and spirals her torso with increasing agitation as the recorded voice of the announcer repeats its commands with mounting irritation. "Sarah will give us a kiss today," he bellows as Carlson puts her hands over her eyes and lifts her elbows outward like tail fins while moaning in the high-pitched whine of a sea mammal.

Among the things that Carlson uncovers for viewers in her solos are the various encryptions and transformations the dancer's body, and her awareness of it, undergo in the act of preparing to perform and in performing. Her performances of the ordinariness of consciousness can, at their best, act to contest traditional conceptions of the body that have served for decades to establish identities for women on the stage in essentialist, ahistorical, or universalist terms. While Duncan's reference to spectral Greek choruses accompanying her has been read as a gesture to legitimize herself as part of the classical sisterhood of noble female performers of antiquity, Carlson uses the solo form with a more postmodern agenda: her ghosts are identity categories, particularly those separating the (female) human and the animal, the domesticated woman and the private one running wild outside social boundaries.

For both artists, the solo serves as a vehicle for the female dancer implicitly to explore cultural dualities that circumscribe women performers. It is an assertion, through performance, of what feminist scholar Elizabeth Grosz referred to as the fact that "bodies have all the explanatory power of minds."[16] Duncan and Carlson demonstrate that the solo is an exemplary place to reveal continuing cultural anxieties about the social categories of the female and the animal through dance. The work of both choreographers focuses on what Grosz has called the "volatile body," the body that is "neither while also being both—the private or the public, self or other, natural or cultural, psychical or social, instinctive or learned, genetically or environmentally determined."[17] For the female dancer the solo form highlights this volatility because it is simultaneously a spectacular and an intimate act.

There is no other form of dance in which this volatile body is so exposed in its delicate negotiation between these dualities as the solo. Here is where the viewer's attention can linger on the single individual steadily enough to see the fragments of herself she works to highlight, connect, or at times suppress as she constructs a stage identity. In addition to her *Animals* series of mostly solo dances, Carlson has also created a series of dances about labor, called The Real People Series. In the solos in this series one of the major markers of domestication for humans—the physical vocabulary of labor—becomes the basis of the dance actions.

Sloss, Kerr, Rosenberg and Moore (1986, 2007), the first dance in The Real People Series, was originally made in 1986 with, and on, four young New York lawyers, and then it was revived and filmed twenty-one years later with the same four men taking their original roles. Set in the small space of a hallway outside a bank of elevators in a New York high-rise office building, the men enact their daily gestures in the law profession as a private little dance of frenzied gesticulations and doglike panting, while remaining confined to a tiny section of carpet. They wear the uniform of their profession—dark suits, white shirts, ties, and dress shoes—but the anomaly of their dancing on the edge of the civilized and the canine recasts their, and our, relationship to legal culture and white-collar labor.

The twenty-one-year hiatus between these two performances reveals a deeper integration of these two identities and a settling in of the distinct gesture of labor into the life vocabularies of each man. The conflation of the identity categories between the animal and human here, however, is both less subtle and more comic than in any of the solos Carlson performs herself—with the exception of one. In this one, "The Dog Inside the Man" in *Animals*, Carlson, dressed in a man's white shirt, tie, and boxer shorts, gives a trained dog a series of commands, which she begins obeying herself, becoming more of a panting, eager-to-perform-and-please canine with each new order. Gender—real for the people and imagined for the animals—is troubling and it matters in Carlson's world of solos. The linking of the four lawyers with imaginary dogs is made much more broadly humorous than Carlson's animal solos because of the clear distinction all of the lawyers display between performing themselves and becoming dogs. They make clear that their focus is on *commanding* the canines more than embodying them. At the same time they also invite laughter to dispel the unease of the momentary inversion of seeing lawyers in three-piece suits pleading for a dog's attention.

The more one views Carlson's solo choreography with or about animals, the more nuanced our understanding becomes of how sharing the stage with animals critically recontextualizes the narratives and intersections of a performer's identities. It prompts a fresh appreciation for the capacity to *be present*—the state of being that is unconditional for animals and such a challenge for the human performer. In a recording of her performance of *Grass/Bird/Rodeo* (1999) at the American Dance Festival at Duke University in 2000, Carlson phrased her affection for the solo form this way: "I'm presenting my personhood. This is me. [When I perform a solo] I'm presenting a dance to be fearlessly myself."[18] The implicit idea here of her solos as a basis of understanding herself—meanings and thoughts—not only reverses the false assertion that the mind is *dis*embodied and that thinking transcends feeling, neither of which Carlson believes, but also affirms feelings as part of making meaning and knowledge. This is very much in the spirit of the philosopher John Dewey, whose book *Art as Experience* expounded the eponymous theory formulated in the early twentieth century and was the pedagogical foundation of Carlson's own college training in the University of Arizona's dance program. Much of her solo work is, in fact, about experience on display—hers with the animals. Instead of representing what she imagines this experience to be, she offers it only mildly mediated and lets us look for ourselves within the special frame the stage provides.

Carlson's solo performance strategy is reminiscent tactically of that of another turn-of-the-century art force, the theatrical performer and frequent soloist Adah Menken, about whom cultural studies scholar Daphne Brooks has written, "Menken offered spectators a body which was a text of multiple social and historical inscriptions which doubled and covered over each other."[19] Whereas the primary categories Menken's work illuminated were those of personal issues of racial and gender identification, Carlson, like Duncan and Menken, uses the fecundity of solo performance as a site in which to pair uncomfortable dualities, and in the instance of Carlson this is often the human with the animal, the socialized female partnered literally with a live animal or, as in "Bird," the detritus of its proxy. However, in the work of all three female artists the solo becomes a fragile yet subversive means of revealing the cultural currents of the time—Duncan's strategy now reconnected to the art form she launched.

"Bird," as represented through archival video documentation, begins with Carlson standing before the camera on the empty stage of PS 122, framed by a microphone in front of her and the bare stage behind. A brilliant blue scrim hangs on the back wall, its expanse of open sky broken by strings of white clouds. Carlson is in costume (part of a costume) and she is talking about dancing—talking *as part* of dancing—as "Bird" begins.[20] She wears a sequined bra, glittery G-string, silver high heels, flesh-colored stockings, a huge headdress of tall white feathers, and half-trousers of molting white chicken feathers on one leg. In radical juxtaposition to this flashy showgirl attire, however, Carlson wears no makeup, her hair is messy, and she speaks to the audience in a tone of comfortable intimacy about the prosaic memories that influenced her making of this dance.

So even in these opening moments of her solo, a shadowy twin solo of Carlson examining and subverting representations of women, animals, and spectacular performance conventions unfolds simultaneously. Revealing a flair for what Russian literary critic Mikhail Bakhtin calls the Carnivalesque—a literary mode that subverts and liberates the assumptions of the dominant style or atmosphere through humor and chaos, so that social hierarchies of everyday life, their solemnities and pieties and etiquettes, are profaned and overturned by normally suppressed voices and energies—Carlson's showgirl costume in "Bird" is a masterpiece of excess.[21] The huge feathered headdress she wears is a familiar article of the burlesque dancer's costume, but the other two costume parts, a massive feathered wing and one feathered pant-leg that keeps shedding feathers, add a dimension of the decaying and macabre, reminding us that the bird had to die in order for this fetishizing costume of feathers framing flesh to be constructed. "I told the costume designer LaRue that I wanted to be part bird and part burlesque dancer," Carlson explains to her audience as she dresses on stage in the American Dance Festival recording. The audience laughs, but this is a duality at the heart of so many nineteenth- and twentieth-century images of the commodified female body, from the winged insect sylphs of Romantic ballet to the swans of classical ballet to the feathered women of Las Vegas revues, that the laughter fades quickly. "I resent myself for liking this costume so much," she adds, further complicating her relationship to the image she presents so that its irony is mediated by this confession of the guilty pleasure it gives her. The convention of a striptease, of course, is that the female body is marketed as a commodity through the act of undressing, yet paradoxically getting closer to unavailability each time another item of clothing is removed, but in "Bird" Carlson does the inverse—she adds rather than subtracts items of clothing, assembles rather than uncovers.

As she describes the genesis of "Bird" to the camera for the PS 122 documentary that is the best archival record of this dance, Carlson's costume and choreography gradually acquire more detail and context. Excusing herself, she steps away from the microphone and returns with a sequined glove while continuing to talk about a childhood memory of seeing a New York City Ballet performance at Ravinia where the conventions of performance were shattered when the conductor restarted a section of Balanchine's *Who Cares?* after the dancers got off tempo. "I remember adrenaline rushing through me as I heard the conductor's tap, tap, tap and saw the dancers all run back to restart the ballet," Carlson says, as she slides on her glove and then fastens the huge feathered headdress of a Las Vegas showgirl on her head.

She is deliberately showing us Carlson the artist performing publicly while channeling her private self through childhood memories. "It was a seminal experience of glimpsing a window into the form [of dance] and realizing it was a set of principles, rules, I was following."[22] Carlson's solos contain a similar kind of interruption—a rupture in the flow of the performance where she steps out of her performance persona and back closer to the "offstage" Ann. As she speaks these words we notice how in her costuming and actions Carlson discloses simultaneously the process of revealing and becoming—of disclosure and concealment—that is nested in all of her solo dances.

In the PS 122 video of "Bird," Carlson never stops talking while adding the pieces of her costume. Next she describes a dance lecture-demonstration she saw years earlier in which the choreographer Murray Louis offered his definition of dance as any conscious movement—including washing the dishes. "So I could be dancing all the time," Carlson said, miming washing dishes with exaggerated solemnity. With each story recounted and each piece of costuming she adds, Carlson is using the solo form in "Bird" to expose the permeability of identity categories and the critical way that these categories inform each other. Many of her major solos use the form to question what happens if we read the intersections of human and animal identification at their threshold. Carlson is performing the practice of everyday life—appropriating symbols and traditions from the popular culture tropes of women as animals—to comment on the discomfort of this depiction.

We recognize her costume as the fragments of a burlesque dancer's costume. Yet the warm confessional tone of Carlson's chat with the audience as she adds each item of her costume is scaled diametrically opposite to this flashy, calculated packaging of glamour. The choreography itself, like the costume, is a compilation of a showgirl's seductive strutting, sliced through with the stumbling gait of a wounded animal. This becomes even more uncomfortable to watch when Carlson cuts loose with the piercing cry of a male game bird summoning its mate. We realize with a jolt that the subject has become object as Carlson uses the solo form to represent to her audiences the nuances of these subcultures in American life—strip revues and wild-bird hunting—practices she finds so intriguing and disturbing.

Madame 710 exists at the intersection of these two series of Carlson's dances about animals and labor, respectively. In this remarkable piece Carlson quiets and softens her presence into the silent bulk of a dairy cow, the

Madame 710 of the title who is also her partner in the dance. Sharing a small white room, its floor covered with fresh hay, Carlson signifies her own physiological proximity to the newly washed black-and-white female Holstein by dancing nude, clad only in a clear plastic raincoat filled with dollar bills in the hood, sleeves, and hem. (fig. 3.2)

While her fleshly pink knees and legs, back, and loose breasts are like those of Madame 710, Carlson's addition of the "cash" to her own portrayal of a "cow" suggests a repurposing of her body into the consumption equivalent of the dairy cow. She lumbers through the straw, her arms held oddly in front of her like short legs, and at times she suddenly hurls herself onto her side with the blunt effort of an exhausted large animal needing rest, or a fatigued dairy farmer.

De Certeau's concept of the practice of everyday life as a means to examine the ways in which people appropriate cultural symbols so that "the subject is marked as a series of (potential) messages or inscriptions from or of the social (Other)" offers a useful lens for regarding the dairy cow, and now Carlson as well, as just such marked subjects.[23] There is a frank beauty in the implied fecundity of both females in Carlson's dance, as she presents her own nudity with an uneroticized matter-of-factness, moving about the small room seemingly indifferent to her confinement in a manner that closely approximates that of Madame 710.

As filmed by Carlson's colleague, video artist Mary Ellen Strom, *Madame 710* is enchanting yet disturbing. It enacts a mini-narrative of historical models of animal representation in performance, at the same time commenting ironically on the marketing of female bodies across species. In the first part of the work's three sections, we glimpse only Madame 710's hindquarters, torso, and udder. These are the marketed parts of her body that supply leather, meat, and milk. Carlson's own costume reminds us of this utility of the animal body but always presented as headless because her hood filled with dollar bills also almost totally hides her own head and face from view. In doing this, Carlson provides us an invitation to rethink what Chaudhuri calls "Zooesis," the effect of having art activity happening with animals present in traditionally human-only performance genres (like dance).[24]

As long as it is only Madame 710's body Carlson is dancing with, next to, and behind, the tone of the work is light and humorous, with Carlson

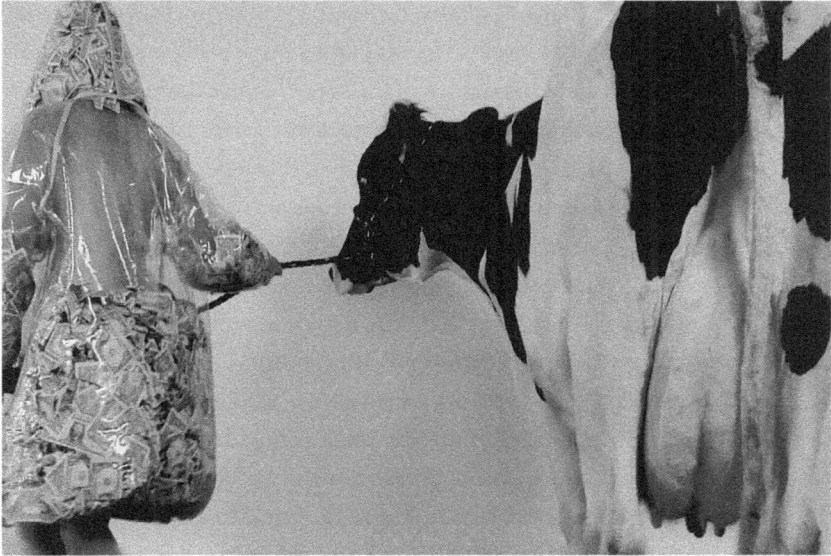

3.2. Ann Carlson costumed in a money-filled clear plastic raincoat with Madame 710, her dairy cow partner in *Madame 710*. Photograph by Mary Ellen Strom. Courtesy of Mary Ellen Strom.

3.3. Ann Carlson in a face-to-face moment with Madame 710 in *Madame 710*. Photograph by Mary Ellen Strom. Courtesy of Mary Ellen Strom.

not doing much more than co-inhabiting the space with the bulky Madame. However, in the second section when Madame's huge black-and-white cow *head* first comes into view, the nature of the solo changes dramatically. Now Carlson quiets her gestures to the smallest postures of attention, gently leaning her head against Madame's brow and holding that pose almost reverently. As she does so, we read emotional connection and responsiveness in the way the cow seems to be gazing back at Carlson, serenely meeting her eye to eye. As her huge lids slowly close and open—blinking in a gesture that cat owners call a visual "kiss"—Madame acquires a soul, according to Chaudhuri's analysis of what face-to-face human-animal encounters produce. (fig. 3.3)

Indeed, the intimacy of Carlson's contact with Madame's face invites anthropomorphism, which Chaudhuri identifies as the idea that animals have emotions and that the expression of emotions is not unique to humans.[25] The prominence of Madame's face and head is critical to Carlson's portrayal of her emotions. In their final head-to-head pose with each other, Madame slowly folds her ears forward and then back as Carlson stays locked in this face-to-face pose. The effect is like a fluttering embrace with Madame's suddenly expressive ears caressing as if they were arms.

Carlson's choreography in all of these solos has succeeded in connecting the life of the mind to the life of the body, repositioning "human" and "animal" literally and metaphorically, as one of many modulations of the psychic interior of the body. In the process she reawakens our awareness of how incision and inscription actively produce that body and that what we do to animals is removed only by degree from what we do to ourselves and to our deputy stage images. Her remarkable solos are cautionary tales about the reality and liabilities of having cultural beliefs, as well as social values and practices, etched upon our bodies.

Like those of Duncan and Menken, Carlson's works prod us into this understanding through her deployment of the hidden narratives that lie within finely wrought solos. Like a series of discrete artists' books, Carlson's works preserve the ephemera of a dance coming into being, the layers of citation and memory in its making, as well as constituting the artifact of the work itself. Her solos make beautifully complex the function of performance as a site where the process of coming into visibility, in this instance for some of the least culturally visible beings, is negotiated, remembered, performed.

The rich implicit narratives of Carlson's solos with animals are tender but compelling reminders of how the act of performing fractures but also re-unites us, affording the solitary dancer the possibility of never really dancing alone.

Notes

1. Isadora Duncan, "The Dance of the Greeks," in *Isadora Duncan: The Art of the Dance* (1928), ed. Sheldon Cheney (New York: Theatre Art Books, 1969), 96.

2. Ann Daly, *Done into Dance: Isadora Duncan in America* (Bloomington: Indiana University Press, 1995), 20.

3. Quoted in "Trailblazers of Modern Dance," *Great Performances*, text by Elizabeth Kendall, dir. Emile Ardolino, WNET-TV, New York, 1979.

4. Ann Carlson, interview by the author, Stanford, California, April 7, 2010.

5. Ibid.

6. Ann Carlson, interview by Irene Borger, in *Force of Curiosity* (Los Angeles: California Institute of the Arts, 1999), 61.

7. Carlson, quoted in Borger, *Force of Curiosity*, 50.

8. Michel de Certeau, *The Practice of Everyday Life* (Berkeley: University of California Press, 1984).

9. Ann Carlson, postperformance talk, Dance Theater Workshop, New York, February 13, 1998.

10. Carlson, in Borger, *Force of Curiosity*, 44.

11. Carlson, postperformance talk.

12. Una Chaudhuri, "(De)Facing the Animals: Zooesis and Performance," *TDR*, Special Issue on Animals and Performance, vol. 51, no. 1 (2007): 10.

13. Ibid.

14. Carlson, in Borger, *Force of Curiosity*, 56.

15. Dance Theater Workshop, documentary DVD, February 2002.

16. Elizabeth Grosz, *Volatile Bodies: Toward a Corporeal Feminism* (Bloomington: Indiana University Press, 1994), vii.

17. Ibid., 23.

18. Ann Carlson, *Grass/Bird/Rodeo*, program, American Dance Festival, Durham, North Carolina, June 2000.

19. Daphne Brooks, *Bodies in Dissent: Spectacular Performances of Race and Freedom, 1850–1919* (Durham, N.C.: Duke University Press, 2006), 160.

20. Ann Carlson, "Bird" from *Grass/Bird/Rodeo*, program, PS 122, New York, February 10–20, 2000.

21. Michael Gardiner, "Bakhtin's Carnival: Utopia as Critique," in *Bakhtin: Carnival and Other Subjects: Selected Papers from the Fifth International Bakhtin Conference, University of Manchester, July 1991,* ed. David Shepherd, *Critical Studies,* vol. 3, no. 3, and vol. 4, nos. 1–2 (Amsterdam: Rodopi, 1993): 20–48.

22. Carlson, in Borger, *Force of Curiosity,* 44–45.

23. De Certeau, quoted in Grosz, *Volatile Bodies,* 119.

24. Chaudhuri, "(De)Facing the Animals," 8–20.

25. Ibid., 12.

four

Aesthetics of Early Modernist Solo Dance in Central Europe

Karl Toepfer

Modern dance in Europe established itself as a distinctive aesthetic experience in the early twentieth century primarily through solo dancing. Audiences became aware of a new relation between body and movement as a result of seeing concerts featuring a lone woman performing a program of dances designed to reveal the power of physical movement to define or amplify her unique personality. Dance became "modern" insofar as it presented a woman who moved "alone" in time and space and "free" of any membership in a communal or social context. Until the early 1920s, modern dance attracted audiences largely through solo dances by women whose movements constructed a unique "personality" that associated the dancer with exceptional power to transcend the moral codes or constraints imposed on the movement of the female body. Audiences granted solo dancers permission to move and display themselves in seductive ways that were otherwise inappropriate anywhere in public except on a stage. By attending solo-dance concerts, audiences sought an expanded understanding of the erotic power of the female body; they sought an intensified insight into women as sexual beings. In turn, solo dancers attempted to differentiate themselves by developing erotic "brands," so to speak, that associated a particular idea of seductive movement or female eroticism not so much with the dancer herself but with her distinctive access to knowledge of female sexuality. Yet solo dancers revealed privileged access to knowledge of female erotic power as much by aligning their movements and displays with mythic images of femininity as with any new way of looking at the relation between movement and female sexuality. What made early solo dance modern, then, was its critique of mythic images of femininity, its ambivalent attitude toward mythic images as models of female sexuality.

Early solo modern dance may be defined as an escalating or at least intensely competitive measure of a woman's capacity to "dare," to determine thresholds of daring. In 1905, Mata Hari (Margarethe van Zelle, 1877–1917) began impressing audiences in Holland and Germany with exotic dances in which, attired in splendid "Asian" costumes vaguely ascribed to her presumed Indonesian heritage, she voluptuously disrobed and displayed her nakedness, often in an unconventional way, such as exposing her pubic region while leaves covered her breasts (fig. 4.1). Her choreography was apparently rudimentary and did little to reveal the expressive potential of movement, and although she experimented with "new" types of dances, such as an "Egyptian ballet" (1913) and a Salome production (1912), she always relied on a familiar vocabulary of "voluptuous" movement: much undulation of the arms, swaying of the hips, sudden thrusts and lurches, violent pivots, and sweeping or arcing strides, with the head held high, proudly, brazenly. She was not one to dramatize superior balance or elegant poise through skillful coordination of upper-body movement with intricate foot- or legwork. Instead, she paid great attention to creating an elaborate scene filled with luxurious details—large plants, orchidaceous flowers, oriental rugs, plush curtains, glittering vases, and mysterious bric-a-brac—that together produced a curious synthesis of jungle and opulent domestic interior.[1]

Because of censorship laws that prevented nonaristocratic audiences from being "invited" to attend her performances, and because she could not expand her audience, aristocratic or not, without sharing with uninvited

4.1. Mata Hari, ca. 1905.

audiences some idea of what they were missing, Mata Hari made innovative use of photography to construct an alluring image of herself as a dancer. Postcards and newspaper images of her posing in her Asian costumes in luxuriant studios circulated throughout Europe. The erotic charm of these pictures almost immediately shaped a powerful public perception of solo modern dance to a large extent quite detached from any actual experience of dance in performance. Moreover, pictures of Mata Hari in her dance poses precipitated an interest in images of her without her "masks": images of her "real" or at any rate her manifold self.

Soon she was modeling fashions, posing on horseback for equestrian events, commissioning glossy portraits of herself, and most interesting of all, having herself photographed performing dances outdoors, in wooded spaces and lush gardens—dances indeed designed exclusively for the camera.[2] Photography subordinated dance to the image of the dancer, so much so that it could retard innovation in choreography, for if anything innovation and complexity of movement undermined the capacity of photography to stabilize perception of the dancer. As long as photography defined solo dance as a primarily pictorial experience, innovation in dance emerged primarily through exotic (that is, "revealing") costumes and accessories, theatrical decor, and flamboyant props, all of which aligned modern dance with an archaic, mythic, and "foreign" image of woman, who, because she belonged to history and to a presumably more relaxed moral climate, could move more freely and more freely awaken desire.

Far more daring and far more imaginative in her thinking about dancing and photography than anyone else of her time, yet far less acknowledged for her contribution than so many "pioneers" of modern dance, was Adoree Villany. Possibly of Hungarian origin, she began her performance career in Germany around 1905 with programs of "ancient" dances evoking Egyptian, Persian, Roman, and Old Testament themes, including the apparently obligatory Salome dance. These she performed throughout Germany and in Holland, Belgium, Vienna, and Prague. Like other solo dancers of the time, she equated the "reform" of dance with images from the ancient world because antiquity offered a view of women who could move and display themselves in a manner that appeared free of the physical constraints imposed on women by nineteenth-century fashion and codified most extravagantly by the rigid and obsessive regulation of female movement in ballet.

In 1908, however, she started to experiment with nudity in the performance of her "Apis" Egyptian dance and in pieces of a more abstract or allegorical significance and of a more melancholy mood, such as "Pain," "Despair," and "The Awakening of Night." At the same time, she began photographing herself performing all of her dances and showing the manifold identity she projected when assuming different poses, movements, costumes, and moods. She understood before anyone that nudity was the key to focusing perception on movement because nudity "freed" the body from the "unnatural" constraints of Christian anxiety toward the destructive or disruptive power of female physical beauty. Villany herself possessed a slender, athletic body, whose beauty hardly diminished when performing her improvised, pantomimic, and often awkward movements. She uniquely understood the expressive capacity of the head, torso, and hands to strengthen dance, and she saw how photographs of movements in succession could deepen appreciation of dance in a way that neither a single image of dance nor observing the dance on the stage could.

Nudity, however, was for her the necessary condition for allowing dance to stir deeper, darker, and more complex emotions. In 1911 Munich police arrested her for performing "absolutely naked" before an "invited" audience. She contested the charges in court and won acquittal, after many members of the Munich artistic and scholarly elite testified on her behalf. She then brought her nude dancing to Paris, where the police of course arrested her for indecency, and the French court, although charmed by her intrepid determination to contest the justice of the proceedings, nevertheless remained unmoved by her defense of artistic freedom, perhaps because in Paris she was not able to summon the support of artists and intellectuals who would testify on behalf of a woman who brought with her such a Teutonic-Jewish (nonballetic) approach to dance.[3] By the time the court had decided that she could not perform naked in France, she had published in Paris but written in German a grandiose, opulent book, *Tanz-Reform und Pseudo-Moral*, offered as "critical-satirical reflections on my life and stage works," but in reality a complex treatise on the role of female solo dance in transforming social consciousness.

The book is immensely entertaining, partly because the author discloses a pervasive sense of humor in regard to her detractors, skeptics, and prosecutors. While she made hardly any reference to other solo dancers, Villany did describe her own dances in greater detail than other dancers had done, and she accompanied her descriptions with numerous photographs to show both the range of possibilities for modern solo dance and the evolution of her aesthetic in relation to a larger examination of the social environment in which she cultivated her art. She discussed the differences between audiences in different cities, deciphered moral codes that encumbered the development of dance art and physical health, described the practical difficulties of pursuing a career in dance, inserted magazine interviews with herself, and proposed methods and exercises for strengthening the health of the body. The large appendix to the book also included an extensive collection of reviews from all over Europe that gave the most comprehensive description of a modern dancer's performances that anyone had ever bothered to assemble up to that time (or well beyond). It is an eccentric book. The author mixes expansive historical erudition with gossipy anecdotes of her theatrical adventures in European cities; she publishes glamorous photographs of herself modeling and dancing, along with cartoons and caricatures of herself that appeared in the popular press. She even included the scenario for a 1910 dance-pantomime dramatizing the hallucinatory effect of opium, as a woman (Villany) transforms herself into an avenging panther that kills the man who betrayed her.

Yet despite the abundance of fascinating material in the book, Villany revealed hardly anything of her personal life. By doing so, she implied that dance as an art had little to do with revealing the self of the dancer; dance had no great value as a disclosure of autobiographical experience. For precisely this reason, nudity enjoyed special significance in dance. The nakedness of the dancer did not create a more transparent or clarifying "exposure" of the dancer's personality; nakedness did not establish higher or greater magnitudes of vulnerability, strength, purity, or moral ambiguity in the dancer. For Villany, nudity in dance was an entirely aesthetic phenomenon: it was the revelation of a beautiful form in motion, and this form achieved its most intense beauty when it incarnated abstract moods, such as Despair in her eponymous work.[4]

A similar sensibility informed the solo performance aesthetic of Olga Desmond (1890–1960), a German from East Prussia. She began her performance career in 1906 at the London Pavilion when she appeared as the only woman in a four-person team of models; her male partners were athletes, with bodies excellently trained for wrestling and boxing. The team performed *tableaux vivants* of famous artworks and mythic scenes, apparently with musical accompaniment. The law allowed them to perform these scenes nearly nude as long as they did not move and drew the curtain to conceal the movements they made in reaching the next pose.[5] The success of the team was immense. What the spectator saw was a mysterious, disconcertingly vivid image of "living marble," bodies coated with white powder and posed on pedestals or, relief-like, against "stone" walls. So expertly constructed was the tension between stone and flesh that the spectator longed

4.2. Olga Desmond and Adolf Salge as "living statues" in *Conquered*, 1908.

to see the bodies move, to see them freed from a fixed, idealized, yet almost monumentally indecisive condition between life and death (fig. 4.2). Desmond grasped this profound audience hunger to see the movement of bodies frozen by their ideality.

When she returned to Germany, she developed a partnership with one of her colleagues in the London venture, Adolf Salge, and changed her name from Olga Sellin to Olga Desmond. With Salge, she continued to perform living statues, and they incorporated three more male athletes into their series of incarnations of popular (mostly German) paintings and mythic-allegorical figures. In February 1908, however, in Berlin, Desmond began introducing solo dances between tableaux, short pieces set to music by Gounod, Chopin, and Offenbach, in which she fluttered and skittered about the stage clad in simple diaphanous tunics. At the time, advertising that a program of living-statue scenes also contained dances was enough to attract a strong audience. Desmond was entirely self-taught as a dancer, and she apparently realized that she could not sustain audience attention unless she did more than present herself as a pretty body that offered a relaxing contrast to the comparatively somber tone of the living statue scenes. In Berlin she made the acquaintance of Karl Vanselow (1877–1959), who became her husband. Vanselow edited a glamorous magazine dedicated to glorifying nudism and social-sexual reform, *Die Schönheit,* as well as other publications devoted to sexual enlightenment, eroticism, and physical beauty. He was an encouraging spirit, but it is doubtful that he exerted a Svengali-like influence over Desmond. Rather, Desmond saw that through him she gained access to a cosmopolitan audience with whom she could win great favor in spite of her limited education and ability to meet expectations of artistic daring.

In May 1908 she introduced the piece that made her a star of the German dance culture, *Der Schwertertanz* (Sword Dance). In this piece, apparently accompanied by improvised piano music, Desmond appeared completely nude except for a small crown, an arm bracelet, and a jeweled girdle belt that somewhat covered her pubic zone. She moved in an improvised fashion between two pairs of "swords," although these actually looked more like upward pointed spearheads (fig. 4.3). While the movements did not follow a rigid choreography, Desmond moved in a rigid manner, with arms raised or spread, as if to emphasize the muscular stability of her body and its regal power in relation to swords pointed at or around her rather than held by her. The piece created a sensation that brought Desmond and Salge (and Vanselow, the producer) invitations to present *Schönheit* "evenings" elsewhere in Germany and even in St. Petersburg. *Der Schwertertanz* owed its success to its brilliant combination of very simple choreography and a very simple scenic device: the juxtaposition of the four erect spearheads with the naked contours of the female body and the consequent blurring of the distinction between the phallic and the vulvic. The piece evoked an archaic, Teutonic heritage; it exuded a distinctly Nordic aura, a kind of pre-Christian, Viking image of a mythic woman, a Norn, a Valkyrie, as if glimpsed at some tribal nocturnal bonfire or ritual. *Der Schwertertanz* moved solo dance away from its excessive reliance on Mediterranean and Asian motifs. In a Northern European context, Desmond's piece freed solo modern dance and the nakedness associated with it from assuming a "foreign" or "alien" origin. Simple though the choreography and conception were, the piece was exceptionally imaginative in making transparent the racial consciousness that conditioned

4.3. Olga Desmond in *Schwertertanz* (Sword Dance), the first of a sequence of twelve photographs depicting the dance, 1910. Courtesy of Jorn Runge.

perception of why it was important or artistic to see white women dancing alone and sometimes naked.

Lacking any dance, gymnastic, or gestural education, Desmond was unable to build upon the remarkable achievement of *Der Schwertertanz* and establish a performance persona deploying variations on the bold image of Teutonic womanhood she introduced in that piece. She could not create manifold incarnations of a basic, evolving, solitary female archetype, for, indeed, she apparently saw *Der Schwertertanz* as the culmination of a performance aesthetic imposed upon her rather than developed by her. With Salge, she published in 1910 a marvelous portfolio of photographs depicting her and him in various living-statue poses. The book documented beautifully the eerie but monumental effect of nude living bodies emulating idealized sculptures. But as long as she remained a partner of Salge, she remained attached to the living-statue performance aesthetic; that is, she remained a component in a male idealization of the body.

Even if *Der Schwertertanz* showed her own capacity to move the living-statue aesthetic to a new level and to transform into dance the Teutonic fascination with an uncertain distinction between living flesh and a "dead," sculptured idealization of it, the piece still found its place within the living-statue repertory and depended on that repertory to establish its heritage, its reference to an opportunity defined and given by men. Her relationship with Vanselow freed her from the living-statue aesthetic, but the "plastic improvisations" she devised for the *Schönheit* "evenings" never produced any impression of her as vivid or alluring as performance in *Der Schwertertanz* or the living-statue shows. Her solo dances became more "feminine" insofar as they dispensed with the stillness and steady, concentrated, calculated momentum of *Der Schwertertanz* and became more fluid in her movements, emphasizing the fluttering, looping, gamboling, rotating motions associated with the exuberance of nymphs, graceful Rhine maidens, sweet girls opening themselves to the radiance of a spring meadow, and the revelation of the "purity of German being."[6] A kitsch element began to pervade her dances, which, even though she retained moments of nudity, seemed content to define her in a very narrow way: as a charming, graceful, innocent figure whose solitude on stage appeared as a blessing, as the happiest condition, "free of any compulsion," and free of any dark emotions.[7]

This approach to dance, which she regarded as uniquely "cinematic" and at the same time "folkloric," led to opportunities beginning in 1915 to appear and even star in movies (now lost), although in these she apparently did not dance alone. The important thing, however, was that cinema was the ultimate, happiest freedom from the living-statue aesthetic because for her kind of dance, which was "no dance in the customary sense" it was the ideal "path to beauty," as she titled a 1916 pamphlet (*Mein Weg zur Schönheit*). Nevertheless, in 1919 when she published the little book *Rhythmographik*, designed as a movement notation guide for students to teach themselves how to dance, she described movement tropes by inscribing tiny robotic figures onto music staves so that the movement of hands, arms, and legs unfolded according to rhythmic intervals or beats in a quite mechanistic fashion. Here she abandoned "plastic improvisation" in favor of an analytic, technological approach to dance that recognized the necessity of preventing dance from becoming too fluid, too "feminine."

Yet early modern solo dance borrowed ideas from that which it purported to oppose. One should not underestimate the impact on the evolution of solo dance of Anna Pavlova (1881–1931), the great Russian figure from the world of classical ballet. She was probably not the greatest ballerina of her time in terms of technical skill, physical agility, or choreographic imagination. She danced alone only intermittently in concerts that supported her performances with a corps de ballet and a strong male partner. All of her pieces belonged to the nineteenth-century ballet repertory, and she felt no inclination to challenge any of the rules governing the identity of ballet. Neither did she seek to build her artistic identity around "bold" or "daring" performances; it would never have occurred to her that nudity could add anything to her performances. Yet so powerful were her performances that a huge international audience saw her as beautifully *alone* insofar as she seemed so apart, not only from the glamorous entourage that surrounded her but from mainstream ballet culture.

Her physical beauty was amazing and incredibly photogenic: no one ever took a dull picture of her, and possibly no other personality of the time had so many photos taken of her by so many different photographers. Her beauty cast a tragic or melancholy aura, "something frail and wistful."[8] No one could escape feeling drawn to her, and yet, although she never even seemed aloof, her beauty, always so intensely moving when she danced alone, magnified the dark supposition that being alone is the most beautiful state of being for anyone. Her dancing benefited immensely from the strong emotions her beauty awakened. Pavlova was a wonderfully *dramatic* dancer. That is to say, she knew how to construct an emotional architecture for dances, concerts, ballets, repertories, and tours. Even when her choreographers appeared to lack imagination, she could nevertheless make pieces exciting through her skill at mobilizing people and theatrical resources on behalf of a memorable dramatic, emotional experience.

Although she achieved fame in St. Petersburg through the performance of lead roles in full-evening ballets, like *Sleeping Beauty, Giselle,* and *Swan Lake,* she sustained and amplified her greatness when in 1909 she broke away from the "official" Russian ballet, established her own company, and began presenting concert programs of extracts from the traditional ballet repertory, small ballets she herself commissioned, and "divertissements"—short solo pieces that she alone danced. What audiences saw was not a ballet, but Ballet, a series of pieces that featured Pavlova performing with the corps de ballet, with a male partner in a pas de deux, or by herself. They saw her dance in various beautiful and often exotic costumes from different cultures; they saw her extraordinary ability to evoke different moods or emotional conditions; and they saw how masterfully she integrated music with her movement, as if, as the great music critic Ernest Newman observed in 1912, her movement gave life to the music rather than the other way around:

> When others dance, it is they who seem to be rendering the immaterial into the material; when Pavlova dances, she refines movement and gesture so far down to their pure essence that it is the music that seems in comparison slow and heavy with burden of mere crude matter in it. The thing would be unbelievable had not one seen it. . . . [In Chopin's C-sharp minor Waltz] one was amazed at the fidelity with which every nuance in the rhythm, the colour, or even the tonal intensity of the music had its counterpart in the dancing.[9]

Music for Pavlova was not simply an incidental embellishment or aural translation of a mood or even, as it was for Duncan, an "inspiration" for movement. Tones, melodies, harmonic configurations, rhythmic patterns never failed to stir her nervous system, awakening an incomparably refined power of feeling to move the body with the greatest beauty. This intensely visceral, emotional response of her body to distinct musical elements, sometimes in quite banal music, made even her more mediocre or trivial dances emotionally charged—*dramatic.* Music moved her entire body in the most delicate ways, as George Calderon remarked in the *Times* of London in 1911:

With Pavlova there are no accessory parts. She dances with her feet, her fingers, her neck (how much expression there is in the various inclinings of her head), her smiles, her eyes, her dress. There is nothing left over, not even a personality watching its own evolutions. She is all dance and all drama at the same time.[10]

The dramatic, emotional power of her dancing resulted from a complex, volatile interaction between the intricate physical system of her beautiful body and the intricate abstract system of music. But Pavlova amplified the emotional experience of her dances by linking movement to compressed narratives. Her dances told mostly brief but strong stories, and she did not shun pantomimic gestures to clarify narrative elements. She understood that popular audiences appreciated dance most not when it told an elaborate, familiar, or innovative story from some source outside of dance but when it told a different, contrasting story of the interaction, the conflict, between the beautiful body of the dancer and the music, with body and music striving to possess each other. Her concert programs therefore followed, in the sequencing of pieces, an emotional logic much more complex as a narrative than the full-evening ballets by which the "official" ballet established its seriousness as an art. Indeed, Pavlova freed ballet from its dependence on a particular narrative of social organization, freed it from its dependence on an "official" exclusivity of social classes.

For this reason Pavlova was much more modern than her repertory might suggest. Probably no dancer has ever achieved as much popularity and wealth as she did. She toured incessantly. Millions saw her dance throughout Europe, across the United States, in Central and South America, Japan, China, the Philippines, India, Southeast Asia, Australia, and Egypt. Glamorous and abundant publicity surrounded her no matter where she was. Her image was pervasive in popular consciousness; she endorsed various products; the media sought her opinion on almost any subject, and she answered almost every question with charm, sophistication, and modesty, without ever conveying the impression that anything she said was ever even remotely as important as seeing her dance. And yet, no matter how many popularizing innovations she introduced, Pavlova's refined and worldly personality, image, and performance technique bestowed an aristocratic identity on her and reinforced the perception that no matter how accessible dance became as an art, it remained an aristocratic art, insofar as success in the art resulted from the dancer achieving a rare, privileged relation between music and her physical beauty.

Her success, of course, depended upon a huge production apparatus inaccessible to other dancers: the corps de ballet, an orchestra, stage designers, costumers, choreographers, a theatrical production staff, a dance instruction staff, an administrative staff, accountants, lawyers, servants, publicists. Yet the piece by which her world public most closely identified her was a solo dance that did not depend at all on a large production unit: *The Swan*, which she premiered in St. Petersburg in 1907.[11] The piece was so popular that she danced it in almost every concert until her death, and eventually she even complained about the oppressive audience obsession with seeing her dance it. No other solo dance has ever become so famous, but the reason for its popularity is not hard to understand. *The Swan* is an enduringly moving dance; one can see it again and again and still feel moved by it, as happens when watching a film of the dance on YouTube.[12] The piece is only about two minutes long, danced to "The Swan," from Camille Saint-Saëns's suite *The Carnival of the Animals* (1886), an elegiac tune performed by a cello with piano accompaniment. No theatrical setting was required for her movements. The dance unfolded on an empty stage in which her white tutu and tiara, embellished with white feathers, glowed against a dark background (fig. 4.4).

On pointe, she emerges from the depths of the darkness with her arms and head uplifted. The almost incandescently beautiful dancer conveys an overpowering sense of being alone, struggling against that great darkness, which seems ready to engulf her. Pavlova did not actually emulate the movements of a swan; rather, always on pointe, with her arms swirling and flapping, she made her entire body tremble and shudder as she glided forward, then receded, then glided forward again, glided to her left, glided to her right, glided forward. Michel Fokine's choreography is made quite complex because Pavlova uses so many delicate motions of her fingers and hands, her shoulders, her head, and with different rhythms. She suddenly drops to her knees, in a kind of bow, in which her body momentarily ceases its trembling, then abruptly rises onto pointe and resumes her trembling and gliding, only

4.4. Anna Pavlova in the opening of *The Swan*, Berlin, 1908.
Photograph by Hänse Herrmann.

to sink again, while lifting her face outward, toward the viewer, but yearn-ingly, as if seeing only more darkness. She rises, she recedes, her back to the viewer, but she arches, she gazes upward, she pirouettes, she flinches, she flutters one arm while leaving the other gracefully suspended. The piece is an extraordinary anthology of the emotional nuances provided by the deli-cate movements of so many parts of the body. Pavlova glides backward once more, this time with a kind of swaying motion, then straightens up and ad-vances, trembling, with arms upraised but head tilted, as if resting on the pillow of the shoulder. Abruptly she lifts her head for the last time, opens her arms, her body to the darkness, then sinks to the floor, bows limply, and dies.

The Swan showed that a solo dance could compress an intense, emotional, tragic experience within an astonishingly brief time, and the experience required few resources beyond the body of the dancer. It did much to en-courage audiences to believe in the viability of concerts featuring a series of discrete solo dances. By 1913 solo-dance concerts followed a basic model. A concert contained about a dozen dances in two symmetrical parts, with an intermission separating them. Piano music usually accompanied the dances; most of the music came from the nineteenth-century Romantic repertory, although dancers did use and sometimes commissioned music by contem-porary composers with mostly post-Romantic harmonic inclinations. Most dances lasted between three and six minutes. To change moods from one dance to another frequently required the dancer also to change costume. The pianist might play an interlude to allow the dancer time to make the costume change. The titles of dances often borrowed from the generic name of the piece of music that accompanied the dance, such as "Waltz" or "Gavotte" or "Rondo," if the dancer did not apply her own descriptive name, such as *Der Schwertertanz*, *The Swan*, *Salome*, or *Radha*.

It is difficult to locate a single solo-dance concert at any time in the early modern period in which the dancer constructed the entire concert around a single theme or narrative. At most, a solo dancer might construct a suite of dances related to a single idea, as Ruth St. Denis did with *Radha* (1907) and other "variations" involving the same character impersonation, although *Radha* was the closing work of a program containing several other pieces.

In 1911 Gertrud Leistikow (1885–1948), a German dancer based in Am-sterdam, produced her *Orchestische Tanzspiele*. This consisted of three "dance plays" or "series," of which each series required its own separate performance evening. The first series, *Frauenliebe und Leben im Orient*, involved eight dances in two settings (Women's Tent, Temple), with Leistikow dancing a different role in each dance. In the first dance, she impersonated a Moorish slave and then went on to dance the roles of a bride, a "victorious" woman, a harem guard, a penitent, a mourner, a death dancer, and finally a rapturous nautch (professional dancer of India). The second series, *Adonisfeier*, was somewhat more coherent thematically and purported to dramatize, with nine dances, the ritual worship of Adonis by the ancient Greeks or more precisely, the ritual enactment of Adonis's resurrection from the depths of the earth. The first half of the performance ("Days of Lamentation") involved four somber dances; the second half ("Days of Joy") comprised five dances in an orgiastic or grotesque vein. It is not clear if Leistikow actually performed the third series announced in her 1911 concert program: *Ein byzantinischer Blumengarten* (A Byzantine Flower Garden). The piece, set in the garden of Empress Theodora's palace, presented dances related to symbolic flowers (orchid, lotus), insects (butterfly, gold bug), and a bird (peacock) and contrasted the "excessive pleasures of Byzantine life" with the "ascetic piety" of early Christianity.[13]

In conceiving a trilogy or cycle of evening-length dance concerts devoted to an aspect of ancient eastern Mediterranean religious history, Leistikow disclosed a level of ambition for solo-dance performance that was certainly exceptional for her time but perhaps unimaginable in our own time. Although she seems to have been interested in nude performance before 1914, she achieved "bold" or "daring" elements in her aesthetic insofar as she showed how dance blurred distinctions between conventionally separate modes of experience, the ascetic and the hedonistic, the beautiful and the grotesque, male and female, depression and ecstasy, indeed, between life and death. Her body was quite slender, lithe, and supple, but unlike Pavlova her face lacked charm, and she consistently sought to conceal or veil it in performance or in photographs (fig. 4.5). She loved performing with masks, veils, strange hats, turbans, furs, wigs, stockings, and peculiar dresses and skirts. Her choreography was never complex, and she apparently designed her dances to achieve their climaxes or defining moods with as few distinct movements as possible, with each dance having its own core set of defining movements. Hans Brandenburg noted that her body had "not the slightest trace of excess mass," and this leanness of body corresponded to a lean choreographic economy.[14] She would take a basic position or movement, such as kneeling or swaying or hunching or stepping left foot over the right, and build the entire dance around the movement, as if the movement functioned like a musical key.

A startling example is *Gnossienne* (1924), a four-minute dance set to No. 1 of the eponymous slow, haunting piano pieces by Erik Satie, which contained only two basic movements. The dancer faced the audience and stood still, except for the up-and-down wavelike motion of her arms, borrowed from Javanese traditional dance. Twice during the piece she turned to her left and performed the arm motions in profile. After each profile interval, she turned to her right to face her audience again and take a step toward them. The dancer appears to be in a trance. Although the movements of the arms and body never change their rhythms and the dancer seems to repeat the same movement over and over again from a frontal or a profile position, the piece nevertheless builds to a climax by achieving a kind of hypnotic effect on the spectator, as if "watching a body moving underwater, its arms and hands undulating hypnotically like the tentacles of a luminous aquatic plant, a human anemone."[15] Leistikow's rather dark and certainly sophisticated notion of the "grotesque," distilled in *Gnossienne* but operative even in the 1911 trilogy project, was possible because she was aware of herself in relation to the competing options for establishing oneself as a solo dancer in a European society increasingly eager to see women move alone, more freely, and with greater and greater strangeness.

Long before the manifestation of the solo-dance culture, women could achieve distinction in a solo vein as dancers in nightclubs and cabarets, trapeze artists and tightrope walkers, or acrobats and equestriennes. But these professions, dominated by ancient conventions of performance, were unable to provide women with opportunities to assert their authority to define modernity and to attract serious attention as artists. Dancing solo confirmed the power of the female body to act and move alone, to sustain attention and emotional engagement without the support of partners and groups. The solo-dance concert was a heroic enterprise insofar as heroism entailed a heightened performance of aloneness.

4.5. Gertrud Leistikow in a dance from her cycle *Adonisfeier*, from the concert program *Orchestische Tanzspiele*, 1911.

Dancing solo for an entire concert, however, requires performance skills of considerable sophistication to sustain the interest of any audience. A four-minute solo dance can achieve great impact on an audience to the extent that it is itself alone and "free" of any relation to other dancers or performers. But a series of solo dances by a single performer requires the dancer to have a deep understanding of how a lone, moving body will sustain the attention of different audiences by destabilizing perception of the dancer and exposing a transformative relation between the physical and the metaphysical or abstract, in the sense that the movement of the body transforms the identity of the dancer. Today, neither performers nor audiences seem to believe that a lone dancer can sustain an entire concert of solo dances, even though dancers today enjoy far greater movement education and dance historical awareness than the solo dancers of the early modern period.

At the beginning of the twentieth century, dance audiences did not associate solo dance or modern dance with the display of physical virtuosity or acrobatic agility. Audiences then, wanting to see women move "freely" in relation to cultural regulation and control of the female body, appreciated the idea that dance was modern, not because it provided a new level of physical virtuosity or bodily discipline but because it "revealed" the beauty or expressive potential of a body that moved "naturally" in relation to music or to some dormant, "inner" impulse that otherwise remained hidden from the public. Audiences at that time appreciated that any dance understood as modern did not emerge from a familiar institutional and educational foundation. The solo dancers presented themselves as inventors, largely self-educated, unburdened by movement techniques that subordinated the body to archaic ways of seeing women's functions within the social hierarchies governing, for example, European ballet culture.

Yet solo dancers often relied on the conventions of pantomimic signification they had learned from experience in the theater, or from gestural codes such as Delsarte provided, or from the conventions of "oriental" dance as it was understood at the time. Choreographic imagination was by no means lacking, but dance signified its modernity, not through the performance of difficult physical feats requiring long, elaborate training but by exposing, gracefully or at least impressively, the expressive potential of otherwise "natural" or "accessible" movements. Solo dancers cared as much for exotic or unusual costumes as they did for innovative movement, for the same basic movements performed in different costumes or with different music produced a different emotional ambiance. To be modern meant to be "bold" or "daring," however, and dance never seemed so bold as when the dancer performed in a state of nudity. Barefoot dancing in 1903 initiated an escalating competition among solo dancers to expose more of the body in performance and to challenge the authority of the law to prescribe the limits of what audiences could see of women who felt a dangerous pleasure in letting others see them move naked.

But solo dance was modern insofar as audiences regarded it as an art, which meant that solo dance had to operate in a performance environment independent of cabarets and music halls. As an art, solo dance required the concert hall or the theater, spaces that conveyed a seriousness of purpose and audience focus that audiences did not ascribe to the cabaret. Art entailed the communication of a resonant message and the opening of consciousness to a "foreign" or buried beauty or freedom. Modernity therefore often appeared in the guise of "Asian," biblical, or ancient narrative frameworks that reinforced the perception of modernity as a pre-Christian or non-Christian cultural system. As an artist, the solo dancer extended the notion of "performance" beyond the solo dances themselves; performance ventured into other media, including the publication of books and interviews, innovative use of photography and distribution of the dancer's image, opportunities to model fashions, and appearances in movies. Above all, the solo dancer had to construct a life off the stage that was as interesting as anything she did on stage, for even if audiences did not expect the dancer's art to offer a confessional or autobiographical dimension, they nevertheless depended on the dancer's skill at publicity to indicate the value or uniqueness of her performance.

To produce a concert of ten or twelve distinct solo dances by a single performer involves such physical and mental strain that it is remarkable how unenthusiastic solo dancers were in sharing the burden. It would seem sensible to acquire a partner and produce concerts involving pair dances or alternating solo dances. But such a strategy lacked immediate appeal, and only Pavlova seemed comfortable with it. The popularity in Europe after 1910 of the tango and other seductive social dances perhaps encouraged solo dancers to see the advantages of a performance partner. But suitable partners were apparently not easy to find. By 1913 only Alexander Sacharoff (1886–1963) and Clothilde von Derp (1892–1974) had achieved any notable success as a pair who occasionally performed duets but mostly performed alternate solo dances in an intensely artificial, orchidaceous style. In 1916 Joachim von Seewitz (1891–1966) and Lo Hesse (1889–1983) followed their example for a few years, performing alternate solo dances of perhaps even greater perversity than those of the Sacharoffs.[16]

Yet concerts combining pair dances with alternate solo dances remained uncommon even after the solo-dance concert appeared to have exhausted its potential by 1921. Between 1928 and 1930, Harald Kreutzberg (1902–68) and Yvonne Georgi (1903–75) achieved considerable popularity with this model, but they could not sustain it because of their fundamentally incompatible temperaments. Georgi always hungered to create turbulent dances on a large, even grandiose scale; dancing solo could never satisfy her urge to control the dancing of others. Kreutzberg primarily sought self-sufficiency, discovering, with Georgi, that his satiric, jesterlike, and sometimes grotesque approach to dance worked best when he danced alone. Grete Wiesenthal (1885–1970), whose fame derived largely from her success in dancing Viennese waltzes, attempted in 1928 a brief partnership with the Viennese ballet dancer Toni Birkmeyer (1897–1973), who in 1924 had partnered with Tilly Losch (1903–75). She was another Viennese ballet dancer, remembered as a soloist primarily for her cyclonic *Dance of the Hands* (1924), who had difficulty attracting a stable partner outside the official ballet culture, although her ambitions as a dancer, an actress, and a socialite would hardly allow her to find fulfillment within the hierarchy of a state ballet company.

A Dutch dancer, Irail Gadescow (1897–1970), whose real name was Richard Vogelsang, attempted to emulate the Sacharoff pair model, but he soon complicated it. From 1922 until the late 1920s he was continually busy touring northern and central Europe with a combination of partners. For some concerts, the Norwegian dancer Ellen Sinding (1899–1980) was his partner, until she departed for Norway in 1924 to work in the film industry there. At the same time and until into the mid-1920s, he produced concerts with Ami Schwaninger and also with Magda Bauer, with Bauer sometimes performing with him and Sinding or Schwaninger. By 1925 he had yet another partner, Irma Pumanova, who worked with him until 1928, although he also organized a 1927 Berlin concert with the Dutch dancer Ery Bos (1910–2005). But he and Bos did nothing further together, as she became attached to various ballet companies and then in the early 1930s became a film star. When he could not engage a partner, he would attempt concerts featuring only himself, but these were clearly never as successful as those in which his solo pieces alternated with those of a female soloist.[17] Gadescow performed many of the same solo dances (*Sword Dance, Cymbal Dance, Siamese Dance, Lazzarone, Allegrias,* and so forth) with different partners on his programs, but the female partners brought their own solo repertories, which probably had the beneficial effect of shifting the way audiences viewed his dances, while at the same time encouraging the not so beneficial impression that his dances depended on a female counterpart of no consistency to attract an audience.

The problem with building solo-dance concerts around programs of alternate solo dances by a pair of dancers is that this strategy undermined the authority of solo dance as a genre to establish the authority of the solo dancer. If solo dance is a basis for proving the artistry of the dancer, then the inclination of a solo dancer to share the program with another solo dancer would be an indication that neither dancer alone could produce enough solo work to sustain the interest of an audience and demonstrate the power of solo dance to confirm the heroic aloneness of the modern dancer. While audiences may not have considered this question consciously in regard to the pair model, they very likely wondered why the partner dancers did not perform more dances together, for even the most durable partnerships produced programs in which the solo dancers performed only one or two dances together, as if grudgingly conceding to an audience expectation.

Audiences, however, assume (or desire) that a partnership between a male and female dancer not affiliated with any company arises not just from professional but from personal affinities, from a sexual compatibility, which should be manifested in dances they perform together. But if they perform well together because they feel emotionally close to each other, why, then, would they perform more solo dances than duets in a concert program? More than anything else, this uncertainty of a dancer's emotional relation to a partner of the opposite sex accounts for the rarity of concerts in which male and female dancers alternated solo dances. In 1919 Alexander Sacharoff married Clothilde von Derp, even though he was homosexual. But the marriage assured the stability of the couple's partnership in producing concerts in which they alternated the performance of their solo dances: no other dance couple enjoyed such a long career together, for they continued to collaborate on producing solo dances for their joint concerts into the late 1940s, after which they collaborated with ballet companies.[18]

Women were apparently even less inclined to form partnerships with other women to produce solo-dance concerts. Some experiments in female partnerships occurred in the period 1918–21, most notably Mila Cirul (1901–77) and Ellen Tels (1880–1944) in 1919–20, in Vienna, but Tels quickly realized that she was happier working with group dances and with students. Gertrud Falke (1890–1984) and her sister Ursula (1896–1981), from Hamburg, produced concerts there between 1917 and 1919, but their solo dances never achieved the success of their pair dances, which actually dramatized the tension between them, with Ursula always the darker sister seeking to dispel, eclipse, or absorb the more radiant Gertrud, as if Ursula were the deathly shadow of Gertrud, a "ghostly" mirror of her.[19] This relation between the sisters perhaps indicates why women dancers were reluctant to form partnerships with each other. Audiences were inclined to view a program of alternating solo dances by different women as a competition between them; the spectator invariably compared them with each other, and a dancer could not establish the power of her solos if the program was not complete without the presence of another woman.

By 1920 numerous women had presented solo concerts in Germany or Austria: Sent M'ahesa, Rita Aurel, Grit Hegesa, Suse Elsler, Lisa Abt, Ruth Schwarzkopf, Annie Lieser, Ilse Freude, Chari Lindis, Solveig Oderwald, Gusi Viola, Lucie Hertel, Erna Bertini, Macka Nordberg, Hannelore Ziegler, Hilde Schewior, Beatrice Mariagraete, Hilde Sinoniew, Hedwig Nottebohm, Vera Waldheim, Edith Bielefeld, Nina Schelemskaja, Gertrud Zimmermann, Laura Oesterreich, Olga Samsylova, Hilda Hager, Stella Kramrisch, Maria Ley, Charlotte Bara, to name but some. Even an eight-year-old Brazilian girl, Maryla Gremo (1911–85), enjoyed such success with her solo-dance concerts in Germany that she performed dances in movies—*Satanas* (1919) and *Sehnsucht* (1919)—before joining ballet companies in Germany and then Poland. But by 1920 the solo-dance concert probably contained so many aspirants that competition for audiences must have been intense, along with the pressure to produce innovative and exceptional pieces that would draw increasingly discriminating audiences. In any case, after 1921 solo-dance concerts suddenly declined in popularity, as both dancers and audiences longed for modern dance to unfold on a larger scale, through group dances and interactions between bodies. A larger scale was possible with the emergence of schools focused more on modern dance education than on physical education, most auspiciously with the network of movement "institutes" in numerous European cities founded by Rudolf Laban (1879–1958) between 1919 and 1923 and the school in Dresden started by Mary Wigman (1886–1973) in 1919.

But solo dance was by no means dead as a genre. Indeed, the 1920s provided some of the most fascinating solo dances in the history of dance. Yet these appeared in the context of programs containing ensemble dances, pair dances, or theatrical scenes. Wigman produced her famous *Hexentanz* in 1926, which she had been developing since 1914; Tilly Losch introduced her *Dance of the Hands* in 1924, in which the looping movement of her hands gradually caused her entire body to twist and spiral into an ecstatic convulsion; Anita Berber (1899–1928) performed her lurid and tragic *Kokain* (1921); Gertrud Kraus (1901–77) created her eerie *Guignol* (1929), in which, clad in a long black dress but with her face painted white and her fingers attached to long brass fingernails, she performed a mysterious rocking or swaying dance without ever leaving the pedestal on which she perched, like an ominous, macabre puppet; Gertrud Leistikow performed her hypnotic *Gnossienne* (1924); Grit Hegesa (1891–1972), always preoccupied with the perverse, the luxurious, and the cosmopolitan, began in 1919 a series of cross-gender solo dances in which she attempted to impersonate elegant boys or oriental princes; and Valeska Gert (1892–1978) began in 1919, with *Canaille*, to build her solo repertory of grotesque parodies of degenerate women and then of damaged states of being, such as her sobbing dance, *Kummerlied* (1928).

In Hamburg, Lavinia Schulz (1896–1924) produced, with her husband, Walter Holdt (1899–1924), perhaps the most bizarre solo dances ever. Between 1922 and 1924 they constructed utterly fantastic costumes out of debris and materials they scavenged, and then they developed dances, with original modernistic music by H. H. Stuckenschmidt (1901–88), of such choreographic complexity that Schulz invented several elaborate notation schemes to clarify the relations between movement, space, time, and emotional valence. While much of their inspiration for such a strange vision of figures in motion derived from archaic Nordic mythology, such as the Eddas, the spectator experienced a powerful impression of confronting human identity in its most alien and primeval form, insectoid, reptilian, robotic, genetically convoluted (fig. 4.6).[20]

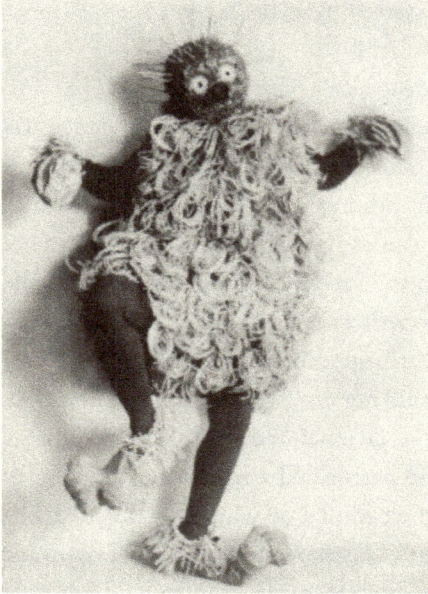

4.6. Lavinia Schulz in the fantastic costume for her *Bibo*, Hamburg, 1924. Photograph by Minya Diez-Dührkoop. Courtesy of the Museum für Kunst und Gewerbe, Hamburg.

But extraordinary solo dances such as these and many others in the 1920s were possible because their creators focused their imaginations on pieces of short duration and did not need to disperse their energies over an entire program of pieces that audiences expected to display the range of possibilities for the solo dancer or the solo dance genre. By 1924 solo dance ceased to define modern dance. It became the work of dancers who felt uncomfortable performing with groups or who lacked the choreographic imagination to produce group dances.

Gret Palucca (1902–93), although she operated a school in Dresden opened in 1925, performed almost entirely in the solo mode throughout the 1920s and 1930s. She toured relentlessly, performing over the years hundreds of solo dances across Germany and Eastern Europe. She was an exuberant performer, famous for her high, long leaps and almost complete inability to project dark or melancholy or even erotically tinged moods. She stripped dance of narrative elements, employed the blandest of costumes, and compelled her audiences to see her dances as purely formal displays of movement devices, such as pivots, lunges, strides, waves, kicks, slides, and swoons.

No dancer offered a more abstract approach to dance; she could produce so many dances because she mostly reconfigured her repertory of movement devices. Dance itself was the only subject of her dances, and it was as if any concert program functioned, cumulatively, to release the spectator from any expectation that dance signify anything more than the beauty of a perfectly executed movement device.

Palucca's aesthetic perhaps anticipated the American "postmodern" efforts of the 1960s to free dance from the weight of referents, metaphor, and alluding to any world outside itself. Perhaps for that reason she exerted far greater influence as a teacher than as a performer. Avant-garde artists like Kandinsky and the Bauhaus clan appreciated her severe formalism, but she presented so many concerts largely because, after 1925 when she discovered her subject and her creative method, her aesthetic never really evolved: the purification of her movements to "essential" abstract forms was for her the greatest freedom and happiness; she could communicate that again and again, and it was not necessary to say anything more.[21]

But Palucca's message was not enough to sustain the solo-dance concert as a preferred medium of modern dance production. One dancer who also remained devoted to the solo-dance concert for her entire career was Edith von Schrenck (1891–1971), but her devotion carried with it an entirely different and perhaps more persuasive message. Born in Riga, she spent her early years in St. Petersburg, where her father was a prominent gynecologist. In St. Petersburg she studied with Claudia Issachenko, a disciple of Delsarte as filtered through the Stebbins-Kallmeyer program of "artistic gymnastics" as well as a former actress for Konstantin Stanislavsky. But she also studied under Dalcroze at Hellerau, with the idea of becoming a teacher of physical education. When the Bolsheviks assumed power in Russia, her family migrated to Munich and was soon in difficult financial circumstances, which motivated Schrenck to perform professionally.

In 1919 she launched her first solo concert tour in Germany. In May that year, as a result of her performance in Frankfurt, she met the writer Waldemar Bonsels (1880–1952), world famous for his children's book *Maja, the Bee* (1912), which made him wealthy. Schrenck and Bonsels became lovers, even though he was already married. In 1907 Bonsels had divorced his first wife, who was the sister of his friend Hans Brandenburg (1885–1968), a major critic and producer in the German modern dance scene. Brandenburg, who had a high estimation of Schrenck's gifts, was a valuable ally of any dancer seeking to build her career. But Brandenburg refused to help Schrenck after he learned of her involvement with Bonsels. In 1920 Schrenck gave birth to their son. For years, Schrenck and Bonsels conducted their romance surreptitiously, but Bonsels never married her, and indeed after the divorce from his second wife in 1926 he married another woman, although marriage never really suited him, for he was a restless "vagabond," always hungry for travel. Schrenck nevertheless continued to love him until his death, although largely through correspondence. He was the great love of her life, and she seems to have developed both her life and her career around her feeling for him.[22]

A dark, tragic spirit pervaded her aesthetic. She was unique among modern dancers in avoiding movements that conveyed a condition of freedom. Occasionally she might begin a dance in a cheerful manner, but then she would drift into a somber or resigned mood. She favored Romantic music in its more serious manifestations: Mussorgsky, Scriabin, Rachmaninoff, Schumann, Grieg, Reger, Chopin. Her recurrent theme was not so much the struggle of the body to gain its freedom as the struggle of the body to exert its strength against an invisible or inner power that threatened her with a destructive freedom, with a fatal release from discipline. She concentrated her movements within a small area of the performance space, usually the center of the stage. She liked hunching and bowing movements (fig. 4.7). She liked lunging, arching, pivoting, swaying, lifting, or sinking movements without leaving an initial point of the stage, relying heavily on her arms, hands, fingers, and head to carry the burden of choreographic engagement, an approach that perhaps achieved its most exciting realization in her dance *Gefesselt* (1919) depicting a woman in bondage, with her hands tied behind her back and an invisible leash preventing her from standing upright or moving farther than a single strenuous lunge. In *Wellen* (1922), though, the movement of combing became the movement of waves.

Despite his displeasure at her involvement with Bonsels, Brandenburg wrote enthusiastically about her dancing in the 1921 edition of his major overview of the new dance culture in Germany, *Der moderne Tanz*, in which he compared Schrenck with Wigman. He contended that Wigman pursued

4.7. Edith von Schrenck, 1925. Photograph by Henri Berssenbrugge. Courtesy of Studie en Documentatie Centrum voor Fotografie, Leiden, The Netherlands.

an "extensive" aesthetic in that she dispersed movement and meaning across bodies, revealing dynamic relations between power and freedom, leader and follower, through group pieces of increasing complexity.[23] Schrenck, on the other hand, adhered to an "intensive" aesthetic, in which she sought to compress as much tension or "otherness" as possible into her body, so that solo dance dramatized the dancer's desire to reconcile competing impulses within her and her failure (or at least unwillingness) to achieve either reconciliation or release from conflict; she could only achieve defeat, or rather the decision to start another dance altogether. Brandenburg thought she was "a group within herself."

For the Dutch critic Werumeus Buning, it seemed as if Schrenck always danced with an invisible partner.[24] She sometimes moved as if catapulted or propelled by the discharge of a coiled up spring within her: she would leap or shoot forward suddenly, then sink, collapse, or stiffen again with gathering tension, as if exhausted by explosive movement or extremely wary of it. She was imaginative in using pauses or stillness or repose in her dances, for these moments invariably conveyed a mood of gathering strength or power—which, however, never seemed to achieve any triumphant or ecstatic release but instead reached a tragic transfiguration, for dance was ultimately about the subjugation of wild and self-destructive impulses.

In *Schmerz* (1922), for example, her movements, which began broadly, crudely, beseechingly, became smaller and smaller, more refined, and slower and slower, continuing even after the music stopped, and then she was still, in the silence. In *Kriegertanz*, later known as *Amazone* (1919–21), the tensions within her assumed voluptuous intensity. She wore a helmet and a very short skirt, which displayed well her wonderfully muscled legs, and she brandished a shield and dagger. The dance contrasted thrusting, stabbing movements with flinching, arching, retreating movements; she gyrated, then stiffened; she bowed or hunched, then darted or exalted; she burrowed behind the shield, then spread her arms wide, as if inviting, taunting her invisible opponent to strike her invincible body; she trembled with anxiety, then sauntered carelessly; she sank to her knees, as if resigned to the death blow from her enemy, then sprang suddenly to tiptoes, with deadly, viper-like violence, striking the fatal blow before her own collapse into deathly stillness.

Schrenck was exceptionally beautiful, and solo dance perhaps made her beauty both greater and more remote or estranging than other presentations of herself. She understood the limit of beauty as a power over others. Her love for Bonsels brought her intense happiness, and her beauty no doubt awakened his love for her. But her beauty was not strong enough to bind them together as a couple beyond a brief moment. That was the powerful message of her solo-dance aesthetic: loving another person is like dancing with an "invisible" partner. Great love is not about sharing a life or uniting with another life; it is a profound estrangement from life, a dark submission or release of one's life to another. That was the motive for Schrenck's determination to remain "disciplined," always to hold something in reserve, and for her refusal to release what seemed so pent up in her. As she remarked in a 1920 letter to Bonsels, "It is better to be alone with my dance than alone with a person."[25]

Her art was perhaps too somber or disillusioning for most dance audiences. She was not outstandingly successful as a solo dancer. Her concerts did fairly well in various German cities, in Holland, and in Vienna, yet they never did well enough to provide more than a humble existence for her and her son. Life remained hard for her, and she frequently appealed to Bonsels for financial help. She tried opening a school in Berlin in 1929, but it soon failed. She never married and never seems to have believed in marriage any more than Bonsels had. In 1941 her son died in the invasion of Ukraine. From then on, life in Berlin became bleaker and she became more religious. After Bonsels's death she lived with her sisters in Munich until her own death. With Schrenck, solo dance no longer had any greater purpose than the revelation that great beauty and monumental love do not bring people together; they estrange you from the world. They make you alone and they make you move not "freely" but as if invaded by a dark, demonic spirit—music that brings you to the "pulsating" limit of your power over your body, your beauty, your desire.

Schrenck admired the solo dancing of Niddy Impekoven, and in a 1924 letter to Bonsels, she even contemplated a partnership with Impekoven to produce a concert program of solo dances, which, however, never occurred. It would have made a fascinating concert, for Impekoven was almost the complete antithesis of Schrenck in her solo-dance aesthetic. Niddy Impekoven (1904–2002) was probably the most successful solo dancer after Pavlova, although Pavlova's concerts in fact always involved her with partners or an ensemble. Yet Pavlova was Impekoven's idol or at least model from childhood, when she saw postcards of the ballerina without ever having seen her dance.

Although Impekoven studied ballet, she actually disliked it, respecting it less as an art and more as a technique that prepared the body to dance in a more effective way than ballet as an art allowed. No dancer was as successful as Impekoven in dancing on her own. She inspired tremendous adulation and adoration across a wide spectrum of audiences, and even people who did not go to dance concerts seemed to love her through the ubiquitous images of her that appeared on postcards. She was an exquisite creature who amplified her exquisiteness through solo dancing. In an ensemble her artistry could never have flourished, for she embodied a delicacy, a fragility, a wispy beauty that gained nothing by being shared with other performers.

Born in Berlin, she grew up in an artistic family who encouraged her precociousness; she gave her first concert when she was six, but her family required her to practice so seriously that she jeopardized her health. She gave her first professional concert in 1918, and from then on she enjoyed success everywhere she performed. The dances she performed at this concert established her uniqueness as a dancer, and she was able to perform them again and again for more than a decade, with audiences throughout the world enchanted by them. She continued to add more dances to her repertory, but the dances from her 1918 concert fixed her image in public consciousness to a far greater degree than she herself thought healthy.

Her most famous dance from the concert was perhaps *Gefangener Vogel*, in which she impersonated a caged bird (fig. 4.8). For her costume she devised wings out of a translucent cloth on which were dyed feathers of different colors. She wore a snug cap that covered her hair. The wings were so skillfully sewn to her mini-dress that they looked as if they grew right out of her body. The image of her as the "captured bird" so charmed the public that it became a subject for numerous artists, especially porcelain figurine makers. In the dance itself, which used music by Bruno Hartl that has probably been heard only when she performed the dance, Impekoven moved on tiptoes, with her arms spread so that the wings fluttered as she glided and turned with the utmost delicacy—yet without ever soaring, without ever flying free of her pedestal, so to speak.

Her choreography was never complex, but she performed it with perfect refinement. She relied heavily on costumes to differentiate her dances and the characters she impersonated, and perhaps no dancer created such

4.8. Niddy Impekoven as the Captured Bird (*Gefangener Vogel*), Munich, ca. 1919. Photograph by Hanns Holdt.

a wide range of memorable figures on stage. In the 1918 debut concert she introduced her series of four "doll" characters: the Rococo Doll, the Erna Pinner Doll, the Lotte Pritzel Doll, and the Käthe Kruse Doll, with each doll accompanied by music of a different composer. Each doll, of course, required a different costume: the Pinner doll, for example, employed a kind of ornamental clown dress, while the Pritzel doll used a vaguely oriental tunic and veiled trousers. (Pritzel's eerie dolls project a perverse and sometimes morbid aura.) In the Pinner Doll dance, Impekoven began by slumbering in an armchair, and then, as if awakened by the pulling of strings on her body, she awoke and started dancing with greater and greater speed, like a dervish, maniacally, as if intoxicated by her own movement, until suddenly she collapsed unconscious onto the chair again.

An armchair was about the only theatrical prop Impekoven ever needed; she always performed against an empty background and conveyed the idea that the character never needed a special context in which to live, for her characters were indeed like figurines that would be charming wherever one put them. She brought figurine characters to life. The scale of performance was always small and filled with peculiar tiny details of costume and movement, especially in the use of her hands and face; for her dance on "the life of a flower," she wore only a simple dress and described the birth, life, and death of the flower mostly with her arms, hands, and face, using her whole body only in the middle of the piece. Her aesthetic was unapologetically ornamental, bordering at times on kitsch, although no one ever accused of her such a transgression of taste. Instead, people persistently ascribed a childlike quality to her persona, even though at the age of fourteen she was already impersonating the frumpy, middle-aged *Münchener Kaffeewärmer*. She made dance simultaneously comic and graceful because she invested a genial sweetness in every gesture. An elfin spirit pervaded her art, an elegant playfulness that audiences associated with exceptional fragility or vulnerability.

Impekoven represented a harmless, nonthreatening feminine innocence at a time when accusations of guilt, shame, corruption, and impurity permeated a European society traumatized by the Great War. She incarnated a purity of being that audiences nostalgically ascribed to the period before the war. Yet she was conscious of an unwholesome dimension to this attitude. In 1922 the journalist Fred Hildenbrandt published a little book of "letters to a dancer," in which he described the turbulent and hardly innocent feelings she provoked in him.[26] Even Hans Frentz, the author of two books about her, idealized her so ardently—and somewhat creepily—that he could not describe her dances with any clarity, so captivated was he, like Hildenbrandt, by her luminous image.[27] Her marriage in 1923 to a prominent physician, Hans Killian (1892–1982), brought a change in her aesthetic, when he introduced her to the music of Bach. Her choreography became somewhat more complex as her costumes became simpler and her new dances became more austere than her early comic pieces, although she never repudiated the early works.

She began dancing in long, satiny gowns of a single color, and it is remarkable how these costumes expanded the colors, so to speak, by which her virginal purity of being manifested itself (fig. 4.9). In one of her Bach dances she moved for much of the time with her eyes closed, then opened them suddenly, as if revelation had struck her through a chord. By 1928 her

4.9. Niddy Impekoven in *Chaconne*, Berlin, 1931.
Photograph by the Robertson Studio.

taste in music was deeply conservative. She built suites of solo dances out of Schumann's *Kinderszenen* and *Carnaval*. Mozart, Haydn, Brahms, Rameau, and Couperin prevailed elsewhere on her programs, although she did turn to Milhaud, Bartók, and Roentgen for a few pieces in which she represented amusing characters in the contemporary world instead of archetypal figurine characters who inhabited a "timeless" zone in the architecture of nostalgic consciousness. Although the scale of her pieces always remained small, she never failed to display considerable variety of mood in her concerts. She did not avoid emotions of melancholy, lament, or even perversity, but these never subverted her dominant angelic gracefulness.

In 1928 Impekoven embarked on a world tour that took her across Europe, then to India, Ceylon, Japan, Hawaii, and the United States. It was so successful that she embarked on another tour in 1930 to Southeast Asia. These tours made her rich. When she returned, however, she grasped that the political situation in Germany would steer her art in a more conservative direction than even she found healthy. She presented her last concerts in 1933–34, when she performed her Bach-inspired "three angels" suite and her cycle of archaic German folk and court dances, which the new regime certainly welcomed. She apparently no longer needed the approval of audiences, no longer felt any great desire to dance, no longer had any urge to restore faith in the feminine purity, playfulness, and innocence that her vast audience associated with her exquisite style of performance. She never established a school to perpetuate her art; she never affiliated with any institution. She retreated to Switzerland with her husband and spent the rest of her long life in comfortable and presumably happy obscurity, waiting until 1955 to publish her memoirs, which in any case covered only her childhood, the most difficult and painful time of her life, starkly contrasting with the sentimental assumptions about childhood held by her audience.[28]

Probably no dancer had fewer illusions about the manipulative relation between performer and audience than Niddy Impekoven. The solo-dance concert began in the early years of the century as a "bold" or "daring" invocation of heroic female identity, moving alone and free of the Christian morality that constrained the modernity of women and calling upon mythic archetypes of "dangerous" femininity. With Impekoven, the solo-dance concert functioned to glorify a small realm of exquisite girlishness, a delicate realm of strange dolls, virginal angels, decorative figurines, and charming folkloric figures, all given life through their creator's pleasure in exalting a Christian dream of innocence.

Modern dance evolved and expanded during the 1920s through ensembles, kinetic interactions between bodies, and movement vocabularies that brought dancers together and distributed modernity of identity among them. Group movement evolved with the growth of schools and companies established by charismatic or ambitious modern dance personalities. With the advent of the Third Reich, group dancing and group movement became an important feature of Nazi educational efforts to inspire "communal" feeling in young people and a unifying concept of German "community," although the Nazis displayed little appreciation for the spectacular achievements of group dancing during the Weimar Republic. After about 1934 it was quite difficult for a dancer to develop a career independent of official institutions and their ideologically oriented goals.

Nevertheless, a daring creator of solo-dance concerts in the Third Reich was Oda Schottmüller (1905–43). She pursued a dual career as a sculptor and dancer. In Berlin she moved in a cosmopolitan circle of artists and intellectuals, which provided her with a busy social life and a strong interest in the operation of social networks. Her involvement with dance arose from her desire to understand the mechanics of group movement. As both a sculptor and a dancer, she was preoccupied with the synthesis of art and technology. She studied under Vera Skoronel (1906–32) at the Trümpy school in Berlin; Skoronel advocated an angular, vehement, machinelike approach to movement that intersected well with Schottmüller's sculptural ambitions, which focused on the making of masks. Her masks were beautiful, eerie, and of astonishing variety. Although she had experimented with masks and movements while a student at Johannes Itten's art school in the early 1930s, Schottmüller did not produce her first solo concert until 1934, and even on that occasion she shared the program with another dancer. She gradually built up her repertory of pieces, so that by 1941 she was able to perform an entire program by herself. Her dances rarely lasted more than four minutes, and many ran for less than two. Between 1934 and 1941 she performed in only five concerts, but these left a deep impression on people who saw them, and her work attracted considerable attention from the German cultural press.

Schottmüller's use of masks fascinated her audience, although she did not wear a mask in all her dances; she was an excellent designer of costumes that made effective use of veils, capes, shawls, scarves, wigs, caps, tunics, and flowing dresses (fig. 4.10). Photographers, including the great dance photographer Siegfried Engelmann, delighted in taking pictures of her wearing her masks, and newspapers delighted in publishing the pictures. Her dances emphasized bizarre, grotesque, macabre, melancholy, or tragic themes. She commissioned composers she knew to write music for her pieces, while other dances received accompaniment from modernist composers such as Bartók, Prokoviev, and Stravinsky. Critics within the Nazi cultural establishment did not fail to notice that her dances recalled the discredited decadence of Ausdruckstanz and lacked basic qualities necessary to align her eerie aesthetic with the Nazi ideal of a heroic German Volksgemeinschaft. She was, however, so well connected socially that she found advocates within the Nazi culture apparatus, including the venerated dance critic Fritz Böhme. Indeed, some Nazi officials thought her pieces appealing enough to assign her to Italy, France, and Holland to dance for soldiers stationed there.

In 1941 a newspaper reviewer, Florian Kienzl, tried to explain the disconcerting enchantment of her dances:

> Oda Schottmüller's dance forms live between realms. She represents both humans and powers, but they are the inspirations of romantic fantasy. Her elegantly formed body plays with masks and magical garments that are not of this world; her movements bind dream and fairy tale. Mimic expression is not present in her, nor can it be pressed into the smoothness of an artificial face. The plastic lines and the painterly colored image reveal her feelings and form them as visions.[29]

Schottmüller's quite obscure career came to an abrupt end, however, when the Gestapo arrested her for collaborating with her friends Harro and Libertas Schulze-Boysen in resistance activities. In 1943 the Gestapo decapitated her and sixteen other friends. But for a person who depended so heavily on friends and an elaborate social network to sustain her career as an artist, producing occasional solo-dance concerts was itself an act of resistance against the regime, against the uniformity of identity imposed by group movement

4.10. Oda Schottmüller wearing a mask she created for *Nachtstück*, Berlin, 1935. Photograph by Madeline Winkler. Courtesy of EMPORE Antikriegsmuseum "Der kleine Soldat" und Archiv Susanne und Dieter Kahl.

and, perhaps, against her basic inclination to find happiness as a member of a group.

Little is known about the choreography of Schottmüller's dances. Yet this deficit is probably less important than it seems. She understood that solo-dance concerts would engage audiences, even when the dances were so short, only through the use of masks, mysterious costumes, and "new" music. By the 1930s so many dancers had created so many solo imaginative dances that it was extremely difficult to introduce pieces built around innovative choreography. Alone, the human body can apply only a very limited vocabulary of movements, without relying on pantomimic gestural codes, to sustain the attention of an audience. Modern dance freed movement from rigid signification systems, but the movement vocabulary for modernity was not large and actually depended on a mechanistic, "technological" or doll-like approach to movement, as Dalcroze, Skoronel, and Impekoven grasped in different ways, when it did more than allow the female body to disclose its potential for voluptuousness and erotic power through "oriental" or "lyrical" forms of movement. The emotional intensity of dances depended above all on the relation of movements to costumes, nudity, masks, props, music, and the physiognomy of the dancer. The same movements changed dramatically when the dancer performed them with different music and a different costume.

Developing solo-dance concerts meant exploring different combinations of relations between movement and the emotional weight borne by choices in costume, color, sound, mask, or accessories. Palucca's totally abstract, antirepresentational approach, in which a constant reconfiguration of movement alone was the object of performance, was a dead end insofar as she saw dance as a freedom from all the emotional complexities that she assumed weighed down the body and oppressed it. On the other hand, how much can one "say" when one is alone? What is the range of feeling that a solitary body can disclose? By 1930 German dance culture had come to the realization that dancing alone revealed an apparently unhealthy desire on the part of the dancer to exclude herself from the larger range of emotions that emerged out of group performances, out of the tensions between bodies. Dancing by oneself signified a fundamental estrangement from the world rather than a "bold" challenge to it.

Yet estrangement constituted a major experience of modernity, the manifestation of a deep disillusionment with the expectation that tensions between bodies could ever be reconciled or that the movement of others could ever make one's self move in a better, freer way. A remarkable example of an enduring commitment to the estranging authority of solo dance was the Estonian dancer Ella Ilbak (1895–1997). She gave her first solo-dance concert in Tallinn in 1918 and produced nothing but solo concerts until she retired from performance in 1967. She never established a school, had any students, or danced with any group. Although she grew up in a cultivated milieu, she came to dance relatively late, studying Isadora Duncan's ideas under Elmerice Parts in Tartu in 1913 before absorbing the Delsarte and Dalcroze philosophies from the Issachenko and Volkonsky schools in St. Petersburg (1915–17), where she became friends with Edith von Schrenck. Although she made friends easily, she was essentially a solitary person, and her attachments to others remained intellectual and pragmatic rather than emotional.[30] Nothing amplified her beauty more than dance, and her beauty was not a thing she cared to lose or entrust to others.

It was obvious that Estonia lacked a large enough dance audience to sustain a career for her as a solo dancer. But it took her a while to develop an international audience. She connected with Schrenck in Munich and presented concerts there and in Leipzig, Dresden, Berlin, and Hamburg. In 1922 she performed at the Théâtre des Champs-Élysées in Paris, then ventured to Brussels, Prague, and Vienna. But then she was back in Estonia, where she had a strong ally in the critic Hanno Kompus (1890–1974), who published detailed and careful analyses of her dances. In 1924 she gave a concert in Stockholm, returned there in 1925 and then posed for the excellent Swedish portrait photographer Henry Goodwin, including for nude photographs, some of which appeared in his 1929 book on portrait photography. She performed almost every year in Estonia up to 1930, after which she apparently appeared there only twice (1932, 1936) up to the outbreak of World War II. Most of her audience was elsewhere, in Paris, London, Budapest, Prague, Helsinki, Sofia, Vienna, Istanbul, German cities, Italy, Egypt, and Palestine.

The outbreak of the war and the subsequent Soviet occupation of Estonia disrupted her success, although she apparently spent most of the war in France. She migrated to Sweden, where she published her memoirs (in Estonian, 1953), which, however, covered her life only up to 1939. Her activities during and after the war remain obscure, although looking at photographs taken in 1924 and 1948, she appears to have attempted after the war to continue the style of performance she had pursued well before the war, and in her costume she preserves an "exotic" image of the solo dancer close to what Mata Hari cultivated in 1905 (figs. 4.11 and 4.12). Through émigré

4.11. Ella Ilbak in costume for *The Flame*, Stockholm, 1924. Photograph by Henry Goodwin. Courtesy of the National Library of Sweden, Maps and Pictures: Goodwin, Henry B., *Portrait of Ella Ilbak*, Gn Ilbak, Ella 22:11.

publishing houses she published two novels in Estonian (1955, 1966), which have recently been republished in Estonia. It is not clear why she migrated to the United States in 1956. She gave a solo-dance concert at a New York City high school in that year, at the age of sixty-one, and then moved to Santa Barbara, California, for several years; the nature of her performances there is not known. Still a remarkably beautiful woman, she gave a final concert in Highland Falls, New York, in 1967, before moving to Pontiac, Michigan, where she spent the next thirty years of her life.

4.12. Ella Ilbak in Sweden, 1948. From Piret Noorhani (ed.), *Kirjad 1952–1961 Ella Ilbak-August Gailit* (Tallinn: Tänapäev, 2009), 57. Courtesy of the Tartu Institute, Dr. Endel Aruju Archive and Library, Toronto, Canada.

From 1918 to 1939 the content of Ilbak's dances was stable. She added or subtracted a few pieces, but her message remained constant. Her concerts provided a romantic vision of female beauty. Reviewers occasionally referred to her as a "blonde idol" or "blonde flame." She shared Schrenck's taste for dark, shadowy music: Scriabin, Rachmaninoff, Debussy, Brahms, Chopin, Sibelius, and Dvorak. But she lacked Schrenck's tragic, masochistic sensibility, even though she attempted her own *Amazon* dance in 1922. For Ilbak, a dance concert demonstrated the power of her beauty to produce a "vision" of female convolution and synthesis of identities. In her early dances she was an Amazon, a page, an odalisque, Melancholia, a witch, Ahastus, a mysterious racial merging of glowing Nordic pallor and dark, Asian sultriness. In her later programs her dances assumed more abstract titles designated by the music that accompanied them—gavotte, march, *capriccioso*, waltz, *dolce con grazia*—but she did not abandon the theme of a body made beautiful by the power of movement to bestow a disconcerting ambiguity on her racial and ethnic identity. Kompus contended that she was a "sculptural" dancer in that she was fond of stretching, reaching, breathing, balancing, and tensing in such a way as to reveal her muscles, which meant that she tended to dance slowly rather than fast.[31]

Yet her most famous piece was *The Flame*, seemingly not a "sculptural" subject, which she probably performed at all of her concerts from about 1920 to 1939, apparently always last on the program. In this piece, with music by Wagner, she wore nothing but a satiny brassiere and loincloth. She began by slumbering on the dance floor until something flickered within her and began to stir her. Gradually her whole body began to vibrate, her arms started to shimmer and undulate like flames, and then they drew her upward. The flame spread through her whole body, causing her to tremble violently. Her entire body undulated with orgasmic rapture, causing her to gyrate and spin and gasp for breath, until the flame began to abate and she slowly plunged to her knees and into a huge stillness. The dance was brazenly masturbatory, narcissistic, the revelation of a woman's supreme pleasure in her own voluptuousness. To dramatize this experience was the perfect reason to dance alone. And as she tried to demonstrate with her lifelong devotion to solo dance, if you cannot dance alone, then you do not have a good reason to dance at all.

Notes

1. Sam Waagenaar, *Mata Hari, niet zo onschuldig* (Bussum: Van Holkema and Warrendorf, 1976), 42–67.

2. Ibid., 83–86.

3. "La danseuse nue," *Le Matin*, May 6, 1913, 5; Georges Claretie, "Gazette des Tribuneaux," *Le Figaro*, May 6, 1913, 5. See also, "To Repeat Dance in Public," *New York Times*, March 2, 1913. On Villany's success in the Munich court, see "Dancer Is Acquitted," *New York Times*, March 10, 1912.

4. Adoree Villany, *Tanz-Reform und Pseudo-Moral: Kritischsatyrische Gedanken aus meinem Bühnen—und Privatleben* (Paris: Published by author, 1912).

5. Jörg E. Runge, *Olga Desmond: Preussens nackte Venus* (Friedland: Steffen, 2009), 14–21. This book provides the most comprehensive description of Desmond's career yet published, but it lacks clarification of her significance as an artist.

6. Olga Desmond, *Mein Weg zur Schönheit* (Berlin: Bücherzentrale, 1916), 12.

7. Ibid., 10–11.

8. Valerian Svetloff, *Anna Pavlova*, trans. A. Grey (Paris: Brunoff, 1922), 92.

9. Keith Money, *Anna Pavlova: Her Life and Art* (New York: Knopf, 1982), 170.

10. "Covent Garden. Mme. Pavlova's Return," *Times* (London), October 30, 1911, 10.

11. John and Roberta Lazzarini, *Pavlova: Repertory of a Legend* (New York: Schirmer, 1980), 89.

12. A YouTube video of *The Swan* is at http://www.youtube.com/watch?v=R3 kPxWUbU5o.

13. Gertrud Leistikow, *Orchestische Tanzspiele*, concert program (Halle: Gebauer-Schwetschke, 1911), 9.

14. Hans Brandenburg, *Der moderne Tanz* (München: Müller, 1921), 167.

15. Karl Toepfer, *Empire of Ecstasy: Nudity and Movement in German Body Culture, 1910–1933* (Berkeley: University of California Press, 1997), 197–98. Marja Braaksma, a Dutch dancer, reconstructed *Gnossienne* for the video *Ein ewiger Kreis* (Amsterdam: V. van Laban, 1991).

16. Toepfer, *Empire of Ecstasy*, 224–33.

17. Wiert W. Fehling, *Irail Gadescov: Danseur célèbre 1894-1970; de opmekelijke carrière van danspioneer Richard Vogelsang* (Den Haag: Eburon, 2007), 139–72.

18. See Patrizia Veroli (ed.), *I Sakharoff: Un mito della danza fra teatro e avanguardie artistiche* (Bologna: Bora, 1991).

19. Nils Jockel, "Die Pioniere des Ausdruckstanzes in Hamburg: 'Ohne jede Affektation,' Gertud und Ursula Falke," in *"Flugkraft in goldene Ferne..." Bühnentanz in Hamburg seit 1900*, ed. Nils Jockel (Hamburg: Museum für Kunst und Gewerbe, 1989), 17–31.

20. The most complete account of Lavinia Schulz and Walter Holdt is Athina Chadzis, *Die expressionistischen Maskentänzer Lavinia Schulz and Walter Holdt* (Frankfurt am Main: Peter Lang, 1998). See also Athina Chadzis, "Die expression-istischen Maskentänzer Lavinia Schulz and Walter Holdt," in *Entfesselt: Expression-ismus in Hamburg um 1920*, ed. Rüdiger Joppien (Hamburg: Museum für Kunst und Gewerbe, 2006), 23–50. Schulz and Holdt lived in great poverty, unable to adapt to the chaotic economic environment of the inflation period. Their extraordinary artistic activities ended when they committed double suicide shortly after the birth of their son.

21. More on Palucca is in Toepfer, *Empire of Ecstasy*, 186–90; Peter Jarchow, *Palucca: Aus ihrem Leben, über ihre Kunst* (Berlin: Henschel, 1997); Huguette Duvoisin und René Radrizzani (eds.), *Gret Palucca: Schriften, Interviews, Tanz-manuskripte* (Basel: Schwabe, 2008).

22. Schrenck's relation to Bonsels, including much of her correspondence to him, receives extensive examination in Lini Hübsch-Pfleger, *Waldemar Bonsels und die Tänzerin Edith von Schrenck* (Wiesbaden: Harrassowitz, 1997).

23. Brandenburg, *Der moderne Tanz*, 202–3.

24. J. W. F. Werumeus Buning, *Dansen en danseressen* (Amsterdam: Querido, 1926), 36.

25. Hübsch-Pfleger, *Waldemar Bonsels*, 12.

26. Fred Hildenbrandt, *Briefe an eine Tänzerin* (Stuttgart-Heilbronn: Seifert, 1922).

27. Hans Frentz, *Niddy Impekoven und ihre Tänze* (Freiburg im Breisgau: Urban, 1930); Hans Frentz, *Weg und Entfaltung Niddy Impekovens* (Leipzig: Weibezahl, 1933).

28. Niddy Impekoven, *Die Geschichte eines Wunderkinds* (Zürich: Rotapfel, 1955).

29. Geertje Andresen, *Oda Schottmüller 1905–1943: Die Tänzerin, Bildhauerin und Nazigegnerin* (Berlin: Lukas, 2005), 255. This book is the most complete compilation of information about Schottmüller.

30. Further information about Ilbak's career is in Ella Ilbak, *Otsekui hirv kisendab, mälestusi ja töekspidamisi* (Lund: Eesti Kirjanike Kooperatiiv, 1953; reprints, 1990, 2009), and Piret Noorhani (ed.), *Kirjad, 1952–1961: Ella Ilbak, August Gailit* (Tal-linn: Tänapäev, 2009). The Estonian Music and Theater Museum contains pictures and newspaper reviews in Estonian of Ilbak's dance concerts.

31. Hanno Kompus, *Maailm on sündinud tantsust* (Tartu, Estonia: Ilmamaa, 1996), 31–36, 52–59.

five

Exotica and Ethereality

The Solo Art of Maud Allan

Julie Malnig

In March 1908 a prominent British critic reported that *The Vision of Salome*, performed by the aesthetic dancer Maud Allan, "was so haunting a fascination that many people cannot keep away from it and return to the Palace to see it night after night."[1] Allan, the Canadian-born, San Francisco-bred "barefoot" dancer who performed in the mode of Isadora Duncan, had the London theatergoing public in thrall for a record-breaking 250 performances. In *The Vision of Salome*, her signature piece, Allan was a striking figure in beaded breastplates, strands of pearls hugging her bare waist, and a translucent skirt revealing her shapely thighs. She dared to plunge herself into a long-standing controversy over theatrical representations of this biblical figure who had become a symbol of female sexual excess and decadence. With *The Vision of Salome*, Allan (and her promoters) knew how to attract and keep her audiences.

Throughout her repertory Allan moved between purity, chastity, and otherworldliness, on the one hand, and sexual provocation on the other.

In slipping in and out of several female cultural ideals of womanhood—the spritely nymph, chaste maiden, and so-called New Woman as well as the *femme fatale*—Allan led her audiences to question their assumptions about female sexuality and identity at a time when Victorian conventions of femininity were under assault. More than a cultural symbol, Allan became a participant in dialogues about women as expressed in the social, intellectual, and aesthetic practices of her day. In a kind of synchronistic relationship with her audiences, Allan embodied many of the beliefs and desires of spectators, who in turn projected them onto her.

Generally in the Dance Studies literature, Maud Allan (1880–1956) has not been held in the same esteem as her better-known and more-documented competitors: Isadora Duncan, Ruth St. Denis, and Loïe Fuller.[2] Recent scholarship on Allan, though, particularly that of Amy Koritz and Judith Walkowitz, makes clear that this trio was indeed a quartet and that Allan was an influential member.[3] Allan was of the first generation of American women solo dancers who broke ranks with the corps de ballet and the lighthearted dance fare characteristic of vaudeville and musical theater dance to forge a new form of art dance.

The reasons for Allan's slide into obscurity, until recently, are several. For one, Allan was primarily popular in England and on the Continent; her British performances were widely reported on by the American press, but by the time she came to the United States in 1910, the so-called Salome craze was on the wane.[4] Also, unlike the case with Duncan, we have rather limited visual and written documentation of Allan's performances. Reviews and articles (and Allan's own writings) provide a sense of the movements she employed but not how she structured dances or what movement qualities she exhibited.[5]

Perhaps another reason for the neglect is that Allan has been considered a Duncan imitator. Allan expanded on the movement vocabulary and style established by Duncan; one of the reasons she added Salome to her repertory, in fact, was to distinguish herself from Duncan and to increase her popularity. Unlike Duncan, though, Allan was more of a popularizer than an innovator. While Duncan performed primarily on elite concert stages, Allan made her mark in the popular theater, where she appealed to a broad range of audiences. Finally, Allan's reputation clearly suffered after a bruising court case instigated by the conservative Parliament member Noël Pemberton-Billing, in 1918. Allan had appeared in a performance of playwright Oscar Wilde's *Salome* produced by the theater impresario J. T. Grein. Although greeted successfully by the public, the production earned the scorn of Pemberton-Billing, who accused Allan and Grein of lewd acts in his right-wing newspaper the *Vigilante*. (The article, by Pemberton-Billings's colleague Harold Spencer, appeared in February 1918 under the headline "The Cult of the Clitoris." It alluded to published rumors about a German blacklist of several thousand "sexual perverts," many of whom had attended her performance.) Allan sued for libel but lost. The publicity was damning though, as it brought to light Allan's previously well-kept secret about her brother Theodore, who had been convicted for murder in 1898.[6] The scandal hovered over Allan for the remainder of her life.

Born in Toronto and raised in San Francisco, Allan, unlike some of her contemporaries, was not trained in dance; like them, though, she had a general disdain for ballet and sought a freer, more expansive movement style. Like Duncan's, Allan's Greek-inspired dances, performed barefoot, conveyed a contemporary view of female comportment; she made lyrical use of her arms, hands, and torso, typically in light, diaphanous dresses or skirts topped with loose bodices and revealing necklines. As one critic wrote of Allan's *Waltz in A Minor*, by Chopin, she wore "a light classic drapery that seems not so much to clothe her as to serve as ambient air wherein she floats."[7] Her rhythmic sense of movement no doubt came from her early training in piano. After attending the San Francisco College of Music she traveled to Berlin, where in 1895 she studied at the Royal College of Music. There she became part of an artistic community consisting of the composer Marcel Remy, the virtuosic pianist Ferruccio Busoni, sculptor Arthur Bock, and other leading figures in the arts. She also became knowledgeable about symbolist art, costume design, and photography.[8] Allan's biographer—Felix Cherniavsky—surmises that her turn to dance was largely pragmatic, since she could not hope to earn a living as a concert pianist.[9]

By 1903 Allan began performing in private and public recitals in Vienna, Berlin, and Liège. These were her first performances of what would become full-length programs consisting of danced interpretations to musical compositions such as *Peer Gynt Suite* (Grieg), *Spring Song* (Mendelssohn), *Melody in F* (Chopin), and *Am Meer* (Schubert). She first presented her Salome dance in 1906 in Vienna, at the age of thirty.[10] Cherniavsky suggests that she yearned for greater attention and remuneration, which may account for the addition of Salome to her repertory. Controversy dogged her dance. In Budapest she was dubbed the "naked dancer," and in Munich the Men's Club for the Fight against Public Immorality lobbied to ban her performances.[11] In 1907, though, when she performed her *Salome* in Marienbad, she had the good fortune to appear before King Edward VII, who is said to have arranged her debut at the Palace Theatre in London. There her manager, Alfred Butt, organized a private matinee recital, in part to prepare the press and help cement her following among the social elite.[12]

In appropriating the character of Salome, Allan drew on an ancient figure who had become a source of fascination for nineteenth-century European artists and intellectuals. The brief biblical account on which these interpretations were based describes King Herod's pleasure in the dance of his step-daughter Salome on the occasion of his wife Herodias's birthday. So taken is Herod with Salome's dancing that he grants her anything she wishes. At Herodias's urging, Salome asks for the head of John the Baptist. Herod releases him from prison, has him executed, and brings his head to Salome. It is a classic story of sexual revenge. Herodias believed she had been wronged by John the Baptist, who declared her union with Herod unlawful. In the nineteenth century Gustave Flaubert's *Salammbô* (1862) and his short novel *Herodias* (1877) set a literary precedent for the depiction of Salome as an object of male desire; at the same time the symbolist artist Gustave Moreau's numerous portraits of Salome presented her as alluring, mysterious, and powerful in her thirst for the head of John the Baptist.[13] Not far from the memories of the British public of 1908, however, was Oscar Wilde's infamous drama *Salome* (1891), in which Sarah Bernhardt was to perform in the nude.[14] The play was banned before its opening in 1892 by an obscure law prohibiting the representation of biblical themes in the theater.[15] With the sinuous and sensuous illustrations of Aubrey Beardsley accompanying the written text, Wilde's play established Salome as a transgressive woman with an assertive will.

Allan was by no means the first to take on the mantle of Salome. Between

1907 and 1910 a "Salomania" swept through Europe and the United States. Loïe Fuller, for example, had already presented a version of Salome called *The Flower Dance* at the Comédie Parisienne in 1895 (with heavy draperies covering most of her body, it did not supply the thrill of Allan's performance).[16] In 1908 the Russian actress and ballerina Ida Rubinstein presented her version of Wilde's *Salome*, which ran afoul of the Russian Orthodox Church for depicting the head of a saint. In New York several dancers and actresses aspired to the role of Salome. *Ziegfeld Follies* star Daisy Peterkin (a.k.a. La Belle Dazie) performed a "Dance of the Seven Veils" in the *Follies of 1907* and became known for creating a profitable school for budding Salomes. Dancer and mimic Gertrude Hoffmann paid homage to Allan in her humorous imitation of Allan's *Vision of Salome* and became wealthy in the process.[17]

Allan's Salome, though, achieved something the others did not: it both aroused and inspired. A reviewer for the London *Times* wrote that "even when crouching over the head of her victim, caressing it or shrinking away from it in horror, she subordinated every gesture and attitude to the conditions of her art."[18] That Allan was able to transform the figure of Salome into a symbol of sexuality, spirituality, and exotica was a significant feat. *The Vision of Salome* was the dance that enticed spectators into the theater. However, it was Allan's handling of an entire range of dances that helped her to succeed in making aesthetic dance appealing to both middle- and upper-class women and men. Various readings of the female body coalesced around Allan's solo performances and became compressed into a singularly potent stage image.

New forms of visual imagery pervaded the culture of late nineteenth-century England and the United States, and those of dance—whether social dance, variety dance, or aesthetic dance—made captivating copy. Improved technology gave rise to commercial advertising in newspapers and magazines as well as illustrated books, billboards, posters, and department-store displays. Cultural historian Martha Banta explains how much of this imagery was associated with women. Her key argument centers on the way that visual and verbal representations (writing, journalism, sculpture, painting) at the turn of the century cast women in symbolic forms as "types." Banta concludes that how these representations were put to use and by whom accounts in large part for how women came to see and measure themselves within their own culture.[19]

One of the most ubiquitous of these images was that of the New Woman. Both a cultural construct and a social reality, the New Woman represented various cultural, social, and political changes that women faced in light of reconsideration of gender assignments at the turn of the century. In both England and the United States, several typologies of the New Woman took root, from the American Gibson girl riding a bicycle to British suffragists interrupting Parliament proceedings from the "ladies gallery."[20] The New Woman, sometimes a marketing tool and often a source of parody, in fact represented real women experiencing a renewed sense of purpose. Women were profiting from increased entry into the workforce, expanded educational opportunities, and a new sense of physical and psychological freedom inspired by suffrage.[21]

The New Woman, though, had not fully supplanted one of the primary nineteenth-century feminine images, that of the so-called ideal woman. Women in the early 1910s were still prey to what was then known as the "separate spheres" ideology (referred to in the United States as the Cult of True Womanhood), which, according to historian Carroll Smith-Rosenberg, "prescribed a female role bounded by kitchen and nursery, overlaid with piety and purity, and crowned with subservience."[22] This doctrine held that women were biologically coded as emotionally superior and thus best suited to the domain of childcare and domestic responsibilities. Men were viewed as reigning over the public, women over the private. This image was translated in other ways, too. The "True Woman" was also a graceful, civilizing agent; she possessed a spiritual capacity that enabled her to check the excesses of male power and aggression. Even though many women were rejecting this identity, others still pressed this representation into service. Many suffragists, for example, clung to the idea that women's greater emotional capacities provided them with "spiritual leadership" to enhance their role in the public sphere.[23] In her solo performances, Maud Allan used her public visibility to present, yet also rework, both of these gendered typologies.

Allan may be viewed as a prototype of the New Woman, as were other modern dance pioneers of the era. Smith-Rosenberg considers Duncan, and by extension Allan, one variety of New Woman, who attempted to be free from bourgeois conventions, seek self-fulfillment, and revel in the "flamboyant presentation of self."[24] Allan was an independent-minded individual, studied music and art seriously, and sought a life of artistic creation. She can be counted among those performers whom theater historian Susan Glenn refers to as the New Women of the popular theater—women who were part of a protofeminist vanguard using the stage to experiment with gender roles and new forms of physical expression.[25] Allan (like Duncan) contributed to the imagemaking of the era in her display of a modern conception of the body. With her bare feet, uncorseted clothing, and rhythmic and seemingly unstrained sense of movement, she intimated liberation from social, physical, and sexual constraints that women were experiencing in their own lives.

By virtue of her carefully constructed solo performances and skillful publicity, Allan attracted a diverse spectrum of the British public. She was revered by middle-class women and became a darling of the nobility, whose participation in the Maud Allan boom was crucial to the perception of her dance as "high art." Historian Judith Walkowitz links Allan's popularity to London's emerging position as a major tourist center and imperial capital. She highlights how Allan's status as a Canadian (although raised in the United States) added to her "exotic" appeal. Walkowitz argues that Allan's performances were part of this increasingly cosmopolitan metropolis where women began to predominate as spectators. Allan, she contends, encouraged "respectable" women to visit a theater such as the Palace, located on the edge of the West End in Soho, an area known for its foreign prostitutes and sex shops.[26] While upper-class women may not have patronized a music hall, Allan's carefully arranged preconcert recitals—private gatherings with selected press and cultural trendsetters—did much to assuage any fears of tawdriness associated with her dancing.

Part of Allan's popularity with her women followers resulted from the kinesthetic rapport she developed with them. Dance historian Sally Banes writes of early modern dancers, "For a woman to show other women her enjoyment of her body was a feminist coup in 1906."[27] Allan seemed to give many women spectators such license and modeled an expressivity that they eagerly sought to replicate. By 1906 women began to shed layers of petticoats and to adopt the shirtwaist (a gauzy, blouse-like shirt worn with a skirt) and the Empire-styled gowns of *couturier* Paul Poiret—styles affirming the idea that clothing could serve an active, moving body. Allan was the theatrical analogue for that moving body. In one instance of this relationship, a London society hostess invited about thirty female guests to a Maud Allan dinner ("undesecrated by the presence of any man") in which the women wore Salome costumes.[28] The extent of the women's identification with Allan's characterization is indicated in this description from a *New York Times* reviewer:

> Dinner was served to an accompaniment of Salome music, tinkled by an orchestra hidden discreetly behind the fortification of palms and flowers, and when the coffee and cigarette stage had been reached some of the most graceful members of the party demonstrated that they had not only succeeded in matching Miss Allan's costume, but had learned some of her captivating steps in movement.[29]

Print culture of the period played a large part in shaping the public response to Allan.[30] Photographs and sketches of her, in her many guises, were abundant in the popular press. One of the more intriguing newspaper articles, designed for female consumption, carried the title "Maud Allan's 'Salome' Dance in Sections" and featured photographs of isolated parts of Allan's hands, arms, and feet. The text and images suggested that Allan's movements were accessible enough that women might practice them in the comfort of their own homes.[31] After the publication of installments of Allan's memoir, *My Life and Dancing*, the *Weekly Dispatch* featured some of the hundreds of letters she received. Her male admirers sent her presents and inquired about her marital status, while both middle-aged and adolescent women wrote of their admiration of her beauty and style.[32]

As a way of catering to Allan's female enthusiasts, the Palace Theatre added matinees that drew celebrities as well as young working women and middle-class matrons. As part of the Salomania one could purchase souvenir statuettes of Maud Allan as well as replicas of her sandals, which were popular with society women, and also beaded necklaces worn as breastplates (see fig. 5.1).[33] At most of her performances, picture postcards of Allan were sold, which, as Walkowitz notes, young working girls coveted and shared with one another.[34] Attendance at Allan's Salome performance had attained such

5.1. Maud Allan as Salome, ca. 1908. Photograph by Foulsham & Banfield. Courtesy of The Jerome Robbins Dance Division, The New York Public Library for the Performing Arts, Astor, Lenox and Tilden Foundations.

cachet that a young bride reportedly brought her entire wedding party to Allan's performance after an elegant dinner at the Savoy Hotel.[35]

In her stage demeanor and physicality, Allan mirrored the New Woman, but she did not always do so in her rhetoric. In her written comments on dance, Allan took a different stance. In *My Life and Dancing*, she safely aligned herself with the separate spheres ideology. She vigorously defended women's education and right to selfhood, yet she opposed suffrage: "As regards the question of votes for women, I believe that a woman can do more from an elevated position in the world of art, by bringing all that makes home beautiful into her husband's and children's lives."[36] She continued that at the risk of offending members of her own sex, "Woman should be the refining, the inspiring, the idealizing element of humanity."[37] Seemingly hypocritical from a woman who herself never married and led an independent life, this suggests that Allan made a shrewd calculation not to alienate a large portion of her female following who still believed in women's innate capacities for nurturing. Her comments also deflected criticism from conservatives, men and women alike, who thought some of her dances were unsuitable for the stage. With this conservative rhetoric Allan placed herself in a middle-of-the-road position lest she become associated with the beliefs and tactics of militant suffragists who were making news at the time.

Another persona that Allan adopted can be described as the woman of spiritualized grace, the pictorial equivalent of the ideology of True Womanhood. This feminized ideal manifested itself in two ways. One was the idea of women possessing qualities of beauty, refinement, and a sense of cultivation associated with the ancient Greeks. There were many cultural precedents for this Greek-inspired ideal: the Greek revivalist movement, which had been in vogue since the early nineteenth century; the 1893 World's Columbian Exposition, based on a neoclassical architectural style; and the renewal of the Olympic Games in 1896.[38] The Hellenistic ideal that permeated late nineteenth-century culture also became synonymous with a modern concept of female beauty and femininity. The classical revival enabled artists to "cloak sensual subjects with respectability," observes cultural historian Lois Banner, and so it served Allan's mission well.[39]

Allan and the reviewers attempting to explain her style drew on this cultural language, which helped to legitimize her dancing in the public eye.

Allan is alternately described as a "Greek maiden, crowned with flowers" and "as Hellenic as a form on a Greek vase."[40] This image might take the form of a nymphlike sprite or patrician-looking woman with a noble air. Photographs of Allan in newspapers and magazines bear this out. In one torso shot of her as Salome, she wears a tiara of pearls and sequined breastplates and her gaze is pensive and almost otherworldly. In another, from her *Spring Song,* she skips lightly, her arms outstretched lyrically, wearing a chiffon tunic and skirt; the title of the review referred to her, in fact, as "a latter-day nymph" (fig. 5.2).[41] In both cases she exudes a sense of elegance and ease.

Allan also drew on two other related traditions that would have been familiar to her women viewers. One was Delsarte, the fashionable movement-training form based on the model of Greek statuary and practiced by middle-class women at the turn of the century. Another was the *poses plastiques,* the British popular entertainment also known as "living pictures," in which amateur women performers struck artistic poses.[42] In each of these traditions, classical allusions signified dance as an embodiment of a timeless beauty created through the techniques of balance, symmetry, and simplicity of line. These concepts enabled Allan to associate her dance with the loftiest of goals. She exhorted her women readers in *My Life and Dancing*:

> A drill sergeant is all very well for soldiers; dumb-bells and elastic exer-
> cisers for raising up lumps of muscles; but a woman who seeks grace of
> movement is best served when she strives to harmonize motion with
> inspiration, be it that of music, or the graceful figure of some picture or
> statue that imagination has endowed with moving life.[43]

Allan, like Duncan, needed to align herself with the exalted tradition of the Greeks to justify her modern dance style.[44] It is also plausible that because of the addition to her repertory of the Salome dance, which contained more than a whiff of late nineteenth-century British decadence, she may have felt a particular need to emphasize a sense of the ethereal.

For a cadre of male writers, journalists, and poets, Allan's embodied translations of music represented the principles of aestheticism and symbolist art come to life. Her solo dances became a plastic, three-dimensional personification of many of the symbolist's core artistic principles. Symbolism, the movement associated with visual artists such as Gustave Moreau, Edward

5.2. Maud Allan in Mendelssohn's *Spring Song*, ca. 1908.
Photograph by Foulsham & Banfield. Courtesy of The Jerome
Robbins Dance Division, The New York Public Library for the
Performing Arts, Astor, Lenox and Tilden Foundations.

Coley Burne-Jones, and Fernand Khnopff, took hold in the late 1880s as a revolt against realism and what was viewed by many as a slavish reliance on naturalistic detail. The symbolists typically depicted allegorical themes and scenes from nature. These images, though, were really the inspiration for the artist's own personal experience, an attempt to look beyond the surface of material things to the hidden and unseen. Women in the symbolist world-view were typically portrayed as somehow beyond the reach of mortal exis-tence. The Pre-Raphaelite painters, whom the symbolists admired, exempli-fied this idea, as in Dante Gabriel Rossetti's *The Blessed Damozel* (1875–79), in which a female figure with a faraway gaze and a billowing scarf wrapped around her neck caresses a bouquet of lilies.[45]

For many writers, Allan seemed to be an exemplar of this divine expres-sion of nature rather than merely its reflection. In Allan's *Spring Song,* per-formed in a style reminiscent of the *poses plastiques,* she mimed picking flowers and basking in the sunlight. It was "poetry in motion," a symbolist expression frequently cited in Allan's reviews. The critic for the *Weekly Dis-patch* said of Allan, "Her long, slender arms are miracles of eloquence."[46] In his poem to Allan, "An Arcadian Idyll," W. L. Courtney, a devotee of Yeats and an author of philosophical texts, wrote, "She lives not in our world of common things, / Nor breathes the common air of mortal men."[47]

Allan and her symbolist-inspired reviewers formed a kind of unspoken alliance. By attaching Allan's dance to the tenets of symbolist art, these critics helped to make the case that new barefoot dance was a part of an ennobling tradition; they could better justify the dance to their readers and the theater-going public by incorporating it into an already existing artistic context. Al-lan herself participated in this practice. She echoes many of these sentiments about her dance philosophy in her writing:

> Dances express emotions and those dances are neither the swaying to
> and fro to a valse measure in a London drawing-room, nor the pirouet-
> ting on one toe of an Austrian ballerina. Such dancing as that is not the
> expression of an immortal soul stirred by all the mystery of existence.[48]

Allan's association with symbolist ideology, in particular the connections be-tween woman-as-nature and spiritual nurturer, also fed into another promi-nent discourse of the day on both sides of the Atlantic: the idea that modern life had grown overly subject to routine as a result of rampant industrialization, commercialism, and a tyrannical work ethic. This disillusionment with modernity and the emphasis on material progress led many people to mysticism, mind-cures of various sorts, and the aestheticism of the Arts and Crafts Movement. The historian J. Jackson Lears describes this response as an "antimodern" one that offered balm to a modern world that had become morally sterile and impotent.[49] Allan's performances, with their poeticism, seeming simplicity, and possibility for a transcendent aesthetic experience, represented an antidote to the harshness of contemporary life. It was an expression of what Lears called "the *fin-de-siècle* yearning for authentic experience—physical, emotional, or spiritual."[50]

The spiritual, the sensual, and the exotic came together most vividly in Allan's *succès de scandale*, *The Vision of Salome*. By the turn of the century, the image of the *femme fatale* prevailed in numerous forms, from the vampire seductresses in Bram Stoker's novel *Dracula* (1897) to Freud's reinterpretation of the myth of Medusa, whose severed head becomes a symbol of male castration anxieties.[51] Salome was one of the most famous of these figures. In the public consciousness, the character of Salome, according to cultural historian Bram Dijkstra, "epitomized the inherent perversity of women; their eternal circularity and their ability to destroy the male's soul even while they remained chaste in body."[52] Many critics and historians have described Salome's predominance in art, literature, and music of the time as a clear representation of male fears of the New Woman.[53] Salome was the New Woman gone wild who threatened male prerogative and power, the threat that many men at the turn of the century felt as a result of the disequilibrium created by women's demands for economic, political, and sexual quality.[54] In her blatant sexual display, Allan clearly played to the traditional idea of the *femme fatale*. How she neutralized this sexuality, though, explains how she quieted a good deal of the controversy over the piece and broadened her appeal.

Salomania went hand in hand with the turn-of-the-century fascination with the East. Orientalism, an ideology derived from a Western, imperialistic worldview, portrayed the East as exotic, primitive, weak, and in need of the stabilizing hand of the West. Depictions of Salome typically emphasized her Oriental "otherness," a combination of the mysterious and the erotic. In "Dancing the Orient for England: Maud Allan's *The Vision of Salome*," dance and literary scholar Amy Koritz, employing the ideas of Edward Said, makes a convincing argument for the way Allan's *Salome* drew on both Edwardian gender concerns and nationalistic interests. Allan's dance, Koritz claims, offered a Western cultural representation of the Orient as "feminized" and upheld a British colonialist notion of superiority by having a Western woman "enact" the East.[55] In equating the East with "essence," Allan dispelled the commonly held assumption that all Eastern dance was licentious and at the same time reinforced the separate spheres ideology of women's innate moral purity and value.

The representation of the East as female colored the language of Allan's critics, detractors as well as supporters, and suggests how Allan managed to bridge the sensual and the ethereal. One British critic said of Allan's *Vision of Salome* that "it was an epitome in itself of Orientalism and yet with scarcely a suggestion of the sensuous."[56] Another reviewer commented on Allan's "provocative posturing" and applauded her ability to dance "in the Eastern manner."[57] This rhetoric presupposed that "Eastern" dance was somehow irrepressibly lustful, yet Allan's skill was in transforming it into a symbolist-like ideal beauty. Part of this had to do with her use of rhythmical, Delsarte-inspired poses, her deliberate manner of movement, and her trancelike, self-absorbed gaze that seemed almost disconnected from her audience.[58] One critic commented that as Allan dances, "no mind is filled with anything but thoughts that are pure, for the dancer is herself the personification of maidenly purity and grace."[59] If viewers had come primed to see a devouring, sex-starved virago, their expectations were surely undercut by Allan's interpretation.

It was in her reworking of the narrative of Salome that Allan departed most dramatically from Oscar Wilde.[60] Wilde's version associated Salome with a nearly perverse sexuality in her fetishistic attachment to the head of John the Baptist and her unbridled, even aggressive, passion.[61] For Wilde, the veil—the *fin-de-siècle* icon suggesting female mystery, sexuality, and exotica—figures prominently. Elaine Showalter writes that "the Oriental woman behind the veil of purdah stood as a figure of sexual secrecy and inaccessibility for Victorian men in the 1880s and 1890s, much as the nun, another veiled woman, had done for Gothic novelists in the 1780s and 1790s."[62] Wilde never describes the dance; in his stage directions he refers to it simply as "the dance of the seven veils." But it is clear that the veil in Wilde's drama reinforced Salome's mysteriousness, and its shedding became synonymous with the unburdening of her sexual desire for John the Baptist.

In her *Vision of Salome*, Allan dispensed with the veil altogether. She was a striking figure with her bejeweled bare torso and beaded tiara from which pearls dangled along the sides of her face.[63] As the lights dimmed, approximating twilight, strains of discordant "Oriental" music sounded. She descended a flight of steps, supposedly of an Egyptian temple, flanked on either side by flickering torches.[64] Her dance before King Herod, though, unlike in Wilde's version, was performed as a dream in which she relived the events that led to the fateful encounter with the severed head of John the Baptist. In Wilde's play Salome caresses and kisses the severed head, prompting a shocked and outraged Herod to have her killed. In Allan's version, this act presumably occurs in her imagination. Of the head, "she was half drawn to it, half repelled," writes one reviewer.[65] Her movements were less overtly provocative than they were tentative, as she ultimately sank to the floor overcome with the realization of her deed.

Perhaps Allan's most significant alteration was her return to the nature of Salome as she was originally conceived in the Bible: an adolescent torn between her duty to her mother and her awareness of her own first sexual stirrings. In Allan's reinterpretation Salome is portrayed as a young innocent doing her mother's bidding and unsuspecting of Herodias's motives. While she does indeed display desire for John the Baptist, this desire is coupled with guilt, remorse, and horror at the action she must carry out. Her "awakening" is not so much a sexual as a spiritual one. Allan writes of Salome in her memoir:

> The awakening is that of her childish heart, the realization of a superior power has so taken possession of her that she is speared on to sacrifice everything, even herself to conquer. . . . What passes in those few moments through this excited, half terror-stricken, half stubborn brain, makes of little Salome a woman![66]

Amy Koritz contends that Allan's own commentary about her dance failed to account for the way that her performance sexualized the spiritual. Koritz writes that Allan's narrative was less one of "provocation of desire" than the expression of desire itself.[67] While this may be true in part, it also seems likely from the descriptions we possess that these desires get undermined by Allan's sense of naiveté, hesitation, and seeming innocence; she reaches for the head, holds it, but immediately recoils as if fearful of that desire.

Although Allan had in a sense "tamed" her Salome, the piece was by no means without its critics and censors. A group known as the Manchester Watch Committee banned a performance of *Salome* when Allan attempted to perform it in that city. Allan also incurred the wrath of Archdeacon Sinclair of London, who objected to the use of a papier-mâché prop to represent the head of Christ's forerunner.[68] Allan's Salome, though, struck a chord with her audiences. For her male viewers, this etherealized *femme fatale* might assuage fears of the New Woman's presumed sexual aggression. For middle- and upper-class women, Salome held out the promise of a demonstrative and positive sexuality that was within their grasp. Other women, too—suffragists and nonsuffragists alike who saw femininity as a source of women's power—felt licensed to enjoy the dance because its sexuality was cloaked in a veneer of modesty and grace.

Although *The Vision of Salome* was the most celebrated dance in Maud Allan's repertory, I conclude with a brief discussion of her dance to the "Funeral March" (*Marche funèbre*) section of Chopin's Sonata No. 2 in B-flat Minor in order to underscore how Allan created a scenography of the body. Her *Funeral March* presented another version of the female self with another kind of veiling. Here, Allan *did* wear a veil, and her appearance was commanding: she was shrouded in a full-length dark chiffon dress, with layers of fabric cascading down her body. Long, loose sleeves hung lightly at her wrists and a trailing head veil covered her shoulders and back. Allan was a vision of intense female mourning, moving slowly and deliberately, "as though overburdened by a weight of woe."[69] Some critics thought the piece was overly macabre. Many, though, seemed to agree that in this dance Allan captured the essence of grief with realism and poignancy.[70]

Encased in billowing fabric, Allan might have seemed an antithetical model to convey women's emerging sense of self. In fact, though, the dance appeared to enable many women spectators to feel greater access to their own emotional lives at a time when they were seeking freedom in other arenas. For male viewers, however, Allan's veiled woman, with its suggestion of

5.3. Maud Allan, veiled, in an unidentified photograph, ca. 1908. Photograph by Apeda Studios, New York. Courtesy of The Jerome Robbins Dance Division, The New York Public Library for the Performing Arts, Astor, Lenox and Tilden Foundations.

impenetrability, was a source of subliminal eroticism (fig. 5.3). She usually presented her Salome dance last on the program; as the penultimate number, then, the *Funeral March* may have served as a sort of "tease," a prolonging of expectation before the final and most talked-about dance, which promised an abundance of bangles, beads, and bare flesh.

In 1910 Allan toured the United States, but by then the Salome fad had peaked and Allan could not reclaim the following she had found in England. After returning to London in 1911 for a reasonably successful season, she went on tour in India. Allan then returned again to the United States, where in 1915 she starred in the silent film *The Rugmaker's Daughter,* which featured excerpts from her Salome dance. In 1916 Allan had planned to perform to a ballet score written for her by Debussy, but because of professional differences with the composer, the piece was never produced. Instead, she presented a dance drama, *Nair, the Slave: A Love Tragedy of the Orient*, that was considered a pale imitation of *Schéhérazade,* which the Ballets Russes had performed a few months earlier.[71]

After 1918 it became difficult for Allan to maintain her once vibrant career. Not only had the appetite for Salomania diminished, but Allan had also lost a good deal of her following after the unfortunate Noël Pemberton-Billing affair. Although her success may have been relatively brief, the role she played in early twentieth-century England cannot be underestimated. Allan's dancing responded to pressing cultural and social issues in a key transitional moment. Elaine Showalter remarks that periods of millennial change tend to be marked by cultural insecurities about gender, and that "the longing for border controls" around the definition of gender becomes more intense.[72] Allan exposed the porousness of these borders, as conventional attitudes of womanhood were breaking down. In her performances Allan managed to create a compelling visual language that aroused the imagination of her audiences, yet eased their anxieties at the same time. In an age of clashing, if not confused, visions of women, Allan's solo performances marked her as an icon of a newly expressive mode of female sexuality.

Notes

1. A. B. [Arthur Bingham] Walkley, "The New Dancer," *Times Literary Supplement*, March 26, 1908, 102, Maud Allan Clipping File, Jerome Robbins Dance Division, New York Public Library for the Performing Arts (hereafter JRDD, NYPL).

2. For Maud Allan's actual birth date, see Lacy McDearmon, "Maud Allan: The Public Record," *Dance Chronicle* 2, no. 2 (1978): 86.

3. See Amy Koritz, "Dancing the Orient for England: Maud Allan's *The Vision of Salome*," in *Meaning in Motion: New Cultural Studies in Dance*, ed. Jane C. Desmond (Durham, N.C.: Duke University Press, 1997), 133–52; and Judith R. Walkowitz, "The *Vision of Salome*: Cosmopolitanism and Erotic Dancing in Central London, 1908–1918," *American Historical Review* 108, no. 2 (April 2003): 337–76. See also Susan A. Glenn, *Female Spectacle: The Theatrical Roots of Modern Feminism* (Cambridge, Mass.: Harvard University Press, 2000); Amy Koritz, *Gendering Bodies/Performing Art: Dance and Literature in Early Twentieth-Century British Culture* (Ann Arbor: University of Michigan Press, 1995); and Felix Cherniavsky, *The Salome Dancer: The Life and Times of Maud Allan* (Toronto: McClelland and Stewart, 1991).

4. Cherniavsky, *Salome Dancer*, 192.

5. Judith Walkowitz asserts that the lack of visual and written descriptions of Allan presents the researcher with challenges in deriving "cultural meanings through nonverbal ephemeral acts." "*Vision of Salome*," 341.

6. The libel trial turned out to be one of the decade's most sensational and reflected

major prewar cultural anxieties over gender issues. Pemberton-Billing attempted to discredit Allan for what author Lucy Bland calls her "sexological knowledge": if Allan knew what the word *clitoris* referred to, she must be a lesbian, viewed at the time as a type of sexual perversion. Lucy Bland, "Maud Allan, *Salome* and the 'Cult of the Clitoris Case,'" in *Sexology in Culture: Labelling Bodies and Desires*, ed. Lucy Bland and Laura Doan (Cambridge, U.K.: Polity Press, 1998): 184–98. For more on the libel trial, see Philip Hoare, *Wilde's Last Stand: Decadence, Conspiracy and the First World War* (London: Duckworth, 1997), 89–96; and Michael Kettle, *Salome's Last Veil: The Libel Case of the Century* (London: Granada, 1977).

7. Walkley, "The New Dancer," 102.

8. Cherniavsky, *Salome Dancer*, 124.

9. Ibid., 12.

10. Some scholars differ on the date of Allan's debut performance of her *Salome*. See McDearmon, "Maud Allan," 89; Felix Cherniavsky, "Maud Allan, Part II: First Steps to a Dancing Career, 1904–1907," *Dance Chronicle* 6, no. 3 (1983): 205.

11. Cherniavsky, *Salome Dancer*, 144, 147.

12. Ibid., 160–62; Walkowitz, "*Vision of Salome*," 342.

13. Udo Kultermann, "The *Dance of the Seven Veils*: Salome and Erotic Culture around 1900," *Artibus et Historiae* 27, no. 53 (2006): 190–91; Bram Dijkstra, *Idols of Perversity: Fantasies of Feminine Evil in Fin-de-Siècle Culture* (New York: Oxford University Press, 1986), 380–81.

14. Kultermann, "*Dance of the Seven Veils*," 195.

15. Ibid.

16. Fuller performed a more elaborate version of *Salome* in 1907 at the Théâtre des Arts in Paris. See McDearmon, "Maud Allan," 88; Walkowitz, "*Vision of Salome*," 351; and Kultermann, "*Dance of the Seven Veils*," 206.

17. Glenn, *Female Spectacle*, 101–6.

18. Cherniavsky, *Salome Dancer*, 164.

19. Martha Banta, *Imaging American Women: Image and Ideals in Cultural History* (New York: Columbia University Press, 1987): xxvii–xxxii.

20. Martha Vicinus, *Independent Women: Work and Community for Single Women 1850–1920* (Chicago: University of Chicago Press, 1985).

21. Ibid., 256.

22. Ibid., 2; Carroll Smith-Rosenberg, *Disorderly Conduct: Visions of Gender in Victorian America* (New York: Oxford University Press, 1985), 193.

23. Vicinus, *Independent Women*, 256. This idea is similar to the ideology of "cultural feminism" prominent in the United States during the height of the feminist movement in the 1970s and early 1980s.

24. Smith-Rosenberg, *Disorderly Conduct*, 177.

25. Glenn, *Female Spectacle*, 6.

26. Walkowitz, *"Vision of Salome,"* 346, 348.

27. Sally Banes, *Dancing Women: Female Bodies on Stage* (London: Routledge, 1998), 99.

28. "Salome Dinner Dance: Tale of London Society Women Dining in Maude [sic] Allan Undress," *New York Times*, August 23, 1908.

29. Ibid.

30. Walkowitz, *"Vision of Salome,"* 341.

31. "Maud Allan's 'Salome' Dance in Sections," undated article, JRDD, NYPL. See Walkowitz, *"Vision of Salome,"* 360–64, for another discussion of Allan's kinesthetic relationship with women spectators.

32. "Letters from Miss Maud Allan's Post-Bag," unidentified clipping, JRDD, NYPL. See also "Touching Missives from Miss Maud Allan's Letter Box," *Weekly Dispatch*, August 30, 1908; and "Marriage Offers for Miss Maud Allan, September 6, 1908," in Walkowitz, *"Vision of Salome,"* 363.

33. Hoare, *Wilde's Last Stand*, 80.

34. Postcard addressed to Miss D. K. James, 87 Brudenell Road, Leeds, Maud Allan Collection, San Francisco Performing Arts Library and Museum, in Walkowitz, *"Vision of Salome,"* 362.

35. "How I Dance: Miss Maud Allan Answers Archdeacon Sinclair," *Weekly Dispatch* (London), 1908 (full date obscured), JRDD, NYPL.

36. Maud Allan, *My Life and Dancing* (London: Everett, 1908), General Books LLC, www.General-Books.net, 43.

37. Ibid., 46.

38. Ann Daly, *Done into Dance: Isadora Duncan in America* (Bloomington: Indiana University Press, 1995), 103.

39. Lois Banner, *American Beauty* (Chicago: University of Chicago Press, 1983), 110.

40. "Maud Allan: The Dancer as She Describes Herself," *Boston Evening Transcript*, December 12, 1908; John Wilstach, "The Art of Maud Allan," *New York Review*, January 30, 1910, JRDD, NYPL.

41. Wilstach, "The Art of Maud Allan"; Maud Allan Reveals Herself as a Latter-Day Nymph," *Musical America*, January 29, 1910, JRDD, NYPL.

42. For more on Delsarte, see Nancy Lee Chalfa Ruyter, *Reformers and Visionaries: The Americanization of the Art of Dance* (New York: Dance Horizons, 1979); on the *poses plastiques*, see John Stokes, *In the Nineties* (Chicago: University of Chicago Press, 1989).

43. Allan, *My Life and Dancing*, 20.

44. Daly, *Done into Dance*, 17.

45. See Robert Goldwater, *Symbolism* (New York: Harper and Row, 1979), 39–43.

46. "How I Dance."

47. W. L. Courtney, "An Arcadian Idyll," in *Maud Allan and Her Art*, publicity portfolio, ca. 1908, *MGYB-Res., JRDD, NYPL.

48. Allan, quoted in Raymond Blathwayt, "Two Visions of Maud Allan," *Black and White*, July 18, 1908, JRDD, NYPL.

49. J. Jackson Lears, *No Place of Grace: Antimodernism and the Transformation of American Culture, 1880–1920* (Chicago: University of Chicago Press, 1981), 4–5.

50. Ibid., xix.

51. Elaine Showalter, *Sexual Anarchy: Gender and Culture at the Fin de Siècle* (New York: Penguin Books, 1990), 145.

52. Dijkstra, *Idols of Perversity*, 384.

53. Glenn, *Female Spectacle*, 97; Showalter, *Sexual Anarchy*, 144–45; Jane Marcus, "Salomé: The Jewish Princess Was a New Woman," *Bulletin of the New York Public Library* (Autumn 1974): 100–2.

54. Ibid., 104–5. Marcus views Wilde's Salome as "a Biblical Hedda Gabler."

55. Koritz, "Dancing the Orient," 141.

56. Blathwayt, "Two Visions of Maud Allan."

57. J. C. F., "Miss Maud Allan's Salome Dance," *Academy*, March 21, 1908.

58. Judith Walkowitz notes that Allan is usually devoid of the "stereotyped dancer's smile." "*Vision of Salome*," 359.

59. "Maud Allan's Art Creates a Sensation," *Musical Courier*, February 2, 1910, JRDD, NYPL.

60. Allan was apparently influenced by modernist director Max Reinhardt's 1903 version of Wilde's *Salome*. See Cherniavsky, *Salome Dancer*, 142, 147.

61. See Walkowitz, "*Vision of Salome*," 351; Glenn, *Female Spectacle*, 97.

62. Showalter, *Sexual Anarchy*, 145.

63. "Maud Allan's Bare Feet Win," *New York Telegraph*, January 21, 1910, JRDD, NYPL.

64. "Maud Allan's Interpretive Dancing Charms London," *Musical America*, April 25, 1908, JRDD, NYPL; Walkley, "The New Dancer," 102.

65. "Maud Allan: The Dancer as She Describes Herself," *Boston Evening Transcript*, December 12, 1908, JRDD, NYPL.

66. Allan, *My Life and Dancing*, 49–50.

67. Koritz, *Gendering Bodies*, 44.

68. "How I Dance."

69. "Maud Allan's Tour Opens Successfully," *Musical Courier*, November 6, 1916, JRDD, NYPL.

70. Ibid.

71. Cherniavsky, *Salome Dancer*, 237. See also Elizabeth Weigand, "*The Rugmaker's Daughter*: Maud Allan's 1915 Silent Film," *Dance Chronicle* 9, no. 2 (1986): 237–51.

72. Showalter, *Sexual Anarchy*, 4.

six

Modernity and Nationalism in Solo Dance in Brazil

The *Bailado* of Eros Volúsia and the
Performance of Luiz de Abreu

Sandra Meyer

The first four decades of the twentieth century witnessed countless transformations in dance in Europe and North America, which reverberated in Asia and South America. One of the most important phenomena of this new dance was found in the composition of the solo. Soloists' search for personal expression was distinguished by the specification of a national or sociocultural context allied to a view of a new dance based on the absorption of aesthetic models from other cultures, such as the Greek in Isadora Duncan, the oriental in Ruth St. Denis, and the African in Katherine Dunham. The stylization of dance in the early twentieth century based on African cultures, unlike the alterity constituted by means of a utopian, late Romantic look at Greek, Indian, or Egyptian culture, had latent sociopolitical implications because of the recent and combative formation of black identity in countries such as Brazil and the United States.

In Brazil in the 1930s and 1940s, the solo dances of Eros Volúsia (Rio de Janeiro, 1914–2004) affirmed a combination of nationalism and modernism imbued with reflections on her own Afro-Brazilian culture. In this period, Brazilian arts expressed issues relevant to national culture without losing sight of the desire to be modern. The modernist movement, triggered by the Semana de Arte Moderna de 1922 (Modern Art Week) organized in the city of São Paulo by a generation of intellectuals and artists who criticized the artistic and literary forms upheld by academic traditions, searched for a creative conscience concerned with portraying Brazilian culture, from its natural qualities to its growing urbanization, while maintaining a connection with the movements of the European vanguardists.

In this context in the 1930s and 1940s, the new dance presented by Volúsia turned to Afro-Brazilian matrices, distinguishing her from other figures of Brazilian dance at the time who followed the ballet tradition. In the same period, American anthropologist and dancer Katherine Dunham (1909–2006) was building a unique vision of Afro-American dance in the syncretic, although segregated, American culture. These choreographers brought to the modern dance scene in their countries representation of Afro-American and Afro-Brazilian culture.

Volúsia's proposal to create a national body was appropriated by the political ideology of the Brazilian government at the time of the Estado Novo (1937–45), one of the most authoritarian periods of the country's history.[1] The regime worked on two essential fronts, culture and education, seeking to "establish the bases of nationality, construct the nation, forge Brazilianness."[2] Mestizo culture became the official representation of nation, and the Brazilian dances of Volúsia revealed the nationalist and modern project idealized by the Estado Novo government. Eros Volúsia was the inventor of a national *bailado*, which realized an "anthropophagic" relation to foreign and domestic cultural references.

The Portuguese term *bailado*, translated from the French *ballet*, was used at the time to refer to both modern dances and ballet. It established itself at a time when ballet was institutionalized in the country with the creation of the first official schools and companies by the theaters in large Brazilian cities. My analysis of the beginnings of the modern dance solo in Brazil relies on a study of Brazilian dance of the 1930s and 1940s by Roberto Pereira (1966–2009), one of the most important dance history researchers in Brazil.[3] I refer as well to the concept of miscegenation that arose from the philosophical and ethical anthropophagic proposals of Oswald de Andrade (1890–1954). One of the main proponents for cultural change during the first four decades of the twentieth century, de Andrade defined his Brazilian cultural activism as anthropophagic, creating an analogy with the tradition of anthropophagic Indians. Published in the magazine *Antropofagia* in 1928, the "Manifesto Antropofágico" proposed feeding off everything that foreigners brought to Brazil, "to suck all the ideas from them and join them to Brazilian ones, thus realizing a rich, creative, unique and proprietary artistic and cultural production."[4] The name of the manifesto was intended to revive metaphorically a belief of some anthropophagic indigenous peoples who devoured their enemies, supposing that they would thus assimilate the enemies' qualities.[5] Written by Oswald de Andrade, with the help of Mário de Andrade and Raul Bopp, the manifesto is the most radical of the entire first phase of the Modernist Movement, because it defends resistance to incorporations made without a proper critical spirit. The proposal was to "devour" foreign cultures and techniques and submit them to critical digestion in our cultural stomach, in order to assimilate them or even vomit them if they were considered improper or undesirable.[6] The concept of anthropophagy was not only a way to react to the constant confrontation with colonizing culture but was also concerned with generating processes of cultural hybridization in Brazil, provoked by the successive waves of immigrants during its history.

The solo dances of Volúsia were seen by theater critics of the time as "typically Brazilian" with an "expressionist" tendency. The dancer, choreographer, and researcher differentiated herself by inserting popular Brazilian dance into the spaces of the elite, such as the Theatro Municipal do Rio de Janeiro. She moved parts of the body that are intrinsic to the corporal culture of Afro-descendents in a way that was unthinkable in the structure of ballet.

In addition to analyzing Volúsia's solo dances and her goal of constructing a national dance based on the miscegenation of European, black, and indigenous cultural elements, with echoes of the nationalist political ideology dominant in this historic period in Brazil, I mean to establish a relationship between this pioneer modern soloist and the solo *Samba do crioulo doido* (2004), by Luiz de Abreu, a Brazilian artist active since the late 1990s in contemporary dance, who analyzes themes important to Eros Volúsia: dance and "Brazilianness." These two Brazilian artists, separated by half a century, reveal different artistic and sociopolitical visions of how to make dance in and about Brazil. The approach of Abreu's work—considering the cultural implications of a colonizer-colonized discourse in contemporary terms—is different. More than finding an identity bounded by an affirmation of Brazilian culture or construction of a national dance, as Volúsia tried to do, Abreu's great interest was to "deconstruct" the national body as a way of criticizing the stereotypical image of the Brazilian body.

The discussion about nationalist issues in Brazil had intensified in the nineteenth century with the beginning of a search for a national identity. The racial factor was broadly discussed at a time when there was strong European immigration. A vision of miscegenation inherited from Romanticism excluded the black and idealized the figure of the Indian. Renato Ortiz explains that before the abolition of slavery, blacks were completely absent from the theoretical formulations of Brazilian thinking.[7] With the end of slavery in Brazil on May 13, 1888, blacks gradually reappeared as important personalities in the Brazilian social dynamic.

Since then, Brazilian miscegenation has been understood as a crossing of three races: the European white, African black, and autochthonous Indian. Nevertheless, the European remained the civilizing element. This barrier was overcome with a shift in the 1930s, according to Ortiz, from an emphasis on race to that of culture, a thesis that was defended in the celebrated work of sociologist Gilberto Freyre (1900–87), *Casa grande e senzala,* published in 1933. The ideology of miscegenation, previously imprisoned in the ambiguities of racist theories, came to be socially diffused, "ritually celebrated in daily relations, or in large events such as carnival and football. What was mestizo became national."[8]

In the 1920s, in what was then the Brazilian capital, Rio de Janeiro, where Volúsia was born and became an artist, greater importance was given to the indicative facts of Brazilian identity in an effort to break with Brazil's colonial "backwardness." Brazil made an effort to establish national values that simultaneously responded to an affirmation of its identity and to the edicts required by modernity, with its ideas of urban progress: "To be modern was to be Brazilian."[9] Historian Monica Velloso reconceptualized Rio de Janeiro modernity, distinguishing it from the idea of an organized cultural movement such as the Semana de Arte Moderna of 1922. What marked the modern gesture in Rio de Janeiro was the persistence of artistic-intellectual production, characterized by spontaneity.[10]

Volúsia took her original and spontaneous solos to the elite theaters. She allied the popular and the erudite, based on study of Brazilian popular dances. She conducted lecture-demonstrations in which she presented discoveries based on research in museums and trips for observation throughout the country, illustrating her talks with the presentation of solo dances of her own creation. One of the most striking talks was that held in Paris, at the Archives Internationales de la Danse, in 1948. Parisian newspapers, such as *Le Matin*, prophesied that Eros would be the second Isadora Duncan of the century.[11] It is interesting to note that *Rites de Passage*, by Katherine Dunham, was created as part of a demonstration reading at an anthropology event and only later would become a repertory piece.[12] The first great solo presentation by the creator of a national *bailado* had been in the Theatro Municipal do Rio de Janeiro, the noblest space on the Brazilian scene, on September 28, 1929. Volúsia, barefoot, danced a "typical" Bahian samba, *Oia a fóia no a*, by Aníbal de Oliveira, accompanied by black musicians playing guitar and drums known as *batuques*. The artist's daring, "until then incompatible with the elite traditions of that stage," inspired an initial silence that was broken by then Brazilian president Washington Luiz, who led a standing ovation after Volúsia's presentation.[13] This, according to historian Salvyano de Paiva, was how the Brazilian *bailado* took its first steps.[14] (fig. 6.1)

Volúsia's presentations provoked heated debate in the Rio de Janeiro press, which questioned the sensuality and Brazilianness of her dance as well as its connections to ballet. Nevertheless, there were no analytical parameters to describe the Brazilianness in the dancer's body, beyond the "highly Brazilian motifs" it extolled.[15] The absence of technical refinement based on ballet, the most important artistic reference, is one of the factors that made it difficult to understand Volúsia's aesthetic proposal. Mário Nunes, in a criticism aimed at Volúsia's presentation of the *bailado* titled *Uirapuru*, with music by the composer Heitor Villa-Lobos (1887–1959), questioned its originality by relating the dance to "something already created—expressionism," alluding to the European movement recently assimilated by Brazilian culture.[16] Soraia Silva countered that this was "a very Brazilian expressionism, based on various popular sources."[17]

6.1. Eros Volúsia dancing a "typical" Bahian samba, *Oia a fóia no a,* September 29, 1929.

In her book *Eu e a dança* (Dance and I) Volúsia defines her choreographies as dramatic, symbolic, and recreational, "all impregnated with a large dose of expressionism."[18] The recreational ones would have an entertaining character, the dramatic ones a tragic-satiric vision, and the symbolic ones a fetishistic or religious appeal, like the dances *Macumba* and *Candomblé.*

Upon defining her dances as expressionist, Volúsia declared, "It is dance with more emotion than movement."[19] The term *expressionism* in Volúsia's dance suggests the idea of a subjective representation of states of the soul of Brazilian people by means of connecting the art of the dance to a modernity recently incorporated in the country. Volúsia's solos prepared the Brazilian cultural environment for the later planting of modern dance in the 1940s, marked by the insertion of techniques, most of which had German influence.

It is possible to see in some critical opinions of the time how much black and indigenous culture was still disdained by the elites in the country. When considering Brazilian dance elevated to an erudite art, the parameters were still dictated by a classical vision, with the pretention of being more Apollonian than Dionysian. According to Mário Nunes, Volúsia's dance was still at a "rehearsal" level, at the service of a "rough and primary" representation "suitable for blacks and Indians," lacking the transposition from popular art to erudite art, something that would go beyond "a purely sexual sensualism to a spiritual plane."[20]

It is known that the seeds of the new twentieth-century Western dance were principally spread by an imagined auteur quality, constructed by soloists such as Duncan, with her look to the Greeks, and St. Denis, with her Indian and Egyptian dances. The idea of exoticism and of the natural body in modern dance requires care not to get lost in generalizations. The imagery related to Duncan's natural-cultural body differs from Katherine Dunham's approach. Volúsia, in turn, also presented specificities in her Afro-Brazilian–inspired corporeality. As Ann Daly observed, even if Duncan's dances proposed spontaneity and liberty, they were far from being "wild," in the sense attributed to archaic cultures: "Although it was 'spontaneous,' her style of movement had a decided sense of flowing, unhurried gentility, compared with the 'spasms' or 'paroxysms' of the African-inspired modern dances."[21] Dunham and Volúsia studied movements closer to the kinetic impulses and the visceral quality of the African rhythms, without losing sight of the need to stylize these dances.

Gilberto Freyre, commenting in his work *Sobrados e Mucamos* (1936) on Carmen Miranda's dance steps—which "were rounded in a dance that was more Bahian than African," and so highly applauded by the "refined international audiences"—speaks of the artist's "sublimation" of the "raw energies of blacks and mulattos."[22] If Dunham and Volúsia caused an impact with their proffered aesthetic, they realized a sublimation process by means of the stylization of African dances. It was not possible to reproduce on stage the visceral nature of the rituals studied by the dancers in their field work.

Volúsia was compared abroad to a "tropical Isadora Duncan" or to an "exotic folkloric dancer from Brazil," as she was presented on her tour in the United States and France.[23] Instead of comparing the Brazilian dancer and Duncan, it is more helpful to think of an analogy that recognizes the various differences between the aesthetic adventures of Katherine Dunham and Eros Volúsia. The reactions to their choreographies by the public and critics were, in a certain way, the same. Dunham tried to "educate" the critics and audience in puritan America about the social and symbolic significance of the African and Caribbean dances, especially concerning the emphasis on the pelvic movements.[24] Sally Banes points out that *Rites de Passage,* one of Dunham's most representative works, included social and ritual Haitian, Cuban, and Brazilian dances as well as dances from the plantations of the southern United States, which together formed an ethnographic kaleidoscope.[25] Ramsay Burt suggests that Dunham has contributed not only to the development of modern dance in the United States, Europe, and Africa but also to the development of the concept of negritude, which has not been sufficiently acknowledged. Burt maintains that in her European tours in the late 1940s and early 1950s, Dunham received affirmation and a level of support "from both black and white intellectuals that she had not found in the United States."[26]

Volúsia forcefully "trans-created" Afro-Brazilian culture.[27] Critic Jayme de Barros, reviewing a performance by dancer Madeleine Rosay, wrote that the "grace" displayed by "Rosay, who was trained in ballet, is a live caricature of Brazilian dance, because it lacked 'Eros' stylization and artistic intuition, blood, soul and brown color." Barros comments that Rosay's "convulsive contortions" did not reach the levels of abstraction achieved by Volúsia.[28] Volusia's passage through "erudite-Brazilian-popular" pathways characterized a new body for dance in her time, a body that was precociously mestizo. Volúsia attended the umbanda centers of Rio de Janeiro in her childhood. The artist took her first dance steps at four years of age, at a *terreiro* (yard or house for Yoruba ceremonies).[29] She described her initiation:

I was a little girl when I had contact with strange dances of the macumba ritual. . . . Attracted by those barbarous rhythms, I wound up taking part in the ceremony. The believers in macumba saw in my eyes, in my physiognomy, in my gestures, a supernatural strength, and submitted me to a baptism.[30]

Critics such as Mário Nunes believed that the "epileptic convulsions" of umbanda presented by Volúsia should be transformed into dance steps, to elevate the sensual impulses to the "spiritual plane" of the toadas and dances of African origin, in order to transform them into a superior art. Undercutting critics such as Nunes, Volúsia's art began to be seen as genuinely Brazilian, associated with the recognition of the mestizo composition of Brazilian culture. (fig. 6.2)

6.2. Eros Volúsia resting after a performance of *No Terreiro de Umbanda*, 1937. Photograph by Raul. Courtesy of the family of Eros Volúsia.

The Afro-Brazilian element of Volúsia's dance cannot be explained solely by the social context, where popular forms came to light through an identity project politically forged by the Estado Novo, but was molded by learning and understanding of the dancer's world ever since her childhood. Certification of the authenticity of Volúsia's dance came through recognition that she did not dance "like the Russian ballerinas . . . she danced with the feeling of Brazilian art. She doesn't stay on the tip of her toes, but her gestures express everything that can be said in terms of art."[31] Nevertheless, it would be a mistake to compare Volúsia's art to the codified forms of ballet, wrote some critics of the time. Volúsia's *bailados* were, for them, "stunning novelties, because they are unprecedented and truly beautiful."[32] In an interview with Brazilian newspapers, Volúsia revealed her understanding of art as a hybrid process, in which archaic, classic, and modern references could combine:

> Pure *ballet* does not exist. Classical ballerinas use all the modern creations, from the materialism of acrobatics, to the spirituality of expressionism. My dance is a mixture of classical, modern and folkloric, as is universal dance today, because, as I said, classical dance no longer exists after Isadora Duncan.

Aware of the renovation brought by dancers like Isadora Duncan, Volúsia inaugurated the figure of the creator-interpreter on the Brazilian scene in the 1930s, conducting an authorial miscegenation of codified elements from ballet and from the popular dances of different regions of the country, such as samba, lundu, maxixe, maracatu, and movements of some indigenous peoples. In a way, popular culture is an erudite category, maintains Roger Chartier in *Cultura popular: Revisitando um conceito historiográfico*.[33] The creation of a new dance by Volúsia did not arise from a vehement denial of ballet, as it had with many of the leading modern dancers. Volúsia rejected a purist dance, whether classical or popular, and conducted an operation of intercultural "devouring" of European, American, and Brazilian references, as the Oswaldian anthropophagy proposed, and which involved an attitude of receptivity and critical choice. Although she did not use the strictly codified steps of ballet in her solos, Volúsia drew from her four years of study of this tradition at the Escola de Bailados of the Theatro Municipal do Rio de

Janeiro. The classical tradition functioned as counterpoint to her polyphonic creation of a new dance. She danced on pointe in a pioneering way in the choreography *Tico-Tico no fubá*, to music from the celebrated popular song by the same name by Zequinha de Abreu. Despite praise from the grande dame of world ballet, Anna Pavlova, Volúsia did not limit herself to the academic environment.[34] She wrote:

> Although [Pavlova's] words were of great encouragement to me, truly consecrated, I felt that I could not limit myself to the academic method, given that my temperament, love for Brazilian rhythm and for dances that express states of the soul, demand from me a greater field of action. It would be absurd to cultivate an international expressive art, when an entire race expected from my body the realization of its soul. My tendency toward Brazilian rhythms was manifest as soon as I took my first dance steps.[35]

The modernist writer Mário de Andrade was dedicated to researching Brazilian culture.[36] He calls attention to the originality of Volúsia's work, set apart from the "old classicism with its academic poses or the vulgar leaps of lyric choreography."[37] Volúsia's dance realized the much coveted anthropophagic dream. It is interesting to emphasize that, like Volúsia, Dunham added her studies of African and Caribbean rituals to her technical references to ballet and the modern dance of Mary Wigman.[38] Thus Dunham too was creating a syncretism in her own technique.[39]

Volúsia traveled through various regions of Brazil to collect bodily movement for the construction of a new dance. Volúsia's study was not bound by the notion of cultural revival, as was the work of Andrade, in an attempt to guarantee the preservation of the originality of the popular expressions. Volúsia sought to transform this material into raw material for national *bailados*, combining the popular and the erudite, a style also adopted by Brazilian music and literature at the time.[40]

In one of her most representative solos, *Cascavelando*, Volúsia conducted a scenic trans-translation of the poem "Samba," by the writer Gilka Machado, her mother, whose poetics were inspired by the dances of the Brazilian *terreiro*.[41] In this choreography the *bailarina*, with the upper portion of her body, "made undulating gestures that recalled the movement of snakes or waves in the sea by means of sinuous gestures, composing a very sensual movement."[42]

Cascavelando recalls the visionary work *Serpentine Dance*, by Loïe Fuller, through its recreation of the metaphor of fluid and undulating movement. The name attributed to Fuller's new dance by her agent, Rud Aronson, could not have been more significant. The term *serpentine* dates back to the mid-eighteenth century, when it was associated with a new aesthetic theory for the representation of landscape, invoking an "undulating" or "serpentine line" along which a painting could organize the visual space of nature.[43] The term *cascavelando*, analogous to *serpentining*, its trajectory recalling the movements of Brazil's *cascavel* rattlesnakes, permeates Gilka's poem and the dance of her daughter, Volúsia. The poem emphasizes the rhythm and corporeality of the Brazilian woman, which come from her mestizo elements and the undulation of the movements of her trunk and pelvis, cadenced by a movement of feet on the floor.[44] (fig. 6.3)

Decades later, Luiz de Abreu would be moved to critique the crystallized image of the sensuality of the Brazilian mulatta as well as the social and political questions linked to blackness. Abreu worked in important Brazilian dance companies such as 1º Ato (Primeiro Ato) and Cisne Negro but is now dedicated to a solo career, focused on black corporeality. Like Eros Volúsia, he had his first contacts with dance at the umbanda *terreiros* in the city of his birth, Araquari, in the interior of the state of Minas Gerais, in 1963. Giving rise over the long term to prejudice and stereotypes, this sinuous corporal identity of the Brazilian woman, especially that of the black and the mestizo, surfaces in Abreu's work as he deconstructs the notion of the National Body in *Samba do crioulo doido* (Samba of the Crazy Creole).[45]

The *Samba do criolo doido* is a solo dance created in 2004 in which Abreu explores how Brazilian society sees the black in the construction of a national identity. He uses a samba song of the same name written in 1968 by Sérgio Porto, ironically combining historical facts from the time of a previous dictatorship, that of Getúlio Vargas, which required composers to write sambas of a historic nature about Brazil.

In his solo dance Abreu makes a frontal attack on the national discourses

6.3. Eros Volúsia in *Cascavelando*, 1937. Photographer unknown. Courtesy of the family of Eros Volúsia.

that inculcate an understanding of black Brazilian corporeality through the representation of stereotypes, as in the commercialization of its eroticism. In Abreu's case, the creation of the work was not aimed at finding a national dance, as Volúsia did, but at working critically with the notions of Brazilian-ness and blackness.

The preeminent question for artists today appears to focus not on the creation of a national dance but, as Micheline Torres emphasizes, on how to "make contemporary dance in Brazil."[46] A further focus is "how to create supports for creation, circulation, research and education of the public."[47] In the text "Cinco questões para pensar nas danças contemporâneas brasileiras como anticorpos à categoria tradicional de corpo brasileiro" (Five questions for thinking of contemporary Brazilian dance as antibodies to the traditional category of the Brazilian body), Christine Greiner calls attention to the fact that the instigating practices of the artists of contemporary dance most active in the country function as "antibodies" to the notion of Brazilian dance "as a concept in general or a monolithic referential block."[48] The mark of Brazilianness that many of these artists present in solo works is tuned more to the flow of meaning coming from their aesthetic experiences than to rules established a priori that are coherent with the image of Brazilian dance or of the Brazilian body, whether in Brazil or abroad. Greiner concludes that there is a notable quantity of solo spectacles in Brazil today, which itself deserves a more detailed study.

Volúsia's research and dance reflected the concepts of culture and dance closely connected to her time, "with notions of the body that are simultane-ously romantic and nationalist and of the *bailado* that intends to be Brazil-ian."[49] Her ideology was a radical manifesto against racial prejudice and the "foreign voice that stifled the word nationality" of the recently discovered Brazilian arts:

> Passing from the apparent immaterialism of the classical ballets to the humanistic Brazilian dances, still bloody from the tragedies of captivity and exile, still hot from contact with the earth, and certainly shocking to the sensibility of any public, principally when it is found disturbed by prejudice that wants to hide, to forget, when it acts suggesting through "cosmopolitan nationalism," when it is found addicted to the comfort of

watching or reproducing the old imports. . . . Brazil is discovering itself, it is finally finding itself.[50]

Today, the contact of many contemporary Brazilian artists with foreign productions, especially from Europe, has reheated the debate about the implications of a colonizer-colonized discourse. In a globalized context, these artists have critically exercised the appropriation of artistic procedures of their own culture and those of other countries, aware of the unstanchable processes of miscegenation and hybridization of our times.

Serge Gruzinski, in "O pensamento mestiço" (Mestizo Thinking), recognizes that there is a mixing of cultures in all periods and that this mixture enriches and forges the creativity of societies, making it more dynamic.[51] The inevitable breaking down of borders and the consequent hybridizations led Néstor Canclini to conclude that all cultures, today (or always), come from the frontier, based on the idea that art develops in relation to other arts.[52] Hybridism operates as a shifting of value, leading the dominant discourse to be decentralized and shifted, with the difference of cultures built agonistically at the frontier, finds Homi Bhabha.[53]

A political look at the country itself is a constant in the most recent production of Brazilian contemporary dance. It is without any idea of a nationalist utopia. In Cascavelando, Eros Volúsia sensually sambas, revealing the forms of her body with a tight dress that imitates snakeskin. It was pure exaltation to a recently discovered Brazilian identity. In Samba do crioulo doido, Luiz de Abreu sambas in the nude, wearing only tall silver high-heeled boots, incurring an ambiguous, androgynous identity. (figs. 6.4 and 6.5) The "anthropophagic devouring" takes place by means of the images imposed on blacks through years of history, which were easily consumed by the foreign eye. Abreu does not call for a national dance. His work involves another representational context, in which the mimesis of this "serpentined" dance seen as "typically Brazilian" is subverted. Flirting with the aesthetic of the performance, Abreu's samba denounces the banality of turning the body-object into an export product "made in Brazil." It is accompanied by the rough voice of Brazilian singer Elza Soares, who repeatedly sings the refrain, "a carne mais barata do mercado é a carne negra" (the cheapest meat in the market is the black meat). In Abreu's words:

6.4. Luiz de Abreu with the furled Brazilian flag in his *Samba do crioulo doido*. Photograph by Gil Grossi. Courtesy of Gil Grossi.

I speak of myself but also of the human being, because the gesture is something common. But I also do not want to make a national dance. I use national symbols because perhaps Brazil is one of the few countries in which the issue of the day, both in the Academy as well as in the bar, is that of Brazil, is identity.[54]

The *Samba do crioulo doido* criticizes the reification of the figure of the mulatta. As sociologist Milton Santos declares, to be black in Brazil "is, thus, frequently, to be the object of a slanted look. The so-called good society appears to believe that there is a predetermined place, down below, for blacks to behave peacefully. Thus, it is both disturbing that they have remained at the base of the social pyramid and that they have 'risen in life.'"[55] Abreu's performance is a sharp political tool that makes us see the "slanted" lens through which we still perceive Afro-Brazilian culture:

6.5. Luiz de Abreu with a Brazilian flag backdrop in his *Samba do crioulo doido*. Photograph by Gil Grossi. Courtesy of Gil Grossi.

The solo discusses the inter-relationship between the body-object constructed by the diaspora and the body-subject that transgresses, affirms and resists; it creates a corporeality that returns to the body-object the subject that was stripped from it during history, together with feelings, values, beliefs, the word and its aesthetic singularities. Samba, carnival, and eroticism constitute elements to which the black Brazilian body is generally associated.[56]

From an ideological perspective, the dance solo, as Eugenia Cassini Ropa maintains, is the undeniable and urgent space of the person and the personality in all her singularity, the place of the revelation of the imaginary and of individual memories and feelings.[57] A soloist acts as if she or he were alone or separated, but the apparent loneliness echoes multiple connections, her subjectivity becomes an echo of the collective. The subjectivity is never solitary or alone.[58] A solo is like a multiple of one, the incarnation of the multiplicity by a single body.[59] While Duncan affirmed that she summed up in herself the spirit of the Greek chorus, sustained by universal principles and filtered by personal means, Volúsia understood her art as the essential expression of the mestizo soul of the Brazilian people. Abreu, in turn, builds fragmented, although recognizable, bodily images that question the objectified "black body." They are two distinct moments of solo dance in Brazil, their relationship with the theme of nationalism and Brazilianness differing, but both are legitimized in their own times and contexts based on a critical view of the aculturation processes of Brazilian society.

Notes

1. See http://educacao.uol.com.br/historia-brasil/ult1689u31.jhtm (accessed January 13, 2010).

2. The strong concentration of power in the federal executive, in place since late 1935, and the alliance between the military hierarchy and sectors of the oligarchies created conditions for the political coup by Getúlio Vargas in 1937, which would come to be known as the Estado Novo. Roberto Pereira, *A formação do Balé Brasileiro* (Rio de Janeiro: Editora FGV, 2003), 275.

3. The book *A formação do Balé Brasileiro* is based on Roberto Pereira's Ph.D. dissertation. His *Eros Volusia: A criadora do bailado nacional* (Rio de Janeiro: Relume Dumará–RIOARTE, 2004) is one of the rarest books about Volúsia's dance in Brazil.

4. Oswald Andrade, *Manifesto Antropofágico*, http://www.passeiweb.com/na_ponta_lingua/livros/resumos_comentarios/m/manifesto_antropofagico (accessed January 15, 2008).

5. Ibid.

6. Suely Rolnik, "Anthropophagie Zombie," *Mouvement*, no. 36–37 (2005): 57.

7. Renato Ortiz, *Cultura brasileira e identidade nacional* (São Paulo: Brasiliense, 1994), 41.

8. Ibid.

9. Monica Velloso, in Laura Cascaes, "Queria bordar teu nome: A dança no teatro de revista," master's thesis, UDESC, Florianópolis, 2009, 145.

10. Monica Velloso, *Modernismo no Rio de Janeiro* (Rio de Janeiro: Ed. Fundação Getulio Vargas, 1996), 31.

11. Pereira, *Eros Volusia*, 104.

12. Sally Banes, *Dancing Women: Female Bodies on Stage* (New York: Routledge, 1998), 150.

13. Pereira, *Eros Volusia*, 27.

14. Ibid.

15. Pereira, *A formação*, 41.

16. Ibid., 235.

17. Soraia Silva, "Corporação lingüística no exercício poético da dança," http://www.eca.usp.br/tfc/geral20042/00/soraia.htm (accessed January 15, 2010).

18. Eros Volúsia, "A criação do bailado nacional," speech presented at the Theatro Ginástico in 1939, in Pereira, *A formação do Balé Brasileiro*, 224.

19. The Brazilian Chinita Ullman (1904–77), educated at the Mary Wigman school in Dresden, created the Academia de Bailado, the first modern dance school in São Paulo. Yanka Rudzka, from Poland, was one of the founders of the Faculdade

de Dança da Universidade Federal da Bahia, in 1956. The Hungarian Maria Duschnes was among those responsible for spreading the Laban method in Brazil.

20. Mário Nunes, in Pereira, *A formação*, 235.

21. Ann Daly, *Done into Dance: Isadora Duncan in America* (Middletown, Conn.: Wesleyan University Press, 1995), 115.

22. Gilberto Freyre, in Pereira, *A formação*, 284.

23. At the time, Eros Volúsia appeared on the cover of *Life* magazine (September 22, 1941), even before Carmen Miranda, to whom she declared she had lent the sinuous movements of her hands and arms. Jane Desmond called attention to the generalizations made about the dance of Carmen Miranda in the United States, her Brazilianness reduced to a Latin stereotype. The complexity of the dances coming from different cultures of Central and South America were seen as "Latin." Jane C. Desmond, ed., *Meaning in Motion: New Cultural Studies of Dance* (Durham, N.C.: Duke University Press, 2006), 42.

24. Banes, *Dancing Women*, 152.

25. Ibid., 152–53.

26. Ramsay Burt, "Katherine Dunham's Floating Island of Negritude: The Katherine Dunham Dance Company in London and Paris in the late 1940s and early 1950s," in *Rethinking Dance History: A Reader*, ed. Alexandra Carter (New York: Routledge, 2004), 104.

27. The writer Haroldo de Campos questioned the idea of a literal translation of one symbolic system for another by using the concept of trans-translation, or trans-creation, as a form of creative translation, a remastication or reimagination of the culture of the other, leading concrete poetry to Oswaldian anthropophagy.

28. Jayme de Barros, in Pereira, *A formação*, 249.

29. Macumba is the generic designation of the syncretic Afro-Brazilian cults derived from religious practices of other African and Amerindian, Catholic, Espírita, and occultist religions. Umbanda, a religion born in Rio de Janeiro in the early twentieth century, pondered Espírita and Banto elements. Volúsia probably attended an umbanda center.

30. Volúsia, in Pereira, *Eros Volusia*, 22.

31. Pereira, *Eros Volusia*, 236.

32. Ibid.

33. Ricardo M. Melo, "Cultura Popular, a short theoretical discussion," http://br.monografias.com/trabalhos/cultura-popular/cultura-popular.shtml (accessed December 15, 2009).

34. This occurred in 1928, the last time Anna Pavlova came with her company to Brazil and the year that marked the entrance of Eros Volúsia, then fourteen, to the Escola de Bailados of the Theatro Municipal do Rio de Janeiro. Pereira, *Eros Volusia*.

35. Volúsia, in Pereira, *Eros Volúsia*, 24.

36. Mário de Andrade between 1934 and 1944 wrote *Danças dramáticas do Brasil*, three volumes that combine his studies of popular music, dance, and Brazilian folklore.

37. Mário de Andrade, in Pereira, *A formação*, 126.

38. Banes, *Dancing Women*, 150.

39. Dunham studied anthropology at the University of Chicago and Northwestern University while working as a dancer and teacher. Banes, *Dancing Women*, 149.

40. Pereira, *Eros Volusia*, 47.

41. Space for the realization of umbanda rituals.

42. Soraia Silva, "Corporação lingüística no exercício poético da dança," http://www.eca.usp.br/tfc/geral20042/00/soraia.htm (accessed January 15, 2010).

43. Giovanni Lista, *Loie Fuller: Danseuse de la Belle Époque* (Paris: Éditions d'Art, 1994), 88.

44. "Shifting her flanks, stamping her feet, shaking her breasts, rolling her eyes, teeth spying at everyone and everything, shining, shining, within the lips—*creola* or *cafuza, cabocla,* or *mulatta, mestizo* or *maroon*—only someone who never saw you dancing, sambaing, on a moonlit night, does not love you, Brazilian woman!" Gilka Machado, *Sublimação* (Rio de Janeiro: Ed. Biblioteca Von-Hager-Gintner, 1938).

45. The term *creole* refers here to a black born in Brazil, or whatever was born or produced in the colonized countries.

46. Micheline Torres is a dancer, choreographer, and performer. She worked for twelve years at Lia Rodrigues Companhia de Danças. Since 2000 she has undertaken her own solo work in dance.

47. Micheline Torres, interview by the American magazine *Scene4*, http://www .sweetandtender.org/wiki/index.php?title=Micheline_Tor-res (accessed January 10, 2010).

48. Christine Greiner, "Cinco questões para pensar nas danças contemporâneas brasileiras como anticorpos à categoria tradicional de corpo brasileiro," in *Húmus*, vol. 2, ed. Sigrid Nora (Caxias do Sul: Lorigraf, 2007), 14.

49. Pereira, *Eros Volusia*, 46.

50. Lecture-demonstration held in 1939 at the Teatro Ginástico, where she began working as a teacher. Pereira, *Eros Volúsia*, 46.

51. Serge Gruzinski, "O Pensamento mestiço," in *La Pensée métisse* (Paris: Fayard, 1999).

52. Néstor García Canclini, *Culturas Híbridas: Estratégias para entrar e sair da modernidade* (São Paulo: EDUSP, 1997).

53. Homi K. Bhabha, *O local da Cultura* (Belo Horizonte: Editora UFMG, 2003).

54. Luiz de Abreu, "My work is the size of my body," interview by Tiago Bartolomeu Costa, http://omelhoranjo.blogspot.com/2006/06/na-primeira-pessoa-ii-luiz-de-abreu.html (accessed January 10, 2010).

55. Milton Santos, *Ser negro no Brasil hoje,* http://www.ige.unicamp.br/~lmelgaco/santos.htm (accessed January 10, 2010).

56. Luiz de Abreu, interview by Victoria Noorthoorn, May 26, 2009, http://www.fundacaobienal.art.br/7bienalmercosul/pt-br/subversao-de-estereotipos-e-convencoes (accessed January 10, 2010).

57. Eugenia Casini Ropa, "O solo de dança no século XX: Entre proposta ideológica e estratégia de sobrevivência," *Urdimento,* no. 12 (2009): 67.

58. Rebecca Schneider, "Unbecoming Solo," in *La Danse en solo,* ed. Claire Rousier (Paris: CND, 2002): 86.

59. Jean-Marie Pradier, "Les Multiples du un," in *La Danse en solo,* 66.

seven

Strange
Heroes

Deborah Jowitt

A spotlight picks him out as he enters. It could be a streetlamp. He is dressed to kill—in more ways than one. Black pegged pants, black shoes, a shirt and tie, a blue-green pinstriped jacket with extravagantly padded shoulders and a nipped-in waist. Daniel Nagrin is performing his solo *Strange Hero* (1948). To a piano transcription of Stan Kenton and Pete Rugolo's "Monotony," he prowls the stage as if he owns it, a cigarette dangling from his lips. But antagonists lurk in the shadows. He turns his head sharply, wheels around to stare in another direction. There is something feral about the interplay between charged slowness and sudden whipping into motion. He lifts the cigarette to his mouth or takes it out with a lazy, almost effete grace. The gesture of pulling a gun (two fingers shooting out from a clenched fist) morphs into a flick of the ash.

The music often repeats the same four-measure phrase, but even though cyclical, it is suspenseful. Its sudden bursts cue him from his cocky, sensual strutting into whirling down to a crouch, rolling, and springing up again. He

7.1. Daniel Nagrin in his *Strange Hero*, 1948. Photograph by Marcus Blechman. Courtesy of the Daniel Nagrin Theater, Film, and Dance Foundation.

punches an invisible adversary and saunters away, shoots another (or perhaps it is the same guy), and kicks him when he is down. Even when a bullet hits him, his bravado does not desert him. Slowly he collapses backward, rises, and starts to walk, is shot again, spins into another fall, half rises—saluting the enemy who has bested him—and continues again and again to be shot. He is still trying to outwit death as the lights fade.

Nagrin's mobster has been likened to a Humphrey Bogart character or someone Mickey Spillane's Mike Hammer had to face down.[1] The mobster would not die, although in an article published in *Dance Magazine* in 1951, the choreographer mentioned being "disgusted" by the mythologizing of violent heroes and wanting to make fun of the image.[2] Seven years later, Nagrin's program note for the dance was simply "The tough guy with a heart of gold."[3] He was still portraying this jazzman-gangster on his solo programs more than thirty years later.

Strange Hero illustrates something integral to Nagrin's way of conceiving his solos. Some are soliloquies addressed to an inner demon; others, such as *Strange Hero*, are monologues, with all that the term implies. They are peopled with invisible friends or enemies, and they make us "see" objects or facets of a landscape. "What distinguishes my work from that of most of my colleagues," he wrote in the 1990s, "is that whatever I do—as a dancer—I do not try to look like something, I am someone *doing* something. I never do abstract dance."[4]

During the 1940s and 1950s, when Nagrin was charting his career and the status of the male dancer in America was still shaky, his success was bolstered by the fact that each "someone" he portrayed could easily be recognized or interpreted as a masculine type.

In the canon of modern dance Nagrin has been considered a loner, something of a maverick, most famous for his solo programs. Born in the Bronx on May 22, 1917, of Russian-Jewish parents, he discovered dancing on his own as a teenager. In a 1976 interview with John Gruen, he said that his first brush with it was trying to master the box step (with an eye to looking suave at high school proms).[5] But he also wrote in one of his books that when he wearied of homework, he would switch on the radio and allow what he heard to set his restless body in motion.[6] In 1964 he dedicated a new solo, *A Gratitude*, to the "dear Armenians" whose music he had listened to on Sunday mornings on station WEVD.[7] Those robust sounds impelled him to living-room dancing wilder than fox trot tunes could inspire. "Suffice it to say," he later wrote, "there were long moments when I would become quite intoxicated with the sheer act of flying over the furniture."[8]

When Nagrin was growing up, male dancers were viewed with suspicion. Performers who had aspirations beyond vaudeville had to develop strategies to masculinize their on stage image. When Ted Shawn teamed up with Ruth St. Denis in 1914, he assumed roles that would complement (and dominate) the exotic women she played; as an Arabian sheik, Egyptian god, or Japanese warrior, he could display his prowess (and, usually, his physique). And it was Shawn who began the campaign to emphasize that dance was, as he put it, "a manly sport, more strenuous than golf or tennis, more exciting than boxing or wrestling and more beneficent than gymnastics."[9] The all-male company he founded in 1933 presented audiences across the country with muscular images—whether of forty-niners, field workers, American Indians, or, in his *Olympiad*, athletes.

Still, dancing was not a career to which families were eager to dedicate their sons. Nagrin was nineteen and a freshman in the City College of New York when, in 1936, he took his first dance class and was instantly hooked. In May of that year he attended all six performances presented at a National Dance Congress held at the 92nd Street Young Men's Hebrew Association and absorbed works by Martha Graham, Doris Humphrey, Charles Weidman, and Hanya Holm, among more than thirty companies and soloists on view.[10] In 1937 he started writing dance reviews for the college newspaper, the *Campus*, in order to be able to secure free tickets to performances.

In his interview with Gruen he recalled that a fellow student asked him why he was trying to become a dancer. He thought about the male modern dancers he had seen perform and replied, "Because I'm going to be dealing with things that the others aren't going to touch."[11] In other words, he knew early on that the "heroes" he wanted to bring to life on stage were not tragic figures from myth and literature, of the sort that José Limón later majestically embodied. Nor was he interested in showing off his virtuosity or his lyricism. Although, like any legendary heroes, the characters he came to create struggled against ideas and obstacles, they usually wore contemporary clothes and knew the rhythms of jazz.

Ray Moses (considered by Nagrin to be his first influential teacher) had been a member of Graham's company under the name of Lilian Ray, and Graham loomed large in Nagrin's early view of dance. Reviewing her December 1937 concert, he showed he had done his homework: she was "the first adult American dancer we had seen in a long time. Here was no pretense, no shallow exoticism, no historical oddities, no pantomimic prettiness. Here was an artist trying painfully to speak of what America and her people are made of."[12]

When he made his performing debut—at the New School for Social Research in an antiwar piece choreographed by Moses in response to the rise of fascism in Europe and the outbreak of the Spanish Civil War—he had been studying dance for only six months. In the mid-1930s, accomplished males available for unpaid modern dance concerts did not grow on trees, and Nagrin was trim and muscular (if not especially flexible) and handsome in a rough-hewn way—blessed with strong cheekbones and a square jaw. Years later Nagrin recalled Moses's brutal drill of marching, being shot down, rolling, rising, and continuing to march "in an unending triangle of death."[13] (Perhaps this early experience fed into *Strange Hero*.) By the time he had graduated from City College in 1940 with a degree in health education, he had already won a year's scholarship to study at the Martha Graham School (1938–39) and appeared at the Alvin Theater in February of 1939 in *The Street* by Anna Sokolow, who had recently left Graham's company.

When Graham did not renew his scholarship, Nagrin primed his body and his understanding of dance by studying ballet (notably with the popular New York teacher Elizaveta Anderson-Ivantzova), and he learned the nitty-gritty of show business during the summer of 1940, when he was hired to perform at a resort in the Poconos run by the International Ladies' Garment Workers Union. With the Depression still hanging on, the three-month job was a welcome one. Unity House treated its vacationers to weekly variety nights, music concerts, revues, and plays. Another dancer hired by choreographer Esther Junger for the 1940 season, Sue Remos, got Nagrin fired up about jazz via her collection of phonograph records, and the two of them choreographed a flirtatious duet, *Rhumba Suite*, to Xavier Cugat's "Elube Chango" (which they performed around New York with Fanya Chochem's American Dance Group and in a revue by the American Youth Theatre).[14]

Jazz was to prove an abiding interest and source for Nagrin, and in 1942, from that summer's Unity House choreographer, Helen Tamiris, he learned ideas and processes that fueled and shaped his creative life.

Although Tamiris (1905–66) had started her performing career in the corps de ballet of the Metropolitan Opera Company and danced in nightclubs, revues, and the prologues in movie houses, she had become a socially conscious modern dance choreographer to reckon with. Nagrin had seen her concert work, including *So Long Brethren* (1937), for the all-female Tamiris and her Group she had established in 1930, and *Adelante* (1939), which centered on the Spanish Civil War (both dances made under the auspices of the Works Progress Administration's Federal Dance Project). He had reviewed *Adelante* for the *Campus*, calling it "an essentially honest and convincing work."[15]

The most profound insight Tamiris gave him, he later wrote, and italicized, "was the *need to discover the inner life that fired up the motions.*"[16] The first solo he had thrown together as an audition piece simply showed off all his skills to date ("To be so rich and so poor at the same time!" he sighed during his 1976 solo *Ruminations*).[17] During the summer of 1942 at Unity House he began choreographing *Rhumba Bum* (perhaps a spinoff from his duet with Remos), which he remembered as "the first dance I worked on independently."[18] Tamiris suggested to him "that if I began from an acting premise, *when I was dancing,* most of the technical problems would fall into place."[19] She also introduced him to the writings of Konstantin Stanislavsky about truth in performing. When he later taught in colleges, he recommended that his students read the Russian actor-director's *My Life in Art.*[20]

Tamiris was a beauty and a powerhouse of a dancer, with a mass of redgold curls and muscular legs. She was approximately a dozen years older than Nagrin. She became his mentor, he became her partner on and offstage, and in 1946 they married. There is a wonderful photograph of the two of them in "My Days Have Been So Wondrous Free" from her group work *Liberty Song,* one of several numbers shown in their 1942 engagements at the Rainbow Room. Side by side, their feet planted in a diagonal stride, their gazes toward some distant horizon, their faces alight, they brace a pole bearing a large American flag.[21] For his performing with Tamiris, Nagrin was included in *New York Times* dance critic John Martin's Honor Roll for 1941–42, along with dancers and choreographers far more seasoned than he.[22]

Nagrin met Tamiris near a turning point in both their lives. There was a war going on. In 1942, despite having been classified as 4F because of his poor eyesight, Nagrin was drafted into the air force, and in 1943 Tamiris turned her attention to Broadway, where a large audience could be reached and a decent living made.

Nagrin's military career did not last long; a doctor noticed his limited vision and got him an honorable discharge. And by August 1943, when he was free to join Tamiris at Green Mansions, another summer resort, he had a new solo of his own to add to the bill. He had been assigned to a Special Services unit charged with providing entertainment to the troops stationed at Keesler Field in Biloxi, Mississippi. A board of well-known writers contributed ideas for sketches, including one about Hitler in his paper-hanging days that Nagrin found "crude . . . written by Kaufman and Hart no less!"[23]

The letters written by Private Daniel Nagrin to the woman he addressed variously as "Dearest," "Puss," "Golden Haired One," and "Toots" regale her with his choreographic exploits. One project that came his way involved the statue of Prometheus in Rockefeller Plaza coming to life and somehow ending up in the Rainbow Room. "I got an idea that is beautiful hoke," he wrote Tamiris: one of the comics in the unit would have a drunken bit in which he provokes the statue (Nagrin, his body gilded) into "a wild joyous dance."[24] After the performance, Nagrin gloated. "Some people insist that it was *the* sensation of the evening and the best thing in a none-too-good show." But he also conceded that "of course it's not really a good number, choreographically speaking!"[25]

He was confident that he knew what constituted good choreography. Barton Mumaw, a leading member of Ted Shawn's Men Dancers, was also in Special Forces, and Nagrin was one of four men backing Mumaw in a "Mechanical Ballet" (conceived as part of a 1942 show for air mechanics called *High Flight* and, according to Mumaw, actually from Shawn's *Labor Symphony*).[26] Mumaw, like Shawn, Nagrin noted, "tries to push the men into the 'pictures' he wants." Also: "I think I'd have used a much more realistic use of mechanics than to characterize them as cogs—wheels & machines, i.e. Our approach would have used humans."[27]

The solo he was working on presaged some of his richer, more complex character studies. A soldier enters, wearing fatigues and carrying an open Coke bottle; he spots a jukebox, digs some coins out of his pocket, and—like young Danny Nagrin in his parents' living room—starts bouncing around to the music of a swing orchestra. In an ebullient letter to Tamiris, Nagrin described how he mimes playing the instruments. First he is a "boogie-woogie pianist strutting," then he becomes a trumpeter, other players, the bandmaster. Finally, he launches into "spins & fuller dancing, all leading to the ecstasy of that wonderful step I stole from Vivian Cherry but changed it [to?] a slide. This is the peak—at this point things are so high that the coke water comes out of the bottle sprinkling me—I stop—look up at the sky— put my hand out to see if it's raining—It is! I run off."[28]

As *Private Johnny Jukebox*, the solo, along with *Rhumba Bum*, appeared in one of the revues Tamiris choreographed at Green Mansions and, renamed *GI Jukebox*, was included in the patriotic 1944 revue *The People's Bandwagon*, which toured movie theaters in twenty-five cities as part of the campaign to reelect Franklin Roosevelt. In March of 1944 Nagrin premiered his *John Brown* (also called *Landscape with Three Figures, 1859*), to a score by Genevieve Pitot, on a program of works by Tamiris and her group at Manhattan's Central High School of Needle Trades (now the Fashion Institute of Technology), an affordable auditorium for modern dance concerts. Nagrin structured the piece as portraits (linked with text spoken by him) of a slaveholder, a slave trying to escape, and Brown himself—a farmer turned fiery abolitionist. The evening attests to his stamina. He also appeared in five duets with Tamiris, another duet, a trio, four group numbers, and *No Hidin' Place*, a new solo that Tamiris had created for him.

John Brown was the last solo Nagrin made for himself until 1948. He followed Tamiris to Broadway, where he assisted her on ten of the musicals she choreographed between 1944 and 1955, performed in five, and became a different kind of solo dancer.

In *Up in Central Park* (1945) he played a character listed in the program as "Daniel" and starred in "The Skating Ballet" (the centerpiece of a Currier and Ives scene). In *Annie Get Your Gun* the following year, he appeared as "Wild Horse," the spirit leader of an eponymous "Ceremonial Dance" that segued into Ethel Merman's whooping rendition of "I'm an Indian Too." A striking photo shows him in face paint and what Walter Terry described as "a paucity of clothing"—a loincloth, breastplate, and armbands, plus a headpiece simulating a Mohawk, which sprouted feathers and a long black horsetail.[29] (fig. 7.2) "It's a brutal filthy dance we created," wrote Nagrin to Tamiris shortly after returning from England, where he had been staging the dances for the London production of *Annie* (she had then gone off to Hollywood to work on the movie version of *Up in Central Park*). "To do it daily

7.2. Daniel Nagrin as "Wild Horse" in *Annie Get Your Gun*, 1946, autographed Capezio ad. Photograph by Vandamm Studio. Courtesy of the Daniel Nagrin Theater, Film, and Dance Foundation.

everything must stand and wait upon it."[30] Barton Mumaw, to whom Nagrin taught Wild Horse's solo for the touring company of *Annie*, described admiringly in his autobiography the three leaps with which Nagrin entered and a movement that Mumaw had never seen before—one with which Nagrin was to stun viewers in later dances: kneeling, he would lean back, circle his arms powerfully, and hoist himself to a standing position by rolling over his arched feet to the tips of his toes; you would have thought he owned the sky.[31]

He also had meaty parts in the revue *Touch and Go* (1949), especially in the big dance number called "Under the Sleeping Volcano" and as Laertes in Jean and Walter Kerr's *Hamlet* spoof, a sketch called "Great Dane a-Comin.'" The peak of his Broadway acclaim, however, came in 1955 with *Plain and Fancy*. For that he received fifth billing, played two contrasting characters (the Amish Samuel Zook—featured in "By Lantern Light"—and Mambo Joe in "The Carnival Ballet"), and won a Donaldson Award for Best Male Dancer of the Year. Maurice Zolotow of *Theatre Arts* dubbed him "the most exciting male dancer of the musical stage since Gene Kelly."[32] You can see his charisma in a flamboyant little love-and-death trio (with Miriam Pandor and Florence Lessing) that Tamiris choreographed for a show within the 1952 Bing Crosby movie *Just for You*.[33] While Jane Wyman (somewhat improbably) plucks a guitar and sings, Nagrin, as a Mexican peasant with ambitions to be a bullfighter, dances like a coiled spring—exhilarated, proud, heedless.

But however rewarding the commercial work was, Nagrin chafed at it: "On Broadway, I had seen so many beautiful, daring gestures and ideas fold under the iron law of show business; everything had to be a smash, go over big. Everybody had their fingers in the artistic pie and some of those fingers were not very clean."[34] It was in a rented space over a grocery store in Croton-on-Hudson, where he and Tamiris had bought a house, that he created *Strange Hero* and *Spanish Dance* in 1948. By 1951 he had made two more solos, *Man of Action* and *Dance in the Sun*, and performed these, along with some group works, on various programs (some of them shared) at New York theaters. He had also begun his long-standing collaboration with pianist Sylvia Marshall, who accompanied him—live or on tape—for many of the "Dance Portraits" programs he put together.

Some people felt that the pantomimic aspects of some of these early works were antithetical to modern dance's emphasis on powerful abstractions and universalities. After praising his performing, *Dance Magazine* critic Doris Hering tempered her enthusiasm: "His many Broadway assignments have, however, taken their toll. There is a tendency to gloss over moments of choreographic aridity by injecting facile device, instead of digging deeply into himself to find solutions."[35] Wounded, Nagrin did not create another solo until 1954 with the exuberant *Man Dancing*, but bounced emphatically back in 1957 with *Indeterminate Figure, Three Happy Men*, and *Jazz Three Ways* and, in 1958, premiered *With My Eye and With My Hand* and *A Dancer Prepares*. In an article announcing upcoming events, including Nagrin's first full solo program in 1958 at the YM-YWHA's Kaufmann Auditorium, John Martin wrote, "Mr. Nagrin is one of the most serious and gifted artists in the modern dance field," and "Mr. Nagrin is definitely a realist, with his eye on the present scene, but an artistic penetration considerably deeper than that might imply."[36]

Different though they are in tone, these solos share certain stylistic traits. Even in Nagrin's least narrative vignettes, he was always a particular person (or persons) dancing. And there was never any doubt that these were masculine characters—unless as a man, remembering a woman, he allowed his body briefly to take on her gestures. In the 1950s he played "guys" with whom audiences of the day could identify, but in order to develop complex personas, he avoided trumpeting manliness in the way that Shawn had done earlier. Later, in one of his extraordinarily wise books aimed at dancers, choreographers, teachers, and students, he notes, "It is sad when a woman tries to appear female when that is what she is, and so it is when a man tries to appear manly—whatever that is."[37]

He had learned this early in Mme Anderson-Ivantzova's ballet classes. The only man in her studio, he had felt foolish doing a sequence of flowery *balancés* in waltz-time. "So I taught myself to do it like a 'man.' I was heroic, grand, big and stiffly proud in the carriage of the head. In time, when I had less to fear about who I was, I learned to float as well as to stamp and pound."[38] And his viewpoint in later years was that "the great female dancers carry with the most fragile gesture the implication of thunder. The great male dancers allow themselves passive, floating, gentle movements."[39]

Floating may not have come easily to him, however. Like a number of men of his generation who came to dance late or had careers interrupted by military service during World War II, Nagrin lacked the technical fluency of the male dancers coming of age later in the twentieth century. His feet rarely pointed fully, and when he kicked a leg to the side, it stopped well below his hips. His finesse lay elsewhere—in his power, his command of dynamics, the clarity of his focus, and the deftness of his hands. He could shrug his shoulders and wriggle his hips when he slipped into the music of Jimmy Yancey or Nat "King" Cole or Thelonious Monk, as he did in *Jazz in Three Ways* (later part of his Jazz Changes program), but his lightest steps were precise in the way they struck the floor, brushed it, or skittered over it. He managed his strength like a tiger, able to move from stillness into an explosion of energy.

Too, the modern dance styles that Nagrin grew up with encoded conflict within their approach to the dancing body. For Doris Humphrey, movement arose in the tension between falling and recovering; for Martha Graham, the body responded to emotion by contracting and releasing (or expanding). Building his dances like little dramas, Nagrin sought to discover obstacles, external or internal, to be grappled with. "Onstage," he wrote, "anything that does not contain its own opposite is a bore. A fall contains a compelling excitement when it is resisted. The dream enclosed in the most beautiful leap is a sustained stillness."[40]

In *Spanish Dance*—one of his finest works, which he said much later was "the one I loved doing the most and where I felt I belonged"—the obstacle might have been in part the imprisoning space.[41] Like the score Pitot composed for it, the solo captured the brooding intensity of flamenco, the feeling of tension building to the breaking point and then flashing out like a knife. Nagrin began it profiled in a spotlight, dressed all in black except for a red neckerchief—proud in his stance, motionless as the music began. As he gradually expanded his first deliberate movements into lunges, turns, and drops to his knees, you could see rhythms akin to those of flamenco—its slow wail, its chatter of heels—but they made no sound.

Although the inspiration for *Dance in the Sun* was simply a glorious autumn-gold tree seen on a country walk, Nagrin deepened its atmosphere of wonder and delight by creating an inner battle of sorts. In his book *The Six Questions*, hoping to clarify for students the useful practice of breaking down their work into "beats" (something he had learned to do in acting classes with Sanford Meisner), he revealed what was running through his mind when he performed the solo. A described action, such as "The legs like a clock or a slow-motion seesaw," is followed by *"Taking a long breath, sensing a new burst of trying to leave the limits of my skin to merge with the sky and the tree."*[42]

Even when he filtered a specific character through his own persona, he made stylistic decisions that allied the guy on stage with recognizable stereotypes and matched his obstacles with universal ones. The minute he appeared in *Man of Action,* wearing a fedora and an unbuttoned raincoat, hustling this way and that, checking for rain, and consulting his watch, he could be identified as a city-dweller caught in the urban rat race, his progress thwarted by traffic and crowds. He must have liked the fact that Louis Horst, in his review of *Indeterminate Figure,* saw that solo as a comment on a generation's "oscillation between illusion and reality."[43]

The self-involved, pajama-clad man in *Indeterminate Figure* strove to ignore what he should have been struggling to grasp: the disasters looming outside his apartment window (the whistle of a bomb and an explosion initiated the sound effects mixed with Robert Starer's music). In the Cold War climate of the 1950s, with nuclear holocaust a threat, this man dealt with small obstacles: the creaking floorboard, the dripping faucet, the window that would not shut (of all Nagrin's solos, this is the most detailed in terms of pantomime).

For *With My Eye and With My Hand,* Nagrin wrote a program note that encouraged audiences to view it in universal terms, perhaps worrying that he would be seen simply as impersonating a "primitive man" rather than as presenting a study in daily courage. The note began, "A dedication to every man who has hesitated before one of the many thresholds of the unknown."[44] The impetus for the solo, set to a percussion score by Michael Colgrass and Herbert Harris, was atypical. In 1952 Nagrin had landed a well-paying assignment, the choreography for *His Majesty O'Keefe,* a movie starring Burt Lancaster that was filmed in the Fiji Islands.[45] He wrote to Tamiris describing the usual Hollywood arguments and frustrations, including a leading dancer, Archie Savage, who sometimes chose island pleasures over rehearsals. He got a lesson in spear dancing from a posse of elders and decided that for a fearsome ritual, he had better juice up their simple unison line dances with some twists and jumps.[46] On the other hand, a women's gentle *meke* that he told Tamiris he thought "great" found its way into the movie relatively unenhanced.[47]

Overall, Nagrin was intrigued by Fijian culture and rites that he had seen. The man he portrayed in *With My Eye and With My Hand* loped on in a squat, alert to every sound and flash of motion around him. The way he sat cross-legged and clapped his hands implied a ritual. His rippling arms and big jumps suggested a tuning-up of his perceptions, skills, and courage for a solitary hunt. Nagrin showed him tracking, being wounded, and finally splashing restorative cold water over himself.

In 1957, when Nagrin turned forty, the tap soloist Paul Draper ("a lovely gentleman, a great artist, and another canny cat") convinced him that he could tour by himself.[48] By the end of 1958 the five dances already mentioned, plus *Strange Hero, A Dancer Prepares, Three Happy Men* (Peasant, Tradesman, Nobleman), *Figures in a Landscape, Man Dancing,* and *Jazz Three Ways* (variously selected and combined) formed the variegated repertory of the "Dance Portraits" program with which he traveled the country. Several of the solos also appeared on engagements of the short-lived company that Nagrin and Tamiris directed between 1960 and 1963, and he was still performing some of them into his sixties.

He was no stranger to strenuous tours. In 1954, on a program billed as Dance Percussion Trio (his solos were spelled by musical interludes), he, pianist David Shapiro, and percussionist Ronald Gould played thirty-one one-night stands through June and July. From a motel fifty miles east of Kansas City, Missouri, he regaled Tamiris with a typical road story: "The wildest thing yet was yesterday morning performing in a big gym with tiers of arena-like seats. Ronnie said he felt like a gladiator. I felt like a bullfighter taking a bow. We had to walk at least 25 yards to make an entrance each time. The audience, however, was very sweet & considerate. Every time I had to make an entrance in full costume—they would applaud & that filled the space better than wings ever did. In some ways I danced better than at any other time on the tour."[49]

Over the years Nagrin developed solo touring into a science. He traveled light and mostly alone, his tape recorder, tapes, costumes, and makeup fitting into a wheeled trunk. He sent lighting plots feasible for his various sponsors along with the signed contract and served as his own stage manager—collaborating with the available technical help.[50] At the colleges and universities that provided the bulk of his dates, he requested a student assistant to help him backstage.

He was also savvy about promoting himself, writing letters to potential sponsors that took account of their financial limitations and interest and devising strategies for his personal assistant to pursue. His fees were listed in March of 1968 as $600 for a concert, $250 for a lecture-demonstration, and $150 for a master class. Hire him for all three? That will be $750.[51] He alerted presenting organizations to dates he already had in their vicinity and offered a discounted "en route fee."[52]

When Nagrin was touring his solo program, the public's opinion of male dancers may have received a boost from a high-profile 1958 television show, *Dancing Is a Man's Game*, written and co-directed by Gene Kelly, who, as the production's narrator, used sports stars to demonstrate aspects of rhythm, coordination, and physical prowess that he could link to dance.[53] Nagrin knocked that message home in 1960, when he taught a master class at the Culver Military Academy in Indiana. A *Dance Magazine* article revealed, "One three-letter man was heard to whistle under his breath, 'This is tougher than any varsity sport I've ever played.'"[54] And the cadets were reportedly astonished that Nagrin, instead of resting after the class, went to warm up for his performance that evening. Offstage as well as on, he effortlessly projected an image that matched conventional definitions of masculinity.

The 1960s rocked the world of dance as well as American culture at large. The ideas of the choreographers, musicians, and visual artists who banded together under the name of Judson Dance Theater—among them Yvonne Rainer, Steve Paxton, Trisha Brown, and Robert Rauschenberg—fit well into a decade that would see social and political traditions attacked by the Civil Rights Movement, the Women's Movement, and Gay Liberation.

Nagrin did not embrace the more anarchic principles of those who came to be termed postmodernists, although he followed their careers and knew many of them. Phoebe Neville, who had apprenticed with the Tamiris-Nagrin Company, appeared in several of Meredith Monk's pieces, as did Nagrin's second wife, artist Lee Nagrin (Tamiris and Nagrin had separated in 1963, and she died in 1966). However, he approached in his own way the avant-garde mission of querying the nature of performing and breaching the barrier between spectators and performers. Improvisation, increasingly, became a tool.

The first half of the program billed as "Spring '65" consisted of four new solos and short linking pieces. When audience members entered the Kaufmann Concert Hall, Nagrin was already on stage, and they did not get programs until the performance was over. He wore the same T-shirt and pants throughout and switched a tape recorder on and off as needed. He wiped the sweat away between numbers. After performing *A Gratitude*, he told the story of its living-room genesis in his high-school days. And he began with *Path*.

Path turned minimalism into something intense and personal. Anyone seeing the piece only in a film version with a spoken text and music, which was shot with Nagrin in profile on a bluff against a sunset sky, would have trouble imagining the effect of seeing it on a stage, head-on and in silence.[55] Wearing gloves, his arms bent, he held a twelve-foot 2-by-4 in front of him. For more than eight minutes he paced carefully, absorbed in his task—a couple of slow steps forward, some slightly faster steps side and back, a slight suspended pause; then he resumed his path. The pattern was never mechanical; it breathed with him and changed subtly. In the end, he put the board down, took off the gloves, and moved on to the next solo.

The other remarkable dance on that April 1965 program coincided with the ongoing struggle for equal rights in that year of the Freedom March from Selma to Montgomery, Alabama. In *Not Me, But Him*, to music composed and recorded by Cecil Taylor, Nagrin wore a mask designed by Ralph Lee that, however stylized, was the grinning face of a black man. Some saw fear and wariness in his movements, as well as Uncle Tom humbleness and the role of amiable, foolish idler thrust on the African American by white minstrel-show comedians. But in London's *New Statesman* during Nagrin's 1967 tour of England, France, Austria, and Germany, Fernau Hall wrote that "behind the black mask one could imagine another Negro face, and at the end there was Nagrin's own face (corrugated by his experience as an entertainer) confronting the Negro entertainer's mask, in a bitterly ironic conjunction of realities and identities."[56]

The 1961 Cuban missile crisis had brought the Cold War closer to home, and in 1964 the conflict in Vietnam had begun. In 1966 Nagrin began making notes for what would become, two years later, the two-part, sixteen-section "Dance/Theater Collage" called *The Peloponnesian War*. "Here on the one hand," he wrote on August 12, "is history (& it doesn't matter if it's the Peloponnesian War, Carthage & Rome, the Religious Wars of Germany—also 30 yrs. War—or our World Wars) and on the other hand are the daily activities, intensities, doubts, toothbrushing, dreams going on in their relentless way not really paying attention to what is happening, not really learning. What happens on stage should by the parallel track be revealed as idiocy, sheer cruelty, pathetic beauty, obscene, self-centered, heroic."[57]

Influenced by Eastern philosophy and theater forms, many vanguard choreographers of the 1960s were experimenting with time—prolonging it, substituting collage for linear development, and exploring extremes of repetition. *The Peloponnesian War* was rife with theatrical climaxes, but it lasted about two hours and was, in Nagrin's tentative words, "a grab bag of bits"—brilliant, upsetting, funny, tragic, ironic.[58] It showed him as the master of impersonation and theatrical structure that he had become. Throughout the piece, the calm recorded voice of Frank Langella—often dimly heard through an assortment of music and sound effects—read a translation of Thucydides' account of the war between Athens and Sparta, 431–404 B.C., and Nagrin never left the stage, except perhaps during the intermission. With the help of an assistant, he changed clothes and acquired or discarded props in view of the audience.

Into this idiosyncratic, politically charged revue, he stitched scraps of his own past: the hoodlum of *Strange Hero* and the self-centered man from *Indeterminate Figure* appeared; there was a warmup; a showy, awkwardly danced ballet variation; and a collage of all the flashy, charm-oozing steps he had performed on Broadway. Often one vignette segued surprisingly into another. A Russian folk dance involved what looked like a fit and ended with a Red Army–style march. The show-biz number was followed by a rifle drill to music by Archie Shepp (at one point Nagrin fired right at the audience). A maelstrom of turns concluded with his finding a parcel that contained a severed arm.

He performed a catalogue of falls—every kind of death that could be imagined. He appeared as Hitler, as an enigmatic masked woman using her sexuality as a ploy, and as one of us—a man in a drab suit with a theater program. In place of a formal ending, he simply walked through the audience and stood by the exit, where people could talk to him. Or not. A good friend warned "Danny" that he was great but that "you beat the hell out of your audience and not everyone will hold still for it."[59] Her prophecy was not fulfilled. Between 1968 and 1973 Nagrin performed *The Peloponnesian War* 115 times, including in Guam and the Philippines (Part I only), and in several runs in New York at the Cubiculo on West 54th Street, at the WBAI Church, and at the Public Theater.

In 1969 Nagrin experimented with his own version of the indeterminacy practiced by John Cage and other vanguard musicians. In addition to touring *The Peloponnesian War* and fulfilling teaching residences at a number of universities and festivals, he assembled some creative young dancers and for about three and a half years—using techniques he had learned from Joseph Chaikin and his Open Theater as well as from previous acting experiences—he worked with them on various kinds of improvisations, which were then structured to a degree and performed in public. In one of the announcements, he wrote that "the Workgroup tries to find dances, not to make them."[60] The experience fueled his creative thinking as well as enlightening the dancers involved.

In 1977 Nagrin turned sixty. In September of that year, Marcia B. Siegel wrote about his subtly altered, yet undiminished vividness as a performer:

> Something happens when a dancer is no longer young and admits it. When the bloom is gone and the vitality is not so easily tapped, some purer distillation of qualities starts to show through, some essence of the dancer that's more beautiful, more moving than before, maybe because it's so naked and hard won.[61]

Siegel was speaking not only of Nagrin but also of the younger choreographers Cliff Keuter, Elina Mooney, Phoebe Neville, Ze'eva Cohen, and Mariko Sanjo—who had been associated with him in one way or another and who appeared on the gala celebrating his birthday (she guessed all of them to be over thirty-five)—as well as of the brilliant Paul Draper, who at sixty-eight concocted a witty tribute, threading images from Nagrin's solos into his tapping. Nagrin himself appeared as one of a quartet of men in

Keuter's *The Murder of George Keuter*—a generous gesture and one that gave the piece new resonance. He also performed two revealing solos: *Someone*, a finicky jitter of small should-I/shouldn't-I moves (he could almost have been channeling a woman), and *Untitled*, a barely moving study. He stood in silence, thinking, wearing only a jockstrap, looking like a weary athlete trying out poses for a sculptor, putting his knotty, well-tuned body on the line. Once, and only once, he erupted unexpectedly in what could have been fury.[62]

Later, in his book *How to Dance Forever*, Nagrin offered this advice to dancers: "Your power, potency, and potentiality should all be the product of your thirst for living. If you measure them by the yardstick of your chronological age, you're boxed in by limitations designed by you. NO. NO. NO."[63] Being boxed in was not part of his agenda. In spite of his fitness and continued athletic prowess, the fact of aging spurred him to design new kinds of solos. In almost all of them, the character he portrayed was himself: Daniel Nagrin, dancer-choreographer, here and now.

Someone was part of the evening-long *Ruminations* (1976), a rueful, sometimes joyful retrospective glance at his life in dance in which he took informality to new lengths. From the beginning, he made spectators in the Dance Gallery on 14th Street complicit in the goings-on—addressing them, making asides, taking them into his process. Near the end of the evening, he announced that he had made a "dull dance" for intermittent viewing, suggesting that people might set up look/don't-look rhythms and guess what they had seen when they opened their eyes. That launched a series of famous quotations on "Art," which he delivered in a high-toned manner while constantly slipping and falling (a different kind of "strange hero"—felled by aesthetic theories). He also let the audience watch him struggle to choreograph a new solo to Beethoven music. At the very end, he asked what should be done with the bench he had been making during intermissions—hammering and sawing while people walked around. Give it away? Sell it to support his foundation? (More than one admiring New Yorker still owns one of those benches.)

In this relaxed atmosphere, he would often try this or that until a memory surfaced. Then he would slip inside it—recalling, for example, how someone important to him washed dishes; acknowledging his love of flamenco with stamps and finger snaps; sliding, easy and slinky, into piano blues as he rec-ollected afternoons at Unity House with Sue Remos and her jazz records. He offered "a Jewish dance in two parts for those responsible for my Jewish-ness," full of fleeting character sketches of family.[64] The evening was all the richer for the glimpses of him, thinking, fumbling, reconsidering, letting go.

In 1977 he stepped briefly out of his own scenarios to stage and perform Off-Broadway a grim two-hour monologue he had adapted from Albert Ca-mus's *The Fall*. Despite his training and experience in acting, this was a new kind of venture. No dancing. Words, timing, and gesture invoked Camus's egocentric, malicious Parisian attorney with a guilty secret conversing with a sympathetic man he meets in a bar (Ernestine Stodelle wrote in the *New Haven Register* that Nagrin "had supplied details as only a choreographer could").[65]

In May of 1978, however, not dancing became an issue rather than a choice. Having ripped a cartilage, Nagrin submitted to knee surgery and im-mediately made a piece about his recovery (when he presented it in July, at the American Dance Festival, other dancers who had worked with him per-formed his earlier solos). In *Getting Well*, the obstacle was his own changed leg, and, with wit and charm, he patiently, gingerly tested its abilities. By the time he had pattered joyfully around his hospital bed and sunk into his first plié, spectators were ready to cheer for both his actual triumph and his theatrical artistry.[66]

One could posit autobiographical aspects to the acting-dancing solo *Jaca-randa* (1979), for which playwright Sam Shepard wrote the gritty text, giving Nagrin permission to rearrange, layer, or repeat elements. Nagrin performed it for two weeks at St. Clement's Church in Manhattan. The result was com-plex, wise, and disturbing. Pajama-clad and lying on the slanted board that forms a bed, a man awakens to discover that the woman he has spent the night with (a onetime lover) has gone. He moves from dismay into raging to her absent presence. She was always "independent, self-sufficient, and *so* busy" and could "always get along without me." Whipping a pillow and a blue satin sheet around in memory of their encounter and their quarrel, he lurches—torn this way and that, spitting out the words. But by the end, dressed for the day, he is acknowledging in an anguished litany, "I need you.

7.3. Daniel Nagrin at seventy-one. Photograph by Phyllis Steele. Courtesy of Phyllis Steele.

I need you now. I need you in the flesh. I need you in the bone . . . I need you in the breath . . . in the gut . . ."[67]

In 1981 Nagrin made his last solo, a talking-dancing one called *Poems Off the Wall*, which anticipated his sixty-fifth birthday. The following year he accepted a position as a senior lecturer in dance at Arizona State University in Tempe. There he taught full-time for the next ten years—dance technique and improvisation, performance techniques, philosophy of dance, dance history, and jazz styles. Over those years and beyond, while teaching intermittently, receiving two honorary doctorates and several teaching awards, and writing four books (one of them, *Choreography and the Specific Image*, elegantly illustrated with drawings by his third wife, Phyllis Steele-Nagrin), he also coached Shane O'Hara and—in 1994 and again in 2004—members of the José Limón Dance Company in some of his early solos. In a 1992 interview, filmed at Arizona State, he quoted Camus: "It's important not to die young."[68] He taught his last class in January 2008 and died on December 29 of that year at the age of ninety-one. (fig. 7.3)

Notes

The impressions of Daniel Nagrin's dances are based on the author's viewing of live performances by Nagrin and the filmed performances and interviews gathered on seventeen videotape cassettes as The Nagrin Videotape Library of Dance (see nagrin.com for information). Copies are housed in the Jerome Robbins Dance Division of The New York Public Library for the Performing Arts.

1. Susan Reimer and Nancy Reynolds, eds., *Dance of the Twentieth Century: Slide Text and Catalogue* (New York: Picture Dance, 1978), 33–34, cited in Christena L. Schlundt, *Daniel Nagrin: A Chronicle of His Professional Career* (Berkeley: University of California Press, 1997), 30.

2. Daniel Nagrin, "In Quest of a Dance," *Dance Magazine,* September 1951, 23–25.

3. Dance Performance, program, YM-YWHA, New York, March 2, 1958.

4. Daniel Nagrin, *The Six Questions: Acting Technique for Dance Performance* (Pittsburgh: University of Pittsburgh Press, 1997), xv.

5. Daniel Nagrin, interview by John Gruen, *Dance Magazine,* June 1976, 68–71. Tapes of the December 23, 1975, interview are housed in the Oral History Archives of the Jerome Robbins Dance Division, New York Public Library for the Performing Arts (hereafter JRDD, NYPL). Nagrin gave similar information to Jennifer Dunning, "Nagrin on How to Dance Forever," *New York Times,* May 7, 1982.

6. Daniel Nagrin, *Dance and the Specific Image: Improvisation* (Pittsburgh: University of Pittsburgh Press, 1993), 3.

7. John Martin, "Dance," *New York Times,* April 26, 1965, Nagrin clippings, JRDD, NYPL.

8. Daniel Nagrin, *How to Dance Forever: Surviving against the Odds* (New York: William Morrow, 1988), 356.

9. Ted Shawn, "Manly Sport, Not Fine Art, Is Dancing—Shawn," *San Diego Union,* July 18, 1913.

10. Naomi Jackson, *Converging Movements: Modern Dance and Jewish Culture at the 92nd Street Y* (Hanover, N.H.: Wesleyan University Press, 2000), 90–91.

11. Nagrin, interview by Gruen.

12. Daniel Nagrin, "Dance," *Campus,* November 1937, cited in Schlundt, *Daniel Nagrin,* 8.

13. Nagrin, *The Six Questions,* 84.

14. Schlundt, *Daniel Nagrin,* 12.

15. Daniel Nagrin, "Arts Project Suffers from Pink Slips," *Campus,* April 1939.

16. Daniel Nagrin, *Choreography and the Specific Image: Nineteen Essays and a Workbook* (Pittsburgh: University of Pittsburgh Press, 2001), 11.

17. Daniel Nagrin, *Ruminations,* Nagrin Videotape Library of Dances, Cassette #8, JRDD, NYPL. Taped in performance May 22, 1976, at the Dance Gallery, New York.

18. Daniel Nagrin, letter to Christena L. Schlundt, March 1994, quoted in Schlundt, *Daniel Nagrin,* 14.

19. Daniel Nagrin, letter to Christena L. Schlundt, March 23, 1994, quoted in Schlundt, *Daniel Nagrin,* 59.

20. Nagrin, *The Six Questions,* xv.

21. *Rockefeller Center Magazine,* n.d., Nagrin clippings, JRDD, NYPL.

22. John Martin, "The Dance: Honor Roll 2," *New York Times,* August 9, 1942, quoted in Schlundt, *Daniel Nagrin,* 14.

23. Daniel Nagrin, letter to Helen Tamiris, May 12, 1943. All Nagrin's letters to Tamiris are in the Daniel Nagrin Papers, JRDD, NYPL.

24. Nagrin, letter to Tamiris, March 27, 1943.

25. Nagrin, letter to Tamiris, April 4, 1943.

26. Jane Sherman and Barton Mumaw, *Barton Mumaw, Dancer: From Denishawn to Jacob's Pillow and Beyond* (New York: Dance Horizons, 1986), 165.

27. Nagrin, letter to Tamiris, May 1943.

28. Nagrin, letter to Tamiris, April 14, 1943. Dancer Vivian Cherry, along with Nagrin, appeared in four performances of Tamiris's complete *Liberty Song* in January and February 1942.

29. Walter Terry, "Helen Tamiris Acclaimed for 'Annie Get Your Gun' Ballet," *New York Herald Tribune*, June 16, 1946.

30. Nagrin, letter to Tamiris, July 4, 1947.

31. Sherman and Mumaw, *Barton Mumaw*, 301.

32. Daniel Nagrin, biography, Harper Theater Program, 1966, Nagrin clippings, JRDD, NYPL.

33. *Just For You* (1952), Paramount Pictures, based on Stephen Vincent Benét's novel *Famous*, produced by Pat Duggan, directed by Elliott Nugent. The cast included Bing Crosby, Jane Wyman, Ethel Barrymore, and Natalie Wood.

34. Nagrin, *How to Dance Forever*, 224.

35. Doris Hering, "Daniel Nagrin, Donald McKayle with Guest Artists," *Dance Magazine*, July 1951.

36. John Martin, "The Dance: Futures—From Nagrin in March to Graham in April," *New York Times*, February 23, 1958.

37. Nagrin, *The Six Questions*, 19.

38. Nagrin, *Dance and the Specific Image*, 221.

39. Ibid., 222.

40. Nagrin, *Choreography and the Specific Image*, 53.

41. Nagrin, letter to Schlundt, March 1994, quoted in Schlunt, *Daniel Nagrin*, 29.

42. Nagrin, *The Six Questions*, 200.

43. Louis Horst, "Daniel Nagrin, Geoffrey Holder, William Hug Dance Company," *Dance Observer*, December 1957, 153.

44. Nagrin's program note is quoted in Selma Jeanne Cohen, "Daniel Nagrin; 92nd Street 'Y,' New York," *Dance Magazine*, January 1960, a review of Nagrin's November 11, 1959, concert.

45. *His Majesty O'Keefe* (1953), Warner Brothers, produced by Harold Hecht, directed by Byron Haskin. The cast included Burt Lancaster, Joan Rice, Benson Fong, Philip Ahn, and Grant Taylor.

46. Nagrin, letter to Tamiris, July 30, 1952.

47. Nagrin, letter to Tamiris, July 19, 1952.

48. Nagrin, *How to Dance Forever*, 224.

49. Nagrin, letter to Tamiris, July 16, 1954.

50. Schlundt, *Daniel Nagrin*, 63.

51. Randolph Barron, letter to Daniel Nagrin, February 26, 1968, Daniel Nagrin Papers, JRDD, NYPL.

52. Daniel Nagrin, letter to the Dance Department, Allegheny College, September 4, 1969, Daniel Nagrin Papers, JRDD, NYPL.

53. "Dancing Is a Man's Game" was shown on NBC-TV as *Omnibus*'s Christmas show in 1958. Alistair Cooke hosted the production.

54. William J. Martin, "Cadets Discover Dance," *Dance Magazine,* June 1960.

55. *Path* was produced by Ray Garner at Idyllwild Arts Foundation's summer school in 1967. Included in *Four Films,* Nagrin Videotape Library of Dances, Cassette #2, JRDD, NYPL.

56. Fernau Hall, "Ballet: Contrasts," *New Statesman* (London), May 12, 1967.

57. Daniel Nagrin, "War Diary," in *Dancers' Notes,* ed. Marcia B. Siegel, *Dance Perspectives 38* (Summer 1969), 8.

58. Ibid., 3.

59. Margarita Ibbohs, letter to Daniel Nagrin, January 9, 1969, Daniel Nagrin Papers, JRDD, NYPL.

60. Daniel Nagrin, workgroup brochure, Daniel Nagrin Collection, University of California at Riverside, quoted in Schlundt, *Daniel Nagrin*, 72.

61. Marcia B. Siegel, "Long-Run Hero," *Soho Weekly News,* September 22, 1944.

62. Deborah Jowitt, "Happy Birthday, Danny," *Village Voice,* October 3, 1977.

63. Nagrin, *How to Dance Forever*, 223.

64. Nagrin, *Ruminations* (videotape).

65. Ernestine Stodelle, "Nagrin Performs Camus' 'Fall,'" *New Haven Register,* July 24, 1977.

66. Deborah Jowitt, "Come with Summer—and Gone," *Village Voice,* August 21, 1978.

67. Daniel Nagrin, *Jacaranda,* videotaped in performance by Johannes Holub, St. Clement's Church, New York, June 1979, Nagrin Videotape Library of Dances, Cassette #11, JRDD, NYPL.

68. *Daniel Nagrin: Man of Action,* filmed in 1999 for the Institute for Studies in the Arts at Arizona State University.

eight

Anna Huber

A Conceptual Moment
in Switzerland

Renée E. D'Aoust

Anna Huber's dances begin with a concept; we watch the concept evolve into something centered in the body and yet beyond the body. Huber bases her choreography on ideas integrated with the body, a conceptual approach, rather than on ideas formed out of the body, a movement approach. Because ideas are privileged over the body, her work is an example of what is meant by conceptual art. This existential approach to a visceral medium means that the intention behind Huber's choreography gives rise to structured dances. I contend that funding practices in Europe deepen the possibilities of Huber's conceptual approach.

An ultra-contemporary Swiss choreographer and soloist, Anna Huber was born in 1965, is originally from Bern, and trained as a dancer in Switzerland. While employed as a dancer by the State Theater of Cottbus in Germany (Staatstheater Cottbus), Huber was given studio space and production support and was encouraged to choreograph.[1] Without this support, she would not have considered her career: "I never planned to be a soloist. I never planned to be a choreographer," she says.[2] After many years of financial support in Berlin, Huber is now funded primarily in Switzerland. In addition to numerous other awards, she won the Ellys Gregor-Price in 2001 from the Mary Wigman-Gesellschaft in Cologne, Germany; the prestigious Hans Reinhart-Ring in 2002 (the first contemporary female dancer and choreographer to win this Swiss theater award); and, that same year, a Swiss critics' prize for choreography from the *Tanz der Dinge*.[3]

Although Huber resists being placed within any school or tradition because she does not want audiences predisposed to think of her in a certain way, it is helpful to acknowledge that there is a tradition of the solo dancer in German-speaking countries in Europe.[4] Ausdruckstanz, or the dance of expression, was popularized by Mary Wigman and made Wigman and other German soloists familiar, although still challenging, to audiences up through the 1930s.[5] But technique and form were "qualities not always associated with the practitioners of Ausdruckstanz"; the focus was on expression.[6] In Huber's early career, the contemporary Swiss clown Dimitri called her a "contemporary Mary Wigman . . . [but Huber] has no conscious connection to expressionist dance."[7]

Huber's background places her in a tradition of performers in German-speaking countries that allows for a readier reception of choreography resisting easy categorization. This history may be why the scholar Ramsay Burt suggests that "European audiences for innovative dance and live art seem prepared to take the time to experience and appreciate slow, demanding, and experimental work."[8] To analyze Huber's experimental work, I start with *unsichtbarst* (literally, most invisible), created in 1998 and recorded on DVD.[9]

Huber writes that her idea for *unsichtbarst* was to investigate "ways of seeing and of being seen."[10] Christina Thurner, a professor in the Institute of Theater Studies at the University of Bern, reviewed *unsichtbarst* for *Neue Zürcher Zeitung*:

It is significant that [Huber] first performed [*unsichtbarst*] in a museum [at the National Gallery in Berlin's Hamburger Bahnhof]. . . . The dancer makes the impression of being some kind of contemporary art figure— but not in the sense of something polished and beautiful—intended to be put on display for all to admire; she seems much more like a living sculpture searching for structure with . . . incredible precision.[11]

Huber is petite, but with a powerful, unshakable presence. She has cropped blond hair, a charming smile, and a body that is thin and taut. Her angular motions do not look friable; her body is pliant and lean without being hard and brittle.

In *unsichtbarst* the dancer is movable sculpture, and we see a living piece of sculpture *thinking*. While Huber emphasizes activity, she also emphasizes nonactivity; nonactivity embraces the existence of ideas. Huber sculpts the body, yet the container of the sculpture (her body) also receives our projected ideas. Because the body does not move constantly but is simply present, the dancer's physical presence becomes an abstraction. Huber does not impose meaning but allows meaning to be created by the audience through her presence. Even when she employs stillness, there is a sense of motion, but it is the motion of thought. This juxtaposition and exploration of contrasts continues to show in her work today.

unsichtbarst uses an electronic score by Wolfgang Bley-Borkowski and therefore the body is not the only medium we experience. Yet the piece begins when Huber, wearing funky and clunky wool-felt clogs, slides methodically across the floor and leans her frame forward and back. It is a standing hinge, but with the legs straight; Huber goes far back and far forward, giving the illusion of fall and recovery without the sweeping motion of either. It is as if a bronze Giacometti sculpture started moving. We are not surprised to see the sculpture moving, but we are surprised to realize we thought it *could not* move. The visual artist Simone Meier, writing for *Tages-Anzeiger*, underscores this playful seriousness by suggesting that "what Anna Huber shows doesn't necessarily sound like serious art, but it really is."[12]

In the article "History, Memory, and the Virtual in Current European Dance Practice," Burt suggests that "dances that create a virtual imaginary and those that evoke histories and memories explore theater dance's potential to affect its beholders' experience of temporality."[13] Huber evokes the "virtual imaginary" through the immediacy of form. Her investigation allows a parallel focus on the imaginary sphere in which the audience is as much a partner in the creation of meaning as is the dancer's body and the temporal life of the dance. But the creation of meaning begins within the performer herself, within her ideas, before the body moves. In conceptual dance, whether technology is embraced or not, concepts are detached from emotional expression but commonly accessible to all.

At the end of *unsichtbarst*, Huber unceremoniously pulls down her pant-leg and the arms of a tight-fitting, long-sleeved black shirt. She stands, looks straight out, and walks off. She's impenetrable, detached. The audience takes time before realizing the piece has ended; there is no sound before the clapping begins. This emptiness created after so much meditative focus allows an opening for possibility; it is as if the ideas Huber uses prior to choreographing movement recur in the still space after the dance finishes.

The ability to create another dimension through performance is what makes Huber's work grounded in the present while her approach remains existential. Eva Bucher, writing for *Neue Luzerner Zeitung*, reflects this union of seeming contrasts, which continues in Huber's later work and shows in 1998: "It is the way that everything seems to be evolved from a mere moment and oscillates between 'art-ificialty' and 'authenticity' that makes *un-sichtbarst* . . . fascinating."[14]

Huber's 2001 solo *Stück mit Flügel* continues this exploration of the line between artifice and authenticity. *Stück mit Flügel* shows the need to keep on playing or to stick with flying, as a loose translation of "Flügel" suggests, since the word can mean either "wing" or "grand piano" in German.[15] *Stück mit Flügel* begins with two radio-controlled objects buzzing around the stage. The dancer (Huber) and the pianist (Susanne Huber, her sister) sit at the back of the stage directing the radio controls. Huber writes that "for us it's 'a thing'—an object which could be a '*stück mit flügel*': a mountain, a brain, and the moving light, [a] kind of an '*Irrlicht*.'"[16] When I saw Huber perform *Stück mit Flügel* in Verscio, Switzerland, I thought of the electronic "thing" as a radio-controlled brain chased by an electronic egg. It may sound cute, but it does not look kitschy in the least. Brain and egg then having parked, in nonchalant manner Susanne Huber takes her place at the piano.

The score for *Stück mit Flügel* is a combination of sometimes bombastic electronic music by Martin Schütz with piano pieces by György Kurtág,

György Ligeti, and Franz Lizst, played with great sensitivity throughout by Susanne Huber. Press material reports that "before this work, Anna Huber had always refused to use existing compositions."[17] Her earlier "refusal" to use existing compositions was part of her desire to investigate the contemporary world. Huber writes that she "preferred to collaborate with composers and live musicians to create the music in dialogue for specific projects."[18]

Yet the electronic mix in *Stück mit Flügel* at first does not seem in dialogue with the dance as it interacts jarringly with Kurtág, Ligeti, and Lizst; however, that might be the point because the interlacing of musical tones with electronic turbulence drives home the point of disjunction. Does history matter if we identify only with "now"? The sound combinations suggest history matters because these combinations are at first unsettling, yet ultimately the electronic crescendo focuses the senses. There is an embrace of contemporary sound and musical technology; in contrast to the throbbing pulse, stillness is achieved. It is unclear whether stillness results from classical resonance or from the contemporary sound, but it probably comes from a combination of both.

Stück mit Flügel evokes a space for abstract art within dance even more clearly than the earlier *unsichtbarst*. According to Thurner, *Stück mit Flügel* is characterized "by the choreographic inquiry into unusual and surprising movement combinations typical of Anna [Huber], and successfully cultivated by her since her 1995 debut piece . . . *in zwischen räumen*."[19] Nevertheless, she does not live without constraint. When she tries to jump, she looks incredibly awkward. She twitches more than jumps. When she tries to run, her feet are gripped in an antipoint; she lands on heel and crunched toes, not on the soles of her feet.

Instead of showy moves, there are consistent, even predictable steps. The music sweeps. The steps stay the same. Methodical. Are we going somewhere or nowhere at all? Think of an Alexander Calder mobile. Walk under it, and it moves. Take a breath, and Huber moves. In the way Calder used existing materials to create new work, here Huber uses existing pedestrian motions to create new ways of moving combined within a collaboration of sound, lighting, and spatial design.

Then there is her presence: Huber has a disarming way of looking directly into the theater; she lies down, rests her chin on folded hands, and looks out, the way a child might, with an unadorned gaze. She takes us in as we take her in; our interpretations, the meaning we project onto her, are again part of her intention. The pedestrian costumes by Inge Zysk help us to see Huber as human, but this kind of concentration—a Zen focus—would be impossible for the novice.

The choreographer Foofwa d'Imobilité, who works in both Geneva and New York, describes the intensity inherent in Huber's creations, readily apparent in her earlier work: "[Huber] is a unique kind of performer. Her presence and her movements are unconventional. Her way of making art is really odd in a positive way."[20]

Operated by Susanne Huber, the radio-controlled brain returns at the end of *Stück mit Flügel*. Rather than an open ending as we saw with *unsicht-barst*, here we have a bookmarked ending. As Anna Huber stands and slowly revolves, she pulls up the dance floor and wraps it around her like a towel. The radio-controlled brain vrooms up and parks next to her. This electronic framing device shows a development in formality. Yet instead of stepping backward or continuing forward, she begins crossing her legs sideways, stepping outside of expectation.

Just because she resides on the European continent, Huber should not be identified with what critic Joan Acocella describes as "European (theme-heavy, emotionalist, I-can't-take-this-anymore)" dance.[21] But neither is Huber on the western side of Acocella's Atlantic divide with "the American (abstract, formalist, shut-up-and-dance)" crowd.[22] Huber neither gives up nor shuts up. Her unexpected use of an unadorned gaze as a positive affirmation becomes the most surprising element, and as her intention becomes clearer, *Stück mit Flügel* takes you forward.

Burt might suggest that this type of work can "stimulate nonverbal collective memories."[23] Indeed, rather than making an audience passive, memories stimulated by a performer's gentle play help an audience to participate in the creation of art. The projection of memory is an integral part of the ideas used to create Huber's most recent piece, *Eine Frage der Zeit*. This title indicates that we will be dealing with "the matter, the question, of time," but once again it is not necessary to paste a narrative onto the piece.[24] Huber welcomes ideas but frees us from narrative. Her work has become more sophisticated, still deceptively simple yet full of risk. After all, as she suggests, she "prefer[s] opening questions [rather] than answering or giving solutions."[25]

Eine Frage der Zeit premiered on October 29, 2008, in Bern. The performance I saw in Zurich almost one year later showed that the piece extends the boundaries of Huber's previous work. There was collective concentration of the sold-out audience within the warehouse space of Theaterhaus Gessnerallee; Huber has a dedicated following. In *Eine Frage der Zeit* she appears on stage for more than an hour, piecing together fragments of a life: walking, running, stitching. The stitching movement looks as if she is sewing silk thread through her body, either with grand arm motions or with small detailed needlework. One should not take these motions too literally because, although many of them are pedestrian with angular twists, the point is less to reflect daily life than to conceptualize an experience of living. For example, *Eine Frage der Zeit* is reminiscent of the late American writer David Foster Wallace's reflections on "the ambient volume of . . . life's noise."[26] Huber contains the excessive twenty-first-century noise by controlling the volume, using stillness and angularity to create space and reflect time. (fig. 8.1)

Much of the movement in *Eine Frage der Zeit* is again minimalist, even repetitive, and once again Huber extends the boundaries of the stage with diagonal walking, abrupt falls, and in one section, a brief crab walk. Critic Lucie Machac, reviewing the premiere, writes that it is "formally concise but playful, simple but refined, unspectacular but still captivating."[27] The fleeting repetition in *Eine Frage der Zeit* is never relentless and is ultimately optimistic.

As with *Stück mit Flügel*, electronic music is used, in part, to focus the senses. A blast of Martin Schütz's evocative electronic score shocks the system. As is Huber's preference, she and Schütz created in collaboration; they were able to talk extensively about their ideas and their readings on the subjects of memory and of time.[28] While Schütz recorded his musical improvisations in real time, Huber spent hours reviewing videos of herself improvising to shape them into the hour-long piece. Thilo Reuther's atmospheric lighting never hides Huber's power, which at times feels sensual. The unity achieved among music, lighting, dancer, costume, and space itself is also made possible because, as with Schütz, Huber has had a long collaborative relationship with Reuther.[29]

Huber amends the perception of time's passage through her unaffected and genuine presence. While performing, she uses constructed mental images as a way of intentionally creating different qualities and textures of movement.[30] She says, "There must be enough space in the piece for time itself."[31] Although the idea of existentially exploring time sounds serious, there are sustained moments of joy in *Eine Frage der Zeit*. Huber frequently employs ebullient and often continuous movement, making this a rigorous piece for the performer. When she uses the back of her hands to walk, she bends over her legs and steps backward. We are so used to seeing Huber's world move in reverse that when her fingers point up and her palms come forward, it looks as if she is extending a benediction. Now far along in her artistic development, Huber appears to stitch her vertebrae with needle and thread, yet we see only fleeting images because her hands are behind her back. Is she sewing a life back together?

Suddenly, Huber uses absurd humor to jolt the audience out of a serious reverie. It is a total surprise and creates total fun. There is not the abyss here in the way that Acocella suggests Europeans "[have] seen socialism, and they are into something else: apocalypticism."[32] Huber is far too assured to step into the abyss of the fatal nothing. Without forced expression, meaning might become opaque; however, here interpretation of meaning becomes accessible to all. Nascent in the early *unsichtbarst*, this approach is sophisticated in the later *Eine Frage der Zeit*. In an unassuming, nonaggressive manner, like a good friend who can teach us to view our lives anew, Huber with physical stillness quiets for us the musical-crescendo noise of our daily lives.

Huber creates what avant-garde American writer Lance Olsen calls "possibility spaces," which are "where everything can and should be attempted, felt, thought."[33] He suggests "the difference between art and entertainment":

Art deliberately slows and complicates perception so you can re-think and re-feel language, narrativity, experience [while] entertainment deliberately speeds and simplifies perception so you don't have to think about or feel very much of anything at all.[34]

8.1. Anna Huber in *Eine Frage der Zeit*, 2008. Photograph by Caroline Minjolle. Courtesy of Anna Huber.

If we replace the word *language* with *dance* and apply it to a reading of Huber, we have dance that "deliberately slows and complicates perception," thereby making us rethink and redefine our definitions of dance and the use of our imagination while viewing it.[35] We are involved in the creation of the "possibility space" not only while it is being performed but also thereafter.[36]

Huber creates these "possibility spaces" because of the long process of creating the work. That long process is made possible because of her consistent funding, which allows her to start with an idea and then proceed to choreography. It makes all the difference to her conceptual process, which has its roots in thought outside the dance studio. While one does not need funding to maintain such an approach, having it means that the choreographer can take risks over the course of an entire career that may not otherwise be possible.

Huber's work underscores how the process of choreographing in Switzerland and other European countries differs from the way solo performance and choreography is created in the United States. Her funding includes studio space and production support. The availability of funding in Switzerland and in Germany changes the way work is conceived in the first place because it allows time for ideas to germinate and for work to develop. For example, long collaborative processes with other artists are possible, as has been the case for Huber with Schütz. In addition, the reason we see ideas in action is because Huber has spent so much time developing those mental images that she uses in conjunction with the choreographed movement.

Critic Gia Kourlas suggests that the creation of work in the United States and in Europe differs because of differences in intangible courage, with European choreographers possessing more courage lately than those in the United States. Kourlas proposes the following:

> European dance community stretches beyond culture and country. . . . Europe is becoming what New York used to be. In Europe, innovation flows like water from one country to the next. The work, while varied in quality, has an undeniable energy that has only partly to do with financing and resources.[37]

I contend that the courage to experiment in Europe is a direct result of the financial support a choreographer like Huber receives. The length of time needed to develop ideas is possible because she receives money to create her art. It is easier to have "energy" when one has health insurance, a safety net of sorts in jobs and funding within the arts, and the time to develop ideas without risk of losing funding support. If an artist can count on steady employment from inside the arts and also has health insurance, that artist might be better able to find the courage to take the risks to which Kourlas refers. For example, in Switzerland, health insurance coverage is required by law, purchased privately yet regulated to be affordable.[38]

In 2007 Huber became an artist-in-residence at Dampfzentrale, Bern, a cultural venue with performance and studio space that is located in a converted steam factory situated along the River Aare. In addition to numerous grants, she receives long-term funding in Switzerland from three organizations: Kultur Stadt Bern (the city of Bern), Amt für Kultur des Kantons

Bern (the Bern canton), and the Pro Helvetia Swiss Cultural Foundation (a national-level organization). These are cultural funding organizations at the city, canton, and national level. All three organizations agree to support one company: in this case, Anna Huber's. A so-called cooperative funding agreement requires a certain number of performances at home and abroad, two new works in a three-year period, and written reports.[39] Huber is the first contemporary choreographer to receive this kind of funding in Bern, and the funding has just been extended through 2012. Although Huber finds she has a lot of administrative work to do, this is nothing compared to the juggling act of choreographers in the United States, who often have to fund all aspects of their art, leaving little time and space to process ideas prior to developing choreography.

Although this funding structure is relatively new to Switzerland, it appears to be a successful effort to establish specific support for dance.[40] Foofwa d'Imobilité writes, "In Switzerland, I am able to pay dancers and collaborators and an administration in a way that would be unimaginable in the States . . . unless I did something more commercial."[41] The organization Reso, Dance Network Switzerland, was itself formed only in 2006 to support and promote dance in Switzerland.[42] Typical of Swiss pragmatism, before forming Reso, in 2002 "Projekt Tanz" began analyzing "the existing funding system [and it also] brought dance onto the cultural political agenda and instigated pilot projects."[43]

Yet some people do not think funding disparities between the United States and Europe make a difference in the creation, or quality, of work. Anouk van Dijk, a choreographer based in Belgium, writes, "In my view most of the European 'conceptual dance' wave, for instance, is repeating— in a lot less interesting way even—what was shown 20 or even 30 years ago in the U.S."[44] I disagree. The ideas Huber explores in her work show how we might engage ourselves with concepts before aggressively moving; conceptual work helps us to slow down. This is a radical departure from the narcissistic moment and an affirmation of the value of detachment. It stems from Huber's preference "to work in contrasts, in contradictions. I search for the friction rather than harmony."[45] What results, though, often feels quieting rather than abrasive or unnerving. Simply put, this process is made possible because Huber has the money to spend time thinking and then to put those ideas into the body. Particularly in *Eine Frage der Zeit*, she intentionally uses her imagination to create qualities of movement; this intention, the idea impulse that occurs before movement, is observable.

In *No Fixed Points* Nancy Reynolds and Malcolm McCormick suggest a possible term for postmodernists who are less interested in revolt: "With so many realignments being made by choreographers, a new designation—'new postmodernism'—perhaps seem[s] fitting."[46] In a "new postmodernist" vein, Huber can be pedestrian, suddenly appear elegant, and then be more focused on form or stillness than on expression. Rather than angry or rebellious, her new postmodern approach is spare and simple and Zen. The lack of anger and revolt may be connected to stable funding, too. In any case, speaking of choreographic endeavors as "possibility spaces" might resolve some of the assumptions made by placing labels on what is essentially an existential manner of working, although Huber says that "my work is seen as abstract, but for me pure abstract movement doesn't exist. I'm looking for transformation and form, and I have to know where all movement comes from."[47]

Huber says she now feels able to "play and experiment more with ideas."[48] In *tasten*, her most recent work, Huber collaborated with two pianists who call themselves klavierduo huber/thomet (Susanne Huber and André Thomet).[49] ("'*Tasten*' has a double meaning in German, being either the keys of a keyboard or the act of touching or groping.")[50] With funding in place for the last three years and the next three years, Huber plans to embrace technology directly, which in the pieces discussed here focused primarily on electronic sound scores. For a work-in-progress, Huber writes, "I now plan to create a new project with a visual artist [Yves Netzhammer] who works in the field of video and animation. This will be a closer approach to new media."[51] It is part of her continuing exploration of possibilities, trying to stretch her boundaries.

We live in an era when entertainment and often art are built by exploiting a "me, me, me" focus. Another intriguing note about Huber as a solo artist and choreographer is that she never focuses solely on the self or on herself. The shapes of the body fascinate her, but the shapes lead to other angular constructions with her head between her knees or under a leg, and the body rises to a crab walk, suggesting that an exploration of movement is privileged over an exploration of emotion. But that movement exploration begins with ideas, with concepts, and the exploration of those concepts and ideas are made possible, are unhurried, because of funding, including studio space and production support. Although she is alone on stage, Huber neither asserts nor denies her individuality.

While she certainly uses and asserts her idiosyncratic movement language, even this does not make her solos excessively individualistic. Huber creates dances that are Zen koans, paradoxes performed as transparent riddles that are open to the solutions of the viewer. The conceptual intelligence behind *unsichtbarst*, *Stück mit Flügel*, and *Eine Frage der Zeit* reflects the thoughtful negotiation required when one decides to live a conscious life.

Notes

1. Anna Huber, "Biography Long," Anna Huber Compagnie. Printed press material and reviews were obtained directly from the Anna Huber Compagnie; also available at http://www.annahuber.net/bin.

2. Anna Huber, interview by the author, Dampfzentrale, Bern, Switzerland, March 15, 2010.

3. Huber, "Biography Long."

4. Nancy Reynolds and Malcolm McCormick, *No Fixed Points: Dance in the Twentieth Century* (New Haven, Conn.: Yale University Press, 2003), 77, 95.

5. Ibid., 77, 104.

6. Ibid., 105.

7. Irene Sieben, "Laudatio for the Dancer and Choreographer Anna Huber," tribute presented at Ring-Celebration, Bern, June 1, 2002, 2–3.

8. Ramsay Burt, "*Trio A* in Europe," *Dance Research Journal* 41, no. 2 (Winter 2009): 25.

9. Anna Huber, e-mail interview by the author, June 15, 2010.

10. Anna Huber, "*unsichtbarst*," press sheet.

11. Christina Thurner, "*unsichtbarst*," *Neue Zürcher Zeitung*, October 17, 1998.

12. Simone Meier, "*unsichtbarst*," *Tages-Anzeiger* (Zürich), n.d.

13. Ramsay Burt, "History, Memory, and the Virtual in Current European Dance Practice," *Dance Chronicle* 32, no. 3 (2009): 445.

14. Eva Bucher, "*unsichtbarst*," *Neue Luzerner Zeitung*, n.d.

15. Anna Huber, "*offene fragen,*" in *Anna Huber Press Book* (Zurich: Pro Helvetia, 2002), 44.

16. Anna Huber, e-mail interview by the author, April 18, 2010.

17. Anna Huber, "*Stück mit Flügel,*" press sheet.

18. Huber, e-mail interview, April 18, 2010.

19. Christina Thurner, "Stück mit Flügel," *Neue Zürcher Zeitung,* April 6, 2001.

20. Foofwa d'Imobilité, e-mail interview by the author, February 16, 2010.

21. Joan Acocella, "Loners: What It Takes to Go Solo," *New Yorker,* December 12, 2005.

22. Ibid.

23. Burt, "History, Memory, and the Virtual," 444.

24. Astrid Andrä, e-mail correspondence with the author, October 29, 2009.

25. Anna Huber, e-mail interview by the author, February 23, 2010.

26. David Foster Wallace, ed., "Introduction," in *The Best American Essays 2007,* series ed. Robert Atwan (Boston: Houghton Mifflin, 2007), xiv.

27. Lucie Machac, *Berner Zeitung BZ,* October 31, 2008.

28. Anna Huber, interview, March 15, 2010.

29. Ibid.

30. Ibid.

31. Ibid., and e-mail follow-up, April 18–19, 2010.

32. Acocella, "Loners."

33. Lance Olsen, "33 Tweets on the Nature of Possibility," closing remarks, In (ter)ventions—Literary Practice at the Edge: A Gathering, Banff Centre, Banff, British Columbia, Canada, February 18–21, 2010.

34. Ibid.

35. Ibid.

36. Ibid.

37. Gia Kourlas, "Critic's Notebook: How New York Lost Its Modern Dance Reign," *New York Times,* September 5, 2005.

38. Doyle McManus, "Switzerland's Example of Universal Health Care," *Los Angeles Times,* October 18, 2009.

39. *Project Dance: Paths to Comprehensive Dance Funding in Switzerland,* Final Report, Federal Office for Culture Pro Helvetia, Swiss Arts Council, Bern, September 2006.

40. Ibid.

41. d'Imobilité, e-mail interview.

42. Reso—Dance Network Switzerland, "Profile," "Cultural Politics," [and] "Creation," Bern, Switzerland, http://www.reso.ch/index.php?id=6&L=1 (accessed November 2, 2009).

43. Ibid.

44. Anouk van Dijk, "The Center of the Dance World? An Online Conversation," *Arts Journal*, December 16, 2005, http://www.artsjournal.com/danceforum /2005/12/the_old_and_the_new.html (accessed August 1, 2009).

45. Anna Huber, e-mail interviews by the author, February 23, 2010, and April 18, 2010.

46. Reynolds and McCormick, *No Fixed Points*, 606.

47. Anna Huber, e-mail interviews, and interview, Bern.

48. Ibid.

49. Ibid.

50. Lucerne Festival, *tasten* description [anon.], http://www.lucernefestival.ch/ en/festivals/festival_in_summer_2010/events/annahuber_compagnie_huber_ thomet/ (accessed April 20, 2010).

51. Anna Huber, e-mail interviews, and interview, Bern.

Contributors

RAMSAY BURT is professor of dance history at De Montfort University, U.K. His books are *The Male Dancer; Alien Bodies; Judson Dance Theater;* and *Writing Dancing Together* (with Valerie Briginshaw). Burt is founder-editor with Susan L. Foster of the series *Discourses in Dance.*

RENÉE E. D'AOUST is the author of *Body of a Dancer* from Etruscan Press. D'Aoust was a 2008 fellow at the National Endowment for the Arts Journalism Institute for Dance Criticism at the American Dance Festival. Her essay "Graham Crackers" was included in Robert Gottlieb's *Reading Dance.*

DEBORAH JOWITT has written a dance column for the *Village Voice* since 1967. Her books include *Time and the Dancing Image* and *Jerome Robbins: His Life, His Theater, His Dance.* She is on the faculty of New York University's Tisch School of the Arts.

JULIE MALNIG is associate professor of performance in the Gallatin School of Individualized Study at New York University and chair of Gallatin's Interdisciplinary Arts Program. She is the author of *Dancing Till Dawn: A Century of Exhibition Ballroom Dance* and editor of *Ballroom, Boogie, Shimmy Sham, Shake: A Social and Popular Dance Reader.*

SANDRA MEYER is a researcher and professor at the Arts Center of the University of the State of Santa Catarina, Brazil. She is co-editor of the following books: *Tubo de Ensaio: Experiências em dança e arte contemporânea* (Test tube: Experiments in contemporary dance and arts); *Coleção Dança Cênica I* (Theater dance series I); and *Seminários de dança: História em movimento—Biografias e Registros em dança* (Dance seminars: History in movement—Biographies and records of dancing). Meyer is the author of *A Dança cênica em Florianópolis* (Theater dance in Florianópolis) and *As Metáforas do corpo em cena* (Metaphors of body in scene).

CARRIE J. PRESTON is assistant professor of English and women's studies at Boston University. Her book *Modernism's Mythic Pose: Gender, Genre, Solo Performance* traces the history of solo forms and the subjectivities they construct with case studies of Isadora Duncan and H.D.

JANICE ROSS, professor in the Drama Department and director of the Dance Division at Stanford University, is the winner of a de la Torre Bueno Award 2008 Special Citation and author of *Anna Halprin: Experience as Dance* and *Moving Lessons: Margaret H'Doubler and the Beginning of Dance in American Education*.

KARL TOEPFER is dean of the College of Humanities and the Arts, San Jose State University, California. Among his other books and articles, his *Empire of Ecstasy: Nudity and Movement in German Body Culture, 1910–1935* has become a fundamental text.

Editor CLAUDIA GITELMAN was associate professor emerita at the Mason Gross School of the Arts, Rutgers University, New Jersey; she was a choreographer and dancer who taught worldwide. Her books are *The Returns of Alwin Nikolais: Bodies, Boundaries and the Dance Canon*, co-edited with Randy Martin; *Liebe Hanya: Mary Wigman's Letters to Hanya Holm*; and *Dancing with Principle: Hanya Holm in Colorado, 1941–1983*.

Editor BARBARA PALFY freelances as a copy editor for dance books and the journals *Dance Chronicle* and *Ballet Review*, among others, after a career as a librarian in the Dance Division of the New York Public Library for the Performing Arts.

The University Press of Florida is the scholarly publishing agency for the State University System of Florida, comprising Florida A&M University, Florida Atlantic University, Florida Gulf Coast University, Florida International University, Florida State University, New College of Florida, University of Central Florida, University of Florida, University of North Florida, University of South Florida, and University of West Florida.

Index

Cultural identity, 8–9, 63, 141. *See also* Abreu, Luiz de; Dunham, Katherine; Ito, Michio; Transnationalism; Volúsia, Eros
Cultural influences, 10–11
Cunningham, Merce, 4

Dadaism, 38, 48–49
Dalcroze. *See* Jaques-Dalcroze, Émile
Daly, Ann, 3, 39, 55, 147
Dance: Afro-American, 142; in Brazil, 154–55, 159n19; demonic, 49–50; stylization of, 141, 147; women's magazines and, 33, 37. *See also* Modern dance; Salome dances; Solo-dance concerts
Debussy, Claude, 38
De Certeau, Michel, *The Practice of Everyday Life*, 58, 68
Delsarte, François, 3, 10, 129, 133
Delsartism, 10, 24
Demonic dances, 49–50
Denby, Edwin, 4
Denishawn company, 14
Desmond, Olga, 78–83; *Conquered*, 79; *Der Schwertertanz*, 80–82, 81; *Rhythmographik*, 83
Dewey, John, *Art as Experience*, 64
Diaghilev, [Sergei], 38
Dijkstra, Bram, 132
D'Imobilité, Foofwa, 192, 197
Doukhobors, 45
Draper, Paul, 176, 180
Dulac, Edmund, 11, 23
Duncan, Isadora: Allan and, 119, 120; approach to music of, 84; Carlson and, 60, 62–63, 65, 70; "The Dance of the Greeks," 55; description of "Art," 10; first American tour of, 10; Greek tradition and, 129, 141, 147; Ito and, 9; as New Woman, 124–25; popularity of, 2; Romantic music and, 39, 40, 41; self-fulfillment and, 34; solos of, 33; speeches to audience, 56; Volúsia on, 150; "What Do Modern Women Want?," 33

Dunham, Katherine, 141, 142, 147, 151; *Rites de Passage*, 145, 148
Dunn, Douglas, 3
Duschnes, Maria, 159n19

East and West, assumed opposition between, 12, 22, 23, 133
Edward VII (king), 122
Eliot, T. S., 16
Engelmann, Siegfried, 110
Eroticism of female dancers: Allan, 135–36, 136; Hari, 74, 75; Ilbak, 114, 116
Estado Novo in Brazil, 142, 150
Estrangement and modernity, 112–13
Europe: funding support for work in, 187–88, 195–98; modern dance in, 73–74
Everyday life, practice of, 58, 67, 68
Exoticism: of Allan, 125; modern dance and, 8, 113, 114, 115, 147. *See also* Orientalism; Salome dances
Expressionism, 45–46, 145–47

Falke, Gertrud, 96
Falke, Ursula, 96
Female solo dancers: bodies of, 55–56; in Europe, 73–74; partnerships between, 95–96; venues for, 90. *See also* Eroticism of female dancers
Femme fatale image, 132, 135
Film work: of Allan, 136; of Desmond, 82–83; of Graham, 14; of Gremo, 96; of Ito, 14–15; of Nagrin, 172, 175–76
Finley, Karen, 4
Flaubert, Gustave, 122
Fokine, Michel, 39, 40, 41, 86
Foster, Hal, 48, 50
Foster, Susan Leigh, 3
Franko, Mark, 15, 16
Frentz, Hans, 106
Freyre, Gilberto, 144, 147–48
Friedman, Susan Stanford, 26

Modern dance: as art, 92–93; authorship of, 3; in Europe, 73–74; group movement and, 109; images of women and, 76; master narrative, 16; nudity and, 92; solos of, 34–38, 98

Modern dance studies, transnational approach to, 26–27

Modernism: abstraction and, 1–2; in Brazil, 141–42, 144–45, 147; definition of, 1; ecstatic performances and, 51; music and, 38–44; orientalism and exoticism of, 26; twentieth-century, 33–34

Modernity: disillusionment with, 131–32; estrangement and, 112–13; impact of, 36–38; movement vocabulary for, 112; perceptions of, 93

Monk, Meredith, 177

Monnier, Mathilde, 35

Moore, Carol-Lynne, 48

Moreau, Gustave, 122, 129, 131

Morosco, Oliver, 12

Morrell, Lady Ottoline, 11

Moses, Ray, 166, 167

Mumaw, Barton, 169, 172

Music: of Duncan, 39, 40, 41, 84; of Huber, 190–91, 193; of Ilbak, 116; of Nagrin, 163, 167, 174, 175; of Nijinsky and Wigman, 38–44; of Pavlova, 84–85; Romantic, 39, 40, 41, 88, 100; of Schrenck, 100. *See also specific composers*

Musical fragmentation, 40–41, 44

Music visualizations, 7–8

Nagrin, Daniel: Broadway career of, 170, *171*, 172; choreography of, 169–70; *Dance in the Sun*, 174–75; "Dance Portraits" program, 176; debut of, 167; film work of, 172, 175–76; Foster and, 3; gala for birthday of, 180–81; *How to Dance Forever*, 181; *Indeterminate Figure*, 175; *Jacaranda*, 182–83; *Jazz in Three Ways*, 174; masculine characters of, 173–74; master classes of, 177; military career of, 168–69; *With My Eye and With*

My Hand, 175, 176; *Not Me, But Him*, 178; *Path*, 178; *The Peloponnesian War*, 179–80; photo of, *183*; *Ruminations*, 181–82; *The Six Questions*, 174–75; solo touring of, 176–77; solo works of, 165, 172–73; *Spanish Dance*, 174; *Strange Hero*, 163–65, *164*; Tamiris and, 167–68, 169, 170, 177; teaching career of, 183; at Unity House, 167, 168, 182

Nagrin, Lee, 177

Nancy, Jean-Luc, 35, 37–38, 51–52

National Endowment for the Arts, 2, 4

Neville, Phoebe, 177, 180

Newman, Ernest, 84

New postmodern approach, 198

New Woman image, 124–25, 128, 132, 135

Nihon buyo, 9, 18–19

Nijinska, Bronislava, 38

Nijinsky, Romola, 31, 32, 33, 40, 44, 45

Nijinsky, Vaslav: aesthetic mysticism of, 45, 50; approach to music of, 38–41, 44; *Diaries*, 33, 44, 45; intensity of performances of, 35–36; modernism and, 33–34; pacifist views of, 44–46; program of solos of, 31, 50–52; psychosis of, 35; spirituality and, 32, 34; stillness, use of, 31–32; Tolstoy and, 34; on working alone, 35

Noh, 9, 14, 17, 18–19, 21

Nolde, Emil, 38

Nudity: of Abreu, 155, *156*, *157*; of Carlson, 60, *61*; of Desmond, 80–81, *81*, 82; modern dance and, 92; in *tableaux vivants*, 78; of Villany, 76, 77, 78

Nunes, Mário, 145, 147, 149

Oliveira, Aníbal de, 145

Olsen, Lance, 194

Orff, Carl, 42

Orientalism: American, 17; flexibility of construct, 14; Ito and, 9, 11, 12, 13, 20, 23–24, 26; of modern dance, 8, 20, 22–23, 26; Salomania and, 132–34; Shawn and, 17–18; St. Denis and, 23, 143, 147

Von Seewitz, Joachim, 93
Von Zoete, Bertha, 43

Walkowitz, Judith, 120, 125, 126
Wallace, David Foster, 193
Wiesenthal, Grete, 43, 94
Wigman, Mary: approach to music of,
38–39, 41–44; Ausdruckstanz, 188;
at Davos sanitorium, 32, 33, 35, 49,
50–52; Drehmonotonie, 43; Ekstatische
Tänze, 41–42, 46–48; Hexentanz, 97;
intensity of performances of, 35–36;
isolation of, 35; modernism and,
33–34; pacifist views of, 46–50; school
started by, 97; Schrenck compared
to, 100–102; spirituality and, 32, 34;
Volúsia and, 151
Wilde, Oscar, Salome, 121, 122, 133–34
Wiley, Hannah, 15

Wilke, Hannah, 59
Williams, Raymond, 36
Women, visual and verbal representations
of, 123–24. See also Eroticism of female
dancers; Female solo dancers; Gender
identity; Photographs
Wong, Yutian, 9, 16, 24–25, 26
World, relationship with and toward,
34–38, 51–52
Wyman, Jane, 172

Yamada, Koscak, 14, 24
Yeats, W. B., 11, 12, 14, 21, 23

Zolotow, Maurice, 172
Zooesis, 68
Zurich Dadaism, 48–49
Zverev, Nicolas, 45
Zysk, Inge, 192